T0285288

Unlike the Rest

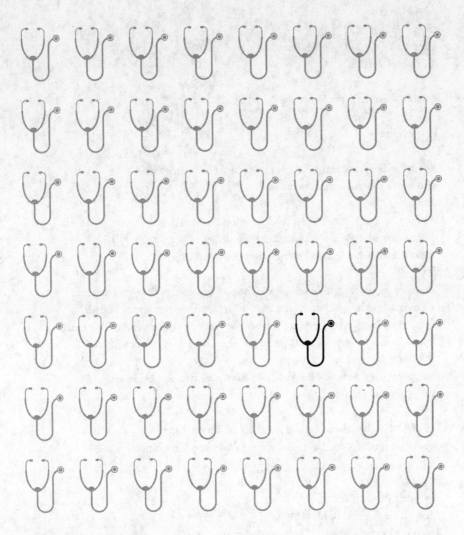

Unlike the Rest

A Doctor's Story

Chika Stacy Oriuwa, MD

HARPERCOLLINS PUBLISHERS LTD

Published by HarperCollins Publishers Ltd

First edition

Unlike the Rest is the author's life story. The patients she describes encountering
as a medical student and psychiatry resident are fictitious but inspired by her
experiences. The scope of medical practice she learns, and learns from, is very real.
Certain names and other details elsewhere in the book have been changed.

Excerpt on page 34 from "The Type," *No Matter the Wreckage* by Sarah Kay.
Write Bloody Publishing.

HarperCollins books may be purchased for educational, business,
or sales promotional use through our Special Markets Department.

HarperCollins Publishers Ltd
Bay Adelaide Centre, East Tower
22 Adelaide Street West, 41st Floor
Toronto, Ontario, Canada
M5H 4E3

www.harpercollins.ca

Library and Archives Canada Cataloguing in Publication is available upon request

ISBN 978-1-4434-6626-4

Printed and bound in the United States of America
24 25 26 27 28 LBC 5 4 3 2 1

For Nmeka, Ezenna, Nkiruka and Dale,
who fill my life with purpose and my heart with love

There is no greater agony than bearing an untold story inside you.

—MAYA ANGELOU, *I Know Why the Caged Bird Sings*

This book contains references to misogyny, racism, suicide and disordered eating. Please read with care.

Introduction

I craned the extension arm of the circular procedure light over my patient's bed, bringing his laceration—a mixture of coagulating blood and fatty, shredded tissue—into bright clarity. He winced in pain as I repositioned his forearm over the sanitary field, atop the blue lining that demarcated the procedural zone.

"That's the last time I drink at the country club," he joked, as I pulled out the minor laceration kit and placed my tools along the border of the metal table. A cutting needle, a needle holder, absorbable sutures and toothed forceps lined the outer edge of the metal tray, waiting to be carefully picked up and used.

He had taken a nasty, drunken tumble, I had learned, down the stairs in the country club. The patient's misadventures had left him with a three-centimetre gash in his forearm, a permanent reminder to know the limits of his inebriation, he bantered.

I threw him a chuckle, but I wasn't there to joke. I was there to work.

I focused my gaze on his wound and approximated how the opposing edges of the laceration would be rejoined, estimating how many sutures I would need to stitch through the tissue, how far apart they should be spaced and which suturing technique would be best.

Simple interrupted sutures, I thought, further examining the depth of the injury. Maybe five or six, but I'd see how the skin came together.

"Just some iodine to clean out the area before we stitch it back up," I said, spraying the open wound with the cool, deep brown solution. It was the second week of my emergency medicine rotation at a major downtown hospital in Toronto as a third-year clinical clerk, and I jumped at every opportunity to practise my surgical skills and turn each cordoned-off patient area in the ER into an operating theatre. I frequently opted for cuts and bruises over broken bones, which never failed to make my skin crawl, and took every chance to broaden my experience in women's health or pediatrics.

I had long known—since the age of three—that I was destined for a career in medicine. Where I would fit in this vast world of diverse specialties was just beginning to declare itself as I dove into the deep end of clinical rotations that defined the last two years of medical school.

At the start of clinical clerkship, in August 2018, I had briefly flirted with the idea of specializing in general surgery after doing a three-week rotation in trauma surgery, followed by plastics and reconstructive surgery. I was particularly fascinated by the challenge of suturing intricate and extensive injuries. One of my favourite patients was an inmate at a local penitentiary who had gotten into a knife fight and had her calf sliced open, right through a detailed tattoo. Over two painstaking hours, a plastic surgery resident and I worked carefully to salvage the tattoo and restore the original image. The experience made me feel like an artist, but instead of using a paintbrush, I held the needle holder and returned a masterpiece to its intended state. I stood back like a proud Picasso as the patient thanked me through tears. It was this moment, and the many clinical encounters to follow, that reaffirmed my long-standing passion for healing.

However, the brutally early morning rounds, the unforgiving culture of the operating room and the back-breaking hours spent standing holding surgical instruments for a grumpy preceptor (also known as an attending doctor, responsible for overseeing our medical training) extinguished my surgical dreams. General surgery wasn't for me, I realized, but I loved the excitement of using surgical skills in the fast-paced environment of the emergency department. Throughout my medical training, I grew to understand that rarely does one leave a specialty or rotation without a skill that can be translated to just about any other area of medicine. Therein lies the importance of committing oneself wholly to the experience and wonder of each specialty, even if it's worlds away from where one finally lands.

"Just making sure that the anesthetic is working—let me know if you feel any pain. Pressure is normal," I said to the patient, as I gently prodded the freshly anesthetized lacerated area with the syringe used to inject the 2 percent lidocaine.

"Only pressure," he responded. We were ready to begin.

I glided the triangular cross-sectioned needle through the layers of my patient's flesh, desperate to balance precision and efficiency within the time-crunched nature of ER work. My preceptor had previously lauded my efforts in creating neat stitches, with the caveat that I needed to work faster and have more confidence in my skills. My frequent requests for someone to double-check my suturing, originally interpreted as prudence, were now seen as insecure pestering.

"You're doing really well, almost done here," I said to my patient, whose witticisms had begun to fade. He was still a tad intoxicated, but the sight of his own blood trickling down his arm had helped speed up the sobering process.

The wound needed only six stitches.

"These should dissolve on their own within ten days or so and won't need to be removed, but I suggest you follow up with your family doctor to make sure you've healed properly." I closed the wound, studying the beautifully opposed edges and the taut but not-too-snug sutures.

"Thanks, Doc," he said, forgetting that I had introduced myself as Chika, a third-year medical student working under the staff emergency physician. I helped him get up from the bed and steady himself.

As I prepared to write my clinical procedure notes into the exam section of the patient's chart, he disappeared through the door and made his way to the exit.

It was a busy December evening in the emergency room of a crowded, century-old hospital, folded into Toronto's core. The department was bustling with patients who groaned from their ailments and bemoaned the exhausting wait to see a physician after being triaged by an ER nurse.

The most urgent patients here were tended to first—those with chest pain and shortness of breath, broken bones, skull-splitting headaches, early pregnancy loss and acute abdominal pain. As third-year clerks, my classmates and I were responsible for taking patient histories, completing physical exams, performing and assisting with minor procedures when appropriate, suggesting orders for the clinical tests and returning to our attendings with a complete picture of our assessment and plan.

The week before starting our clinical clerkships, we had a formal class brunch with the faculty at which we recited the Hippocratic Oath, as a reminder to do no harm as we shouldered our first real clinical responsibilities as medical students. Our desire to uphold the highest standard of medical care was matched only by the fear of disappointing our preceptors, especially as our performance would determine whether we earned a recommendation letter for residency. Without a strong recommendation letter to the specialty of our choice, we would not be a competitive candidate for that residency program and would risk going unmatched (failing to secure a spot within a program/specialty). This daunting pressure was further exacerbated by exams every six to eight weeks that tested our understanding of medical theory through application-based, critical-thinking-style questions. Studying for these exams proved to be challenging, since as clinical clerks we were expected to take call (twenty-six-hour shifts in the hospital, where we often stayed up all night working) every few days on some rotations, working upwards of eighty to one hundred hours a week.

The third year of medical school is often regarded as the hardest year across all four years, and for good reason.

Yet I absolutely adored finally being in the hospital and applying the clinical skills and theory that I had learned in the first two years of medical school. Whizzing through the emergency department that busy December evening, I was completely in my element.

I disposed of the suturing kit in the hazards bin, peeled my powdered yellow surgical gloves off my fingers and grabbed my stethoscope and clipboard as I headed for the nursing station. A series of file holders was affixed to the wall in the south corner, with the most critical patient prioritized at the top. I grabbed the first chart, which belonged to an eleven-year-old girl who had lost feeling and function in her left leg. She was experiencing paresthesia (numbing and tingling) throughout the limb and was waiting in room five down the hall.

The cold dregs of my tea, bought an hour before my shift, gave me a much-needed caffeine bump to make it through the early-evening rush. I dabbed the drips that accidentally splashed onto my blue scrubs and flipped my badge to lay it flat against my chest and display "Chika Oriuwa, Senior Medical Student/Clinical Clerk." My pager and pens hung from the front pocket of my scrubs, completed by a black Littmann stethoscope dangling from my neck. I had all the traditional hallmarks of a physician, at first glance, including a black fanny pack around my waist that held a small notebook for jotting down clinical pearls and a granola bar so I wouldn't pass out after hours on my feet. There was no room in the ER to show any signs of weakness or exhaustion, even if they seemed justified.

I tucked the clipboard under my arm while passing the central waiting room en route to the young girl and her mother, who anxiously stood in the doorway. Like the staff emergency physicians, I kept a pace that was midway between a sprint and a gallop; there were only a few attendings and residents caring for dozens of sick patients, and there was no time to waste. My mind raced with the differential diagnoses (potential conditions that might be afflicting the patient), and the questions and assessments necessary to whittle this list down to the presumptive diagnosis—the true detective work of medicine that made every shift feel exciting.

As I passed the front row of filled seats, I felt a tug on my sleeve.

"Excuse me, excuse me," said an older white woman, possibly in her early to mid-sixties, who was waiting beside her visibly unwell husband. Distracted, I nevertheless turned attentively to the woman and expected her to ask the normal questions that float around the emerg: *When will I be seeing the doctor? How much longer do I have to wait? Have my test results returned?*

"You forgot to clean the vomit off the floor over there," she stated, frustrated, pointing at a puddle of green and brown sick pooled beneath a hunched, writhing patient. "It's been sitting there for hours," she griped, before twisting her face in disgust.

I paused in confusion and shock, struggling to gather the words that fumbled in my mouth.

"Sorry, ma'am, I am one of the senior medical students working with the staff doctors to take care of patients. I'm about to go and see a patient, but I will ask someone to clean that right away," I said, while fixing my stethoscope, which hung precariously from my neck and had nearly fallen off in the hurried rush to my patient's room.

"Oh, apologies, I didn't realize," the woman replied, a flush of surprise blooming across her cheeks. Our discomfort and desire to pretend the exchange had not occurred were mutual.

Unfortunatley, however, it had—breaking not only my stride but also my spirit.

It was clear that she had mistaken the Black woman working in the emergency room as part of the medical team for custodial staff, despite my best efforts to adopt all the recognizable elements of the uniform that distinguishes doctors and nurses.

This is not to imply that there is any shame in doing custodial work—janitorial staff are integral to the functioning and flow of the hospital, and I have immense respect for the work they do, which often goes unnoticed. But I wasn't there to clean the hospital floor. I had spent two years learning an avalanche of medical theory, and four years of pre-med before that, to take care of patients as a clinical clerk and eventually as a practising physician.

I wrestled with the all-too-familiar unease that settled onto my skin—the fear of being seen as an imposter in the medical world, simply playing doctor while the real clinicians got to work. I felt momentarily foolish for believing that a stethoscope and pager would armour me with invincibility against racial stereotyping and implicit bias.

The woman's words echoed through my mind that evening after my shift was done—a seemingly innocuous request, layered in racial micro-aggression, that revealed a schism between who I knew I was and how I was perceived.

It was neither the first, nor the last, nor the worst experience of racism that I faced during my two years of clinical clerkship and beyond. Despite the sanitized and clean-cut nature of a medical career, I had quickly learned that it is not immune to the systemic racism that permeates the fabric of our global society. Many Black doctors have soldiered through the medical-training system in survival mode, placing their heads down and working earnestly toward the coveted MD designation and licensure, climbing the academic ladder, all the while absorbing racism and bias. For many, this was the only way to endure in institutions where they were not only under-represented but often tokenized, marginalized and silenced.

Some, however, feel called to push against a system that can be corrosive to the spirit—risking it all, personally and professionally.

I, throughout my medical journey, became one of those few.

Chapter One

My mother, Nmeka, has a stutter.

Not the kind that afflicts nervous lovers on a first date, but the kind that roars with a thunderous clap. It is a stammer that becomes more pronounced when her temper grows short and English vocabulary feels inadequately expressive; her mother tongue, Igbo, is more helpful to her when her emotions rise like a tide cresting the shoreline. I have come to admire the stutter's familiar cadence and can predict with accuracy when it will rear its head in conversation and just how long it will linger before dissipating. Her voice was the melody of my childhood, her stutter the recurring motif in the soundtrack of my life, and her presence is the most soothing balm to my worldly woes. Nmeka is, and always was, my fiercest protector and the cheerleader of my aspirations.

When I was three years old, I declared to my parents that I wanted to be a doctor. This goal was like a seedling that they watered assiduously, almost feverishly, throughout my life, to the point where it felt as if I might drown in their expectations. This dream was as much my mother's as it was my own, one of the many things I inherited from her beyond our almond eyes, coily hair and love for belting out tone-deaf renditions of Whitney Houston's "Greatest Love of All."

My mother came to Canada in the early 1980s, planting seeds of hope for a life greater than the suffering she had experienced in rural Nigeria. Stories of her childhood were scarce when I was young. I knew only that her father had died when she was ten years old and that her mother raised six children in poverty, alongside her sister wives, in a rural southeastern Nigerian village. There were many nights when my mother and her siblings would split a bowl of eba or gari (dried cassava meal mixed with boiling water), falling asleep to the lullaby of growling stomachs and my grandmother's promises of brighter days ahead. My mother dreamed of immigrating to North America, earning a degree in nursing and becoming a pediatric nurse, a goal that ran parallel to her brother Livinus's of becoming a doctor in the States. Dreaming big and having a sturdy faith in God were among the only things that kept my mother and her siblings alive.

As I grew into early adulthood, the details of her past traumas surfaced in our conversations, adding to the complexity of who I understood my mother to be. When I learned that she had endured abuse at the hands of many men in her life, so much more of who she came to be—as a mother and a woman—suddenly made sense.

When she was introduced to my father, Stephen, in Montreal in the late 1980s, and became pregnant with my older brother, Obata, in late 1989, her academic dreams remained unrealized. But she took the seeds of her own ambitions and sowed them in her children's futures. The next thirty years of my mother's life would follow the familiar pattern of many African Canadian immigrant mothers: willingly taking on jobs requiring manual labour and physical sacrifice, receiving poor financial compensation, struggling to make ends meet for the children, and living under the crushing vestiges of African patriarchy. From nanny to kitchen labourer to personal support worker, my mother never shied away from an opportunity to support her family—no matter how arduous the task or how large a toll it would inevitably take on her physical and psychological health. Her narrative mirrored that of the many racialized support

workers I saw in hospitals and care facilities during my medical training, which often served as a reminder of my mother's sacrifices and the
importance of my own tenacity.

After having three more children, all daughters—my older sister,
Chioma, me and my little sister, Chizoba—she vowed to raise us as
modern women who would move the needle on what was possible. We
could and would be unstoppable embodiments of our ancestors' wildest dreams, the most important ancestor, in her eyes, being my beloved
maternal grandmother, Umumuabuike Obilo.

After years of helping my mother raise her three eldest children, my
grandmother had moved stateside to be with my Uncle Livinus and his
family. When she became gravely ill, she was admitted to the general
medicine ward in a New Jersey hospital where my uncle practised as
a neonatal physician. Upon hearing that my grandmother's health was
rapidly declining, our family travelled to Newark from Toronto on short
notice just days before my tenth birthday in November 2003.

The last time I held my grandmother's hands, they were softer than
I had remembered. Her fragile skin sank under the weight of my fingertips as I willed her to respond to my feeble attempts to rouse her.
She was dying of cancer—and although I had not yet encountered the
death of a loved one, my adolescent mind connected the dots between
my mother's anguished prayers and her mother's silent suffering. Against
the beeping of the vitals monitor, my mother steadied her shaking voice
to beg my grandmother to stay. She was speaking in Igbo, a southeastern
Nigerian dialect, and at nearly ten, I had only just begun to scratch the
surface of learning her mother tongue. My siblings and I had not been
taught the language because of my father's fear that it would pollute our
mastery of English. Yet my mind searched through the Rolodex of Igbo
words I had heard enough times in my parents' conversations to have
firmly cemented in my mind and understanding. "Ndo, Mama, ndo," my
mother said as she wiped away her tears. I knew this phrase; it lingered
in the air just long enough for me to pull its meaning from my memory.

Ndo followed every fall, knee scrape, paper cut and tearful fight with
a friend. It always carried a tune of comfort that only a mother could
render. Roughly translated it means "I'm sorry," but whenever my mother
said it to me, it also conveyed "It will be okay." In that moment, I knew
that despite my mother's assurances that my grandma would survive her
cancer—"through the grace of God," she said—she was really steeling
herself for their final goodbyes.

The rest of my mother's words in that moment escaped me. Some
were muffled by her sobs and the overhead interruption of hospital codes;
others were parts of the Igbo language that were as foreign to me as, no
doubt, expressing the deep, unrelenting pain of watching your mother
die. I wanted desperately to join her in soothing my grandmother as she
stood at the end of this life and on the precipice of the next.

"Grandma, it's Chika . . . You will be okay, I promise," I said, as her eyelids flickered softly in my direction. "Grandma," I repeated, with a more
nudging tone. "It's Chika, Grandma. You will get better." My mother
looked down at me as I grew sullen and discouraged. I had quickly realized that, in my grandmother's final moments, her once firm grasp on the
English language had loosened, and my words crashed to the ground in
the space between us. "Mama, Chika na-agwa gi okwu," said my mother,
bringing my grandmother's attention to the small child at her bedside,
the same child she had cared for while my mother worked long into the
night, the same child who wouldn't let anyone else hold her because there
was no better pacifier than her grandmother's heartbeat, the same child
who now didn't know enough Igbo to say goodbye.

I abandoned my attempt to create a patchwork of words from my
memory that would let my grandma know of my faith in her recovery.
Instead, I searched for the one phrase I was sure my mother had said
to me in Igbo countless times—the one thing I wanted my grandma
to remember as she went to be with the Lord: *I love you.* I scanned the
mental films of my childhood, pausing at moments where I could potentially pull this phrase from my memory. Perhaps it was every night on

the phone, when my mother would call from the group home where she did her night shifts, making sure I felt her love even during her absence. Maybe it was written in our birthday and Valentine's Day cards, in her characteristic cursive writing, on a slight incline sloping across the page, precision abandoned for sincerity. Or maybe it was during those quiet moments when she was home, having weathered the storm of two consecutive shifts and holding her children close in our silent understanding of her sacrifices. Whenever she had said it, I was sure that in this moment I could *will* myself to remember. I would do it for my grandmother, and I would do it in defiance of my father's efforts to keep our English unaccented, untarnished and under the radar of potentially bigoted ears.

But I couldn't find it. Every expression of affection was scrubbed of any Igbo and perfectly packaged in my mother's heavily accented English. I felt a lump begin to swell in my throat, a blend of shame and frustration that sat heavily on my tongue as I offered my parting words. "I . . . I . . . I . . . I love you, Grandma. Ndo . . . I love you, ndo." It did not take me long to realize that I was apologizing not only for her life on earth being cut short, and for the suffering she had endured as a young, widowed mother, and for the lymphoma that riddled her body, but also for my failure to learn her native tongue. For my failure to connect with her in the language that she called home.

Twelve days after my tenth birthday, nine days after I said my farewells at the hospital, on November 24, 2003, my grandmother died. My mother's inconsolable wails could be heard even as I neared the front steps of our home in Brampton, a suburb outside Toronto. She sat in disbelief at our dining room table, sifting through ashen Polaroids and sun-bleached photos of my grandmother. They had always shared a striking resemblance, the kind where you knew with unshakable certainty that they were mother and daughter—the same full, sharp cheekbones and gap-toothed smile. This is not true of my mother and me: her face is rounder and deeper in complexion, and she stands nearly six inches shorter than I do. Yet we have the same eyes—the same windows into our soul, as they say—and this similarity has always reflected the intimate bond we share as mother and child. We have a spiritual understanding of one another. And so, on the crisp Wednesday morning when my grandmother departed this world for the next, I knew—before turning the key in the front door—that a piece of my mother was gone forever.

As I kicked off my winter boots and set my school bag haphazardly in the corner beside the staircase, I turned toward my father, who was standing by the kitchen counter, the cordless phone perched between his left ear and the crest of his shoulder.

"Your grandmother has finally died," he said matter-of-factly to me, as if to demystify my mother's wailing, which had since subsided to quiet sobs, as if I couldn't identify the distinct sound of her heart breaking. After all, the sound of her heart *was* the first thing I had heard in the womb. *"Finally?"* I thought to myself, confused by his peculiar choice of words and his decision to be on the phone in another room instead of by my mother's side. By this age, I had already realized that my father's arms were not the first place I should go to find solace. His tone would often harden at the first sign of vulnerability, and instead of comfort, he would offer lessons on how to be less sensitive and disruptive in other people's lives. My mother's embrace, in contrast, was the safest place on earth. This is why, when her arms were limp with the weight of grief and her speech was a string of barters with God, I realized a time would come when she couldn't be there, and I would need to brave the world alone. The fears that had plagued my childhood innocence, such as spiders and thunderstorms, were replaced that day by a fear that would lead to many anxiety-riddled nights of insomnia, nightmares and panic-filled calls for reassurance: that I could lose my own mother and, ultimately, a piece of myself.

My initial declaration as a toddler that I would pursue medicine was only strengthened in the aftermath of my maternal grandmother's death. I knew that I wanted to help and heal people who suffered, like my grandmother. And yet I didn't understand that the road ahead would require me to push past the impossible.

▼

"Igbos are the most resilient tribe in the nation," my father said to my siblings and me as we gathered in the kitchen for dinner. As per the pecking order, he sat at the head of the chestnut dining table that dominated our dated 1980s-style kitchen. Behind him, the window opened onto a lush green field and freshly raked baseball diamond, our nearby elementary school a dot on the horizon. It was nearing seven o'clock, and Anderson Cooper's voice was murmuring in the background.

We slipped into our usual spots: me beside Chizoba, Chioma beside Obata, and our pup, Pebbles, nestled under the table, waiting for scraps of food to fill her belly. I left a chair open beside me for my mom, who was rarely home for dinner as she was tonight. I loved nothing more than snuggling by her side. She had decided to stay home from work that evening because her feet were starting to swell from back-to-back overnight shifts; after years of manual labour, she lived most days with chronic pain in her knees, feet and back that intermittently debilitated her.

I often marvelled at the strength that my mother possessed. Just a few years earlier, in 2004, she had been diagnosed with ductal carcinoma in situ (abnormal cells within the milk ducts of the breast that are non-invasive) only five months after my grandmother's death. Although it was a pre-invasive form of breast cancer, the terrifying discovery was jarring in the wake of our raw grief.

"Mommy will be fine, Nnem," she would whisper to me assuredly, as I watched my father carefully replace the bandages on her partial mastectomy wounds. "Nnem," in Igbo, is a term of endearment toward daughters that loosely translates to "my mother" in English. "Nnam" is the male correlate meaning "my father." In our culture, children are often seen as possessing the spirit of their ancestors, so I knew that my mother searched for glimpses of my grandmother in my sisters and me, which brought her peace after great loss.

"I am not going anywhere," she promised.

When she returned to work within days of her surgery and soldiered on from radiotherapy appointments to double overnight shifts in the months that followed, it was cemented in my mind that my mother was a real-life superhero. To be her daughter, and inherit this grit, would come to feel like both a blessing and a curse. I would spend much of my adult life trying to strike a balance between calling upon my strength and daring to lean into my softness.

Pebbles pressed her damp nose against my feet and shook me from my thoughts. I crossed my legs on the seat of my chair and watched my mom zip from one corner of the kitchen to the next in a perfectly timed waltz that she had perfected over years of cooking for a family of six. Lovingly, she doled out a spoonful of jollof rice, baked chicken and sautéed kale onto each of our plates. Notes of fried tomatoes, onion, crushed chilis and coriander wafted into the air, filling our nostrils and hearts with a comforting familiarity. The scents reminded me of a place that I had never visited but knew was my home—my mother's village, where the strength of my ancestors originated.

Cherishing the fleeting moments when the jigsaw puzzle of my family was brought together around the dinner table, I took a minute to soak in the elements of the Oriuwa household. Chioma and Obata were distracted with a side conversation about MSN Messenger while fighting over who would take possession of the TV remote before, during and after dinner. And Chizoba, my spunky, downright hilarious little sister, was teeming with giggles at my father's overly animated account of his childhood, which included tales of village wizards and weather-shifters. Our dad raised us to believe that we were the descendants of magical beings. No wonder it felt so easy and natural to dream big dreams.

"My daddy, your grandpapa, was the strongest man in the village when the military troops came to destroy our home," he said, eyes widening for dramatic effect. Chizoba slyly mimicked his facial expression before breaking into laughter. "Seriously, this is your history! You are Igbo children. Even though you are in Canada, you need to learn these things," said my dad, urgently calling for our attention while we tucked into our meals. Nothing brought him greater joy than educating his children about their roots, knowing that without inheriting the language—and being raised as Canadians—the tether that bound us to his home was being worn thin. The balance of this sacrifice for a greater life for his children was a delicate one that haunted him daily.

My father continued to wax poetic, eventually becoming a background murmur that blended with the sound of Wolf Blitzer's *The Situation Room*. I peered over his shoulder to the stove, where sliced plantains simmered in boiling oil, reaching a rich, crisp brown that signalled they were ready to be flipped, scooped and placed on a paper towel for cooling. I feigned attention to his tales while I impatiently awaited the arrival of my favourite side dish and admired how my mother had the energy to execute a flawless Nigerian meal when she was clearly battle-weary.

Over the course of my childhood, by observing the unfair expectations placed on my mother simply because she was a woman, I grew to resent the traditional role of a wife in Nigerian culture.

If I never learn how to cook Nigerian food, I thought to my childhood self, *I'll repel the men who demand that of me, and instead I'll marry someone who finds joy in cooking for our family. Better yet, we could even cook together! But in any case, when I'm a doctor, I will refuse to wake up in the middle of the night to feed a man who is more than capable of feeding himself.* I added this notion to my growing feminist manifesto, right under the mandate that my future husband needed to be an emotional haven for our children.

Often, my father would comment on my lack of interest in cooking Nigerian meals by calling me "domestically illiterate," echoing the taunts of uncles who jeered that "your husband will divorce you for someone who will cook for him, doctor or not." Though annoyed by their jabs, I took them as a compliment and wore them as a badge of pride. "If someone can take my husband because she cooks better than me," I would reply to my male family members, "she can have him."

Of course, I eventually went on to learn how to make meals that I enjoy, and I even found pleasure in the art of cooking, all without the pressure of having to master culinary skills simply to earn a man's fidelity.

My feminist convictions seemed to originate long before I realized that I rejected the patriarchal norms that dominated Igbo and West African culture. The wildfire spirit that burned within me would come to frustrate my parents and other family members who expected me to be a dutiful, dedicated and subservient Nigerian daughter. Instead, I challenged the men in my family, including my father, by requiring respect from elders before I reciprocated it, and I held the men in my life to account for the hurt they caused. This tension was the kindling for many disagreements between my father and me, eventually eroding our relationship for many years before it was healed. Although maladaptive at times, this stubborn trait became the backbone that would eventually lead me to a career of advocacy in medicine decades later.

When the golden-brown plantains were spilled onto the corner of my plate, completing the picturesque home-cooked Nigerian meal that defined my youth, I folded away my mental manifesto and began to indulge my father's stories.

"The Nigerian government tried to eliminate us during the Biafran war," he continued, "yet they failed, and we are now the most prosperous tribe. Therefore, you need to continue the legacy as Igbos here in Canada." My father ended most lectures like this, with a call to action to achieve great things, remain fiercely protective of our Igbo culture, and all the while uphold humility. As my mom placed his meal before him, which usually lulled my dad into a moment of silence, he concluded his pontificating and vowed to pick up where he left off soon. He always did.

Growing up as the daughter of two Nigerian immigrants, there was never a shortage of stories about the Nigerian Civil War, also known as the Biafran war. My parents were children when the war broke out in 1967, and they witnessed the mass genocide of my ancestral tribe, the Igbo people, following their decision to separate from the state of Nigeria and create the independent Republic of Biafra. During the two and a half years of the conflict, nearly two million Igbos died from starvation due to the Nigerian government's state-sanctioned blockade of goods to the Igbo region. Each of my parents lost siblings and extended family members in the war. Thousands of others in my tribe were murdered in cold blood as their communities were decimated.

My father was thirteen when the militia invaded his town. When his village was burned to the ground and his family forced to take refuge in the trenches, he bore the responsibility, as the eldest son, to scavenge for food, seek shelter and keep watch over the movements of the militia. I supposed this was why as an adult he was hardened; emotional vulnerability was the unspoken casualty of the conflict.

As a father, he continued to interpret his role to be that of a strict provider; only once the mortgage was paid and the lights were on could he rest peacefully, believing his duty was complete. Like my mother, he worked exhausting hours, also in health care, as a pharmaceutical technician and part-time nurse. When I sought more from him emotionally, I realized the well of what he had to give had run dry. An "I love you" from his children was met with a frozen stance and a terrified glare, as if he were staring down the barrel of a rebel's gun.

With my mother's assistance, I learned to codify his behaviour into a unique love language. Paying household bills, making inquiries into my academic life and taking trips to the local bookstore for a new novel were equivalent to an embrace, consolation and verbal affirmations of affection.

Though the gap between my father and me seemed expansive, and our mutual stubbornness caused much friction, I took advantage of the only bridge that joined us: our shared love of medicine.

"Daddy, guess what," I said to him, after washing down a mouthful of jollof rice with freshly mixed fruit punch. The dinner table was one of the few places where conversations with my dad remained lighthearted.

"What is it, Nnem?" he replied, eyes heavy with the fatigue that always followed one of my mother's robust meals.

"We got our marks back today, and I got a perfect score on my science test!" I exclaimed, giddy with pride. "My teacher said I'm the first student to have ever done that on her seventh-grade test."

His eyes perked open and twinkled with delight.

After witnessing me dedicate the past two weeks to fervently studying for the test on states of mass and chemical bonding, my dad had been anxiously waiting for the result. Every night prior to the test, I would commandeer the family room table and place my cue cards carefully across the surface like delicate chess pieces. I painstakingly rewrote every detail from my class notes, highlighting key words for memorization and staying up late until the designated pile was committed to memory. My meals were placed in the corner of the room and often devoured well after they had gone cold. I possessed a voracious drive toward perfectionism, considering myself fortunate to deeply love the courses that aligned with the career I aspired to.

My father started to chuckle as he proclaimed, "See? Your good work ethic has paid off. Igbos are the smartest in all the land. And with your tenacity, you will make a good doctor if you keep it up. But you must remain humble in this country, or *they* will destroy your dreams."

Through coded language, and sometimes explicitly, my father reminded his kids about the ever-present threat of anti-Black racism and how it could affect our lives. Having looked for work as a newly landed African immigrant in the 1980s, eventually settling into pharmaceuticals and nursing, he often told us about the prejudice he experienced in the workplace. Superiors and colleagues would downplay his intelligence, take his ideas and snub him for promotions, and peers would mock his thick Nigerian accent. Understandably, these experiences scarred my father. The tragic outcome of this racism was a staunch refusal to pass on to my siblings and me his native language, Igbo, out of fear that our accents would be a scarlet letter of shame and a catalyst for ostracization in Canada. When I entered university and then medical school in later years, I came to learn, painfully, that there was an unequivocal truth in my father's concerns.

My heart warmed at his approval, while my mind wrestled with the contradiction in his advice: celebrate the intelligence that I had been "gifted" as an Igbo but refrain from being seen as audacious. At twelve years old, I was still learning how to strike his balance of pride and modesty. I also questioned how my father had come to this and all his other strongly held conclusions, which seemed based more on subjectivity than on fact. Through many frustrated and impassioned conversations, I learned that he would mentally shut down or just walk away from someone when his opinions were challenged. This left our relationship sadly frayed. Medicine, however, remained as the one enduring tether that held us close.

"I'm so proud of you, Nnem! One day you'll be *Doctor* Chika Oriuwa," squealed my mom, as I envisioned myself wearing a white coat and donning my stethoscope like Dr. Miranda Bailey from *Grey's Anatomy*. As I had yet to meet a real Black female doctor in my community, she was the closest personification I could find of my future self.

I pictured future Chika, like Dr. Bailey, running through the halls of the hospital at the end of a call shift as my name was being paged: "*Dr. Oriuwa. Paging Dr. Oriuwa to the emergency department.*" There, a patient on a stretcher would await, straddling the cusp of life and death, ready for me to swoop in and perform a life-saving measure that was possible only thanks to my years of arduous medical training. My colleagues would celebrate my leadership and agility just as Dr. Bailey's colleagues celebrated hers. I would go home to my loving family and seamlessly transition from doctor to mother and wife, holding together my carefully curated vision of female badassery.

I had it all planned out (minus the dramatic break-ups and make-ups that defined *Grey's Anatomy* storylines). In the nine years that had elapsed since I'd first decided that I wanted to become a doctor, it seemed that every facet of my life had been dedicated to inching me closer to that dream. After I was given Barbie dolls and teddy bears at my fifth birthday party, I assigned them roles as doctors and patients with injuries that I concocted. Treatments were often misaligned—a knee scrape was treated with a cast and a kiss, a tiny bump on the head required neurosurgery—but I remained well-intentioned and devoted.

When I got the game Operation for my eleventh birthday, I refused to surrender the board until my surgical precision had been perfected and I could remove the butterfly from my patient's stomach with ease. Though my friends waited impatiently, I revelled in the triumph of my make-believe surgical mastery.

My siblings and I spent evenings during elementary school summer vacation completing the math workbooks my dad handed us at the end of June and flipping through a hardcover anatomy textbook for kids. I was utterly fascinated by the human body and wanted to know every intricacy of how it functioned, or malfunctioned, and eventually how it could be restored to good health.

As we stood up to clear our plates from dinner, my dad snoozing in his chair at the head of the table, I thanked my mom for a delicious meal and begged her to rest her feet instead of cleaning. "Of course, Nnem," she said, limping from the stove to the fridge as she stacked away Tupperware like Tetris pieces.

My mother would continue to nourish us, in mind, body and spirit, as we grew into young adults who manifested our dreams—and her dreams for us. When the pressures of academia crept in from all sides, as I matriculated through high school and university, she was always nearby with a meal to offer, an ear to listen and a shoulder to cry on.

Chapter Two

At first, the differences were subtle: a notch tighter on my light brown leather belt, an extra fifteen minutes at the gym between anatomy lectures, and the perfectly timed rearrangement of Brussels sprouts on my dinner plate. No one, aside from my university roommates and my mother, seemed to notice.

The first ten pounds shed were the easiest to hide—beneath baggy crewneck sweaters with the McMaster University crest brandished across the chest and oversized joggers that were rolled down twice over my jutting hipbones. The next twenty-five pounds lost necessitated more stealth than I naturally had, but as with all other endeavours in my life, I strove to rise to the occasion.

Almost seventeen years had elapsed since I had declared my toddler-hood aspiration of becoming a doctor, and by the early spring of 2013 I was on the precipice of actualizing this goal. I was a second-year student in my dream undergraduate program, the Bachelor of Health Sciences (Honours) program at McMaster (commonly called "Mac"), tucked away in gritty but blooming Hamilton, Ontario. That summer, I was slated to write the notoriously challenging Medical College Admission Test, the MCAT. Yet this was not the only source of distress in my life.

"My girls and I are heading to Buffalo for some shopping before we start studying for the MCAT," I told my mom, as her worried eyes narrowed on my collarbones, which grew more prominent with each of her visits to Mac.

Explaining away my gaunt appearance should have been relatively easy, even under the anxious radar of an African mother. She knew of my tightly packed schedule, filled with classes that I both adored for the content and loathed because of my drive for academic perfection. I was pacing through a full year of anatomy and physiology, epidemiology, statistics, inquiry (projects on health care systems and biochemistry) and gerontology—with anatomy and physiology my favourite, by far. Absorbing and retaining hundreds of facts about the human body—even the mundane minutiae of cellular pathology that would bore the average person—came as naturally to me as breathing. I spent countless hours poring over my notes in the library, rewriting lectures to consolidate them in my memory, and barely stopping for a moment's rest—or a bite to eat. My MCAT was scheduled for late July. If I were successful, a strong result would allow me to apply to medical school in my third year of undergrad and be admitted early—the coveted third-year acceptance that many Health Sci students pursued. The pressure, both internally and externally, was at an all-time high, and I was too close to my dream to break under it.

But there was more to my frenzied life than colour-coded gastroenterology notes on intestinal pathology and anxiety about timed MCAT practice tests. Underneath my baggy sweater was a body that was withering along with my spirit.

In addition to the school pressure, I had endured the abrupt and turbulent end of a two-year relationship that had been marred by emotional and psychological abuse. That was a story that I'd so far kept secret from my mother. So, no, nothing was okay. In fact, things were as far from okay as they could have been without me being flung off the brink of existence. I was struggling to hold the pieces of my life together in the middle of an emotional storm of guilt, confusion, mounting academic demands and heartbreak. My mother's worry was matched by my own. I didn't recognize the woman in my reflection. How had the confident and outspoken little girl who had graduated high school as valedictorian and gotten into one of the most prestigious pre-med programs in the country wilted into a woman who was vanishing before everyone's eyes? On the surface, I was acing my courses and carving a clear path to becoming a doctor, yet the dark secrets of my struggles were beginning to poke through the veneer of excellence.

"Nnem," she whispered, "you don't look well. Are you okay?"

No, I desperately thought to myself. *I've lost thirty-five pounds in four weeks, and I'm scared.*

"Of course, Mommy," I eventually replied, offering up words of reassurance that the second year of Health Sci was living up to its reputation of being the hardest year of the four. "This is what it takes to get into medical school," I joked. "You know doctors really don't sleep or eat."

I thought a glib explanation would soften her worries, given that we shared the same self-sacrificing commitment to a cause, but I knew she was onto me when her eyes grew weary with concern.

I wanted, more than anything, to tell my mom the truth about my failed relationship and my disordered eating, which had peaked at this crucial moment in my studies. But I couldn't explain to her something that was beyond my own comprehension. I wasn't restricting my food intake to achieve a particular weight goal or body image; my closets weren't lined with magazine clippings of *Vogue* models airbrushed to perfection. Instead, the hunger was soothing in a way I struggled to articulate—and the weight loss simply a byproduct. My relationship had ended very badly—it had taken everything I had to disconnect myself from my ex-boyfriend, and I was struggling to resurface in the aftermath. Losing my first love in such a traumatic way felt like a cosmic punishment for some unclear misstep I'd made, and the feeling of starvation felt like I was making atonement. Maybe if God saw that I was suffering enough,

He would make the pain stop, He would reverse the hands of time. The relics of my strict Catholic upbringing rose up and struck with a vengeance, leaving me repentant and in desperate need of salvation.

So, I developed a nearly fanatical obsession with discipline; every hour of my day was scheduled down to the minute. I tried to balance the tailspin of my life through strict control of my time. My post-lecture evenings were parsed and colour-coded in my agenda: three hours dedicated to annotating anatomy lectures, two hours for preparing biochemistry presentations, thirty to forty-five minutes on the treadmill and an hour or so allotted for researching anti-microbial superbugs. By the time I nestled under the weight of my duvet, curling my exhausted body into the fetal position, the pleas of hunger from my stomach were the only sounds strong enough to drown out my muffled weeping.

As the daughter of a woman whom I regarded as having superhero-like resilience, I felt shame at finding myself lost in the ruins of a relationship. I knew my mother would never tolerate one of her daughters derailing her wellness because of lost love. But being in a relationship that had preyed on my vulnerability and naivety tapped into a well of insecurity that evaded my mother's teachings.

Growing up as a dark-skinned Black girl in the suburb of Brampton, Ontario, I was rarely lauded as conventionally attractive. My fuller lips, broader nose and coarser hair were fodder for ridicule and racist remarks, even from members of my own cultural community. When a white neighbour said his grandmother would die if he brought home a Black girlfriend, and a Black male friend sneered that most men would only date light-skinned Black or white women, I learned that Black girls like me weren't often readily accepted by the world. This sentiment was frequently echoed and amplified in the media I consumed, which socialized me to question the inherent value of Black women everywhere. Throw in a complicated emotional relationship with male figures in my life, and I was all too susceptible to the pull of a man nearly six years my senior.

To spend years feeling undesirable and then fall into the arms of someone who made me feel enchanting was intoxicating. For the first time in my life, a man made me feel seen. If only I had understood that good decisions are rarely made under the influence of any powerful substance.

"Don't worry, Mommy. I'll be fine."

The look on my mother's face was familiar. Over fifteen years earlier, when I was just four years old, my mother had worn that same concerned expression when I first started to develop a peculiar relationship with food. As she always told me, I was a particularly special, yet challenging child from the outset. Despite her best efforts at breastfeeding and supplementing with formula, I struggled to gain weight as an infant, which sparked many anxiety-fuelled visits to my family physician. The doctor would always remark that I was just "a skinny, but healthy baby" and encouraged my mother to keep her worries at bay. As a toddler, I struggled to keep weight on and often straddled the lower percentiles on the children's growth curve. Though her concern was omnipresent, she held on to faith that one day, like my two older siblings, I would fill out and be a chunky, happy kid. That day never came, and my relationship with food only grew more complicated.

During family dinners, I was always the slowest one to eat, so painfully slow that my brother and sister would finish their meals and start to devour mine. My mother would shoo them away and confine me to the table until I finished the plate. My stubbornness led to nightly faceoffs between us; she would ultimately relent and send me, victorious, off to bed. Our family physician continued to assuage my mom's fears and reminded her that I was a healthy kid who would grow at my own pace. Yet when I was about four years old and still quite thin, my mother noticed that I would go through periods of not eating.

"No, Mommy, you have to look at the calories for Cheerios! There are fifteen calories, so that means it's not good for you," I proclaimed, examining the side of the cereal box before placing it back in the cupboard and skipping away. Having decided that I wanted to be a doctor, I turned every meal into an opportunity to debate with my mom on the nutritional stats of each food item—which, at four years old, was information I'd simply made up. My Aunt Amarachi, who often came over to help my mother take care of her small children, burst into laughter. She dubbed me "Doctor Chika" and reassured my mom that "kids say the darndest things, and it's just a phase. If she is hungry, she will eat." I remember them chuckling as my mom attempted to sway me with pieces of fruit and cookies, to no avail.

Over time, her chuckles finally gave way to unease.

"Promise me you'll eat something," my mother said by the doorway, backlit by the bright streetlights of Hamilton.

"*Promise*," I said, squeezing her fingers and assuring her I'd eat more of the food she regularly cooked and delivered. It took me years to reveal to her that many of those meals went unconsumed and were discarded. The irony that she had left an impoverished village in rural Nigeria to have her Canadian daughter willingly throw away perfectly good food was not lost on me and tore into my conscience daily.

But still, I held my cards close.

I had learned many lessons from my mother: how to love unconditionally, how to protect fiercely, how to become unapologetically self-reliant and how to conceal my suffering so as not to burden or frighten those I love. The latter quality became an ingrained trait I carried into my late twenties, until years of therapy sought to reverse the damage.

"We're getting close, guys!" said my girlfriend Kimmy, as my other Mac friends, Liz and Stefania, and I perked up from the hypnotizing hum of her hatchback buzzing down Highway 403 toward Niagara Falls. We were approaching the United States border, brimming with the exhilaration of having finished our second-year exams and the anticipation of our shopping trip in Buffalo, New York. The preceding weeks had been an exhausting stretch of cramming in statistical equations during all-nighters, providing final presentations on the biochemistry of insulin resistance, and committing the brachial nerve plexus to memory. Our minds were still reeling with the information overload needed to pace through the last month of second year, and we all craved a retail cleanse to provide a clean slate for three months of MCAT prep.

Stars and Stripes billowed in the wind as the American flag cut through the crystal-blue May skies. A beam of sunshine refracted through the windows, bathing me in warmth as I revelled in the mental and physical distance from Hamilton and the ghosts that haunted my bedroom.

I shuffled through the mess in my purse—my phone, earphones and a folded envelope that had been pressed into my palms just two hours earlier. "It's not much," my mom had lamented, "but it's all I have. You deserve the world, Nnem." She knew that, unlike my girlfriends, I was planning on window shopping, as my chequing account persistently hovered in the negatives. The envelope contained the last two hundred dollars in her bank account, which she had saved by working a couple of extra night shifts at the group home. Gratitude choked my throat even as I squeezed the packet in my hand and dug under my phone to find my passport.

Kimmy lowered the driver-side window, turned down the music and slowed her car to a stop as we approached the border patrol booth.

"Good morning, ladies. Why are you travelling to the States?" said the officer, as he opened each passport and brought it closer into his focus. He was a middle-aged white man of average height who seemed run down by the repetitive exchange of pleasantries that his job required.

"We're doing some shopping in Buffalo for the weekend," Kimmy replied.

"Uh-huh. And how do you guys know one another?"

"We're all students at McMaster University, in Hamilton, in the Health Sci program!" said Kimmy, with her usual chipper demeanour. She had a magical way of making even the most mundane facts sound charming, a trait that was a good fit with her goal of becoming a pediatrician.

"Interesting. And what do you plan on doing with that?" said the officer, as he closed the last passport and handed the stack back to Kimmy. We passed our respective passports around and waited patiently for his gamut of questions to run its course.

"Well, we all want to be doctors. We're writing the MCAT soon, and so we're doing some retail therapy before we start studying," she replied, as we all happily smiled and chimed "Yup!" in agreement.

The border officer paused, leaned closer toward Kimmy's window and peered over her shoulder at me in the passenger seat. His sunglasses slipped down the bridge of his sweat-slicked nose as his eyes met my own.

"Even *you*?" he said, narrowing his gaze with suspicion.

The car fell silent.

"Um . . . y-yes," I stammered back to him, confused, as my body stiffened.

"Really?" he replied.

I looked at Kimmy and the girls, then back at the officer as my throat tightened and they shifted uncomfortably in their seats. "Yes, I want to be a doctor too. I'm also writing the MCAT," I responded.

We sat in silence for another awkward beat as my eyes locked with the officer's and he raised an eyebrow, thoroughly unconvinced. My mind sharpened to the one lesson that all Black people are taught when encountering law enforcement—be overly cautious, respectful and mild-mannered, or risk untoward hostility. Though angered by his dismissal of my lifelong dream, I kept a soft smile on my face so as not to provoke aggression or further coax his skepticism.

"Really? Mmm . . . Well, all right. Enjoy your trip," he said, gesturing for us to move our car ahead through the gate. Kimmy raised her window as she shifted the gear and rolled cautiously forward. We sat silently for another minute or so, sharing a painful understanding of what had just transpired.

As I was the only Black girl in the car, and the only one interrogated with doubt, it was clear what the officer was trying to imply: A Black female physician? Impossible.

Moments after we pulled away from the American border, I wished I could put the car into reverse and flip the interrogation back on the officer. I would ask him if he knew that I had dreamed of becoming a doctor since I was three years old, despite growing up never seeing a doctor who looked like me practising in my community. I would ask him if he knew that I stayed up studying until 2:00 a.m. throughout the semester, only stopping when physical exhaustion bested my determination to forge a better life for me and my family. I would ask him if he could have weathered the past four months of my life, slowly disappearing before family and friends while also acing the hardest academic year of my undergraduate studies. Through tears, I'm sure, I would ask him how he could be so callous, to strip me of my dignity in front of my girlfriends and take away the one moment of peace and joy that I had had in months.

Instead, we continued our trip, remarking how awkward and idiotic the officer's comments were. I scoured the centre console for some snacks and popped a gummi bear in my mouth, shovelling my rage behind the sugary treat, allowing it to disperse and settle on a cellular level. I had come to learn over my year of disordered eating that momentary junk food binges were both comforting and confusing.

As the car continued humming along the interstate, I daydreamed about the little Black girl from Brampton who dressed up as a doctor every Halloween and spent her spare time reading her father's nursing textbooks. I imagined her angrily protesting the officer's implications and looking around for the nearest Black female doctor to show that her aspirations were possible. She would have been heartbroken to learn that one could not be found nearby.

Travelling down that highway, I promised my younger self that I would get into my dream medical school, become the doctor I was destined to be, and prove him wrong.

It was now mid-October 2013, six months since that shopping trip, three months since writing a brutally tough MCAT, and just two months since I'd found myself. Or, more accurately, saved myself.

Vanessa and I sat under a shared blanket on the carpeted floor of her bedroom, my head nestled onto her shoulder as a YouTube commercial droned on her laptop. The room was nearly dark, with the glow of the screen illuminating our faces. We had known each other since high school, becoming close and then inseparable following graduation. She was Portuguese with Cape Verdean roots; our mutual African ancestry and shared love of books bonded us. After our first year at Mac, we moved—along with our closest friends, Feven, Sara, Chloe and Cassandra—into a comfy six-bedroom university home just a stone's throw from campus, and we still lived there in our third year.

Vanessa and I shared the top floor, a converted attic with sharp, sloping ceilings, and we often snuck into each other's rooms to unpack the happenings in our lives. I would tiptoe to her bedside and ask to borrow something from her unbelievably vast collection of cozy sweaters—they were just baggy enough to hide my thinning frame and simmering secrets. She would frequently creep into my room, prodding me to emerge from the corner of my bed and join the world of the living. If her pleas failed, she would nuzzle beside me in silence.

The summer months that trailed behind us marked a significant period in healing myself from the wounds of second year. I had written my MCAT exam in July, and a week later ceremoniously shaved my heat-damaged tresses to start anew. I finally felt liberated from the shackles of my doomed relationship and the self-destruction that ensued in its wake. As the tufts of natural hair pirouetted toward the bathroom floor, I felt raw, exposed and vulnerable—but free. Shaving my head was a silent revolution, a baptism into my emerging identity as an unapologetic Black woman who would safeguard the sanctity of her mind and body.

Reclaiming and redefining my natural beauty, starting with my natural (not chemically processed) hair, was the beginning of this evolution. Historically, through the efforts of colonialism and slavery, afro-textured hair had been deemed unkempt, unsightly and unprofessional unless manipulated through certain means to assimilate to Eurocentric ideals (for example, chemical relaxers or heat straightening). I, like many other Black women, subscribed to this notion and hid my tresses away in braids, pressings or other styles, to attain social respectability. Countless wide-tooth combs were casualties in the war between my natural hair and me, and I often left the battle with sore arms, cramped fingers and resentment toward my afro. It would be years before I learned how to nurture my hair, realizing that much like me, it did not need to be tamed but held close and loved.

My body, in parallel with my relationship to my hair, had also healed over the summer months. I began seeing an on-campus therapist weekly, unravelling the parts of my mind that connected restrictive eating with control, and learning how to safely cut ties of communication with my ex. Dinners with friends were no longer a series of calculated distractions from my plate but a sacred space of community and nourishment of the body and soul.

When I looked in the mirror, my reflection no longer haunted me—it thanked me.

I drew on this reservoir of strength when my MCAT results were unveiled in the late summer and fell short of what I needed to successfully apply to medical school that year; the coveted third-year Health Sci medical school admission was beyond my grasp. When the web page loaded with my scores, I imagined my mother, grandmother, uncle and father hanging their heads in disappointment. How would I tell them that I had failed in the singular goal that was a lifetime in the making? My heart shattered as tears drenched my sleeves. Devastation and then, eventually, acceptance curled around me. The path forward spelled another year of keeping my GPA strong and competitive while steeling myself to rewrite the MCAT again the following summer. I changed my desktop background to the Japanese proverb "Fall down seven times, stand up eight" and readied myself for the year ahead.

As summer stretched into fall and classes began again, I still retained my habit of picking through Vanessa's wardrobe, finding comfort in the woven threads that clothed me at my lowest, and spending quiet moments together in her room. Occasionally, when my studies intensified and self-doubt crept in, I felt the urge to restrict meals emerge as I craved control over a disorienting schedule. Luckily, my weekly therapy sessions, journalling and checking in with friends kept my disordered eating at bay.

I poked my arm out from under Vanessa's thick, quilted duvet and reached for a bag of freshly popped popcorn before sinking back onto her bedroom floor.

As the YouTube commercial reached its end and the next queued video loaded, spoken-word poet Sarah Kay appeared on the screen and brought the microphone to her lips. The video was grainy, and the wide-angle shot awkwardly cut her lower body out of the frame, but when her voice bellowed through the laptop speakers, I was engulfed in her words and forgot about the visual details.

"Do not mistake yourself for a guardian. Or a muse. Or a promise. Or a victim. Or a snack," she said, punctuating her sentences with dramatic pauses. "You are a woman. Skin and bones. Veins and nerves. Hair and sweat. You are not made of metaphors. Not apologies. Not excuses."

Not apologies, I thought to myself, suspended in that moment. I felt overcome by all the apologies I had doled out in my life.

I'm sorry that I'm not the kind of daughter you envisioned, one who would swallow misogyny and submission without protest.

I'm sorry that I'm not your idea of beautiful.

I'm sorry that my first attempt at the MCAT was unsuccessful. I hope I am still worthy in your eyes.

I'm sorry that I'm crying again. I can't stop crying. Being abandoned in my relationship hurt so badly.

The final *I'm sorry* was an apology to myself, for nearly six months of self-deprecation, restrictive eating and periodic isolation.

I vowed to create a fortress around my self-worth, one that was impenetrable to the effects of anyone who sought to destroy the sanctity of my well-being.

I would no longer turn my body into a reservoir of "sorry"s.

Once Sarah had finished her piece, Vanessa wiped a tear from her eyes as the audience broke into applause. "That . . . was beautiful," she whispered, as she reached for a tissue and giggled at her own emotionality. One of the things I loved most about Vanessa was how easily movies and words moved her to tears. I wished I could reclaim the same emotional softness, but somewhere within the past year the potential for that quality had been damaged. It was in this moment that I realized spoken word could bring me back to myself.

"Wasn't it?" I replied, as goosebumps spread down my forearm.

"Let's watch another," she said, toggling the cursor over the next video.

"This is a good one, get your tissues ready," I joked, as we melted back onto her carpet.

Poetry and writing, like my mother's embrace, had always been the calmest shore for me to find refuge. I wrote my first poem at seven years old, and ever since I'd used creative writing to explore my understanding of the mechanics of humanity, suffering and joy. Dozens of journals filled with diary entries, short stories, poems and reflections lined my bedroom shelves throughout my childhood.

When my maternal grandmother died and I felt helpless to console my mother, I wrote a poem for her from the perspective of my grandma watching over us from heaven. When my mother read it, it was the first time I saw her smile in the days of grief that had enveloped her. When I wrote and performed a poem for Remembrance Day at an elementary school assembly, moving one of the guest military veterans to tears, I understood the power of my words to heal, transcend and restore. The way in which I came to process the world and my place in it has always been through poetry; I viewed myself as a writer and wordsmith before all else.

When I was eight, after a number of summer afternoons spent writing short stories, I briefly abandoned my dream of medicine to instead become an author. "Mommy, I've made a decision! I'm going to be a writer and poet when I grow up. Then maybe I'll be a doctor afterwards," I recall telling her.

My characters ranged from a princess remedying a war-torn kingdom to earthquake survivors trapped under rubble for several days without sustenance. I don't know why I felt compelled to write stories like these, when lighter tales seemed more accessible and age appropriate. I remember, even as a young writer, leaning into the darker, more elusive parts of life. Writing about the beauty of the world seemed easy, yet writing about suffering seemed necessary. Years later, I came to understand that poetry, much like medicine (and my eventual specialty in psychiatry), necessitates an unflinching examination of life—the good, the bad and everything in between.

"Become a doctor first, Nnem, then you can do whatever you want. You will be a brilliant writer one day, I promise," replied my mom, a response that was then repeated (more sternly) by my father when he caught wind of my evolving aspirations.

"You are very good at English, which will help you become a good doctor in this country. But you must stay focused on your mathematics and sciences to become a doctor," said my dad, his tone becoming increasingly dramatic. "When you set up your practice, then you can afford to become a writer. If you focus on becoming a writer first, you'll be poor, I promise you that."

My father always spoke as if everything he stated was fact, even if his pronouncements were based on anecdotal evidence or simply a presumption on his part. Many aspirations of my siblings and me lived and died within my father's convictions.

"And there is nothing worse in this world than being poor. Nothing."

I stared solemnly at him as he crossed his arms and continued to remind me about the requirements for success: all roads led to medicine.

My father inculcated in me not only the unyielding desire to become a physician but also a crippling fear of poverty and financial instability. Even as an adult, I remain haunted by the memories of my dad telling me that purchasing our Christmas presents meant our electricity could potentially be cut. As my mom borrowed money to ensure we all got a small birthday present—often teddy bears, new socks and a chocolate treat—my dad would remind us that the mortgage was due in a few days, and having shelter was the ultimate gift. Living in poverty was akin to not living at all, we were taught, and my parents had not left Nigeria for their children to grow up and barely move the needle on intergenerational progress.

"Fine, I'll become a doctor first. But I'm definitely going to be a writer afterwards," I replied to my parents, hiding my feelings of defeat and frustration. Even as a child, I wanted deeply to exercise autonomy over my life and decisions.

Years later, even as I dutifully followed the path to medicine before writing, I felt a powerful call tugging my soul back to my artistic roots.

Following that night of beautiful poetry in Vanessa's bedroom, I decided to pull out my journal and write a love letter to myself. Sarah Kay's poems were a kind of inverse siren call, beckoning me toward asylum instead of extinction.

Three weeks later, I took the stage at the Toronto Poetry Slam, hosted in the basement of the Drake Hotel, an arts-centric boutique hotel on Queen Street West. Vanessa, Feven, Chloe and Sara came along to support me, thrilled to finally see their best friend reclaiming joy in her life after months of watching her slowly unravel from the girl they knew. My poem was unpolished, unmemorized and torn out of the spine of my journal. It was admittedly mediocre when I think back on it, but also downright courageous and a fresh examination of my healing process.

When we entered the dusky space, the host was on stage giving a final call for poets to sign up for either the open mic or a lottery to compete for a cash prize in the slam rounds. I wended my way through the crowd made up of society's misfits: artists, art-admirers, couples out on a quirky first date, solo adventurers exploring the cultural underbelly of the city, hipsters with taupe-coloured toques and thrifted 1990s sweaters. I signed up for the open mic, not brave enough to compete against the regulars who were seasoned and out for blood. They possessed an air of unflappable confidence in their craft and sat in the front row, studying the literary chops of their competitors. I was paradoxically intimidated and emboldened.

I introduced myself as Chika Stacy, which would later become my pen and stage names. I had never been called just Stacy, my middle name, but there was something freeing about dropping my last name and rebranding my identity. It felt like a challenge to the patriarchy, an opportunity to redefine myself on my own terms.

My performance went by in a blur. It was unspectacular in comparison to the veteran poets who would follow in the competitive rounds, but to me, it felt sensitive and real. The crowd was enthusiastically supportive, almost as if they knew I needed validation on the cusp of my new journey. They snapped and roared, hummed and approved during poetic beats. I smiled into the audience, looking for my friends' faces in the darkened room. Instead, I met the reassuring looks of strangers, eyes transfixed and brows furrowed in careful evaluation of my writing and dynamism.

At the end, they clapped as I handed the mic to the host and crept down the stairs beyond the curtains.

"Let's give another round of applause to Chika Stacy, folks! Shouldn't she come back and compete? Maybe we'll see you next month in the slam rounds!"

I blushed as I scurried back to my seat in the far-left corner, sandwiched between Vanessa and Sara. The ice cubes in my drink were melting as I took several relieving gulps. I felt as though I had just passed a test I'd barely studied for, not necessarily with flying colours, but at least well enough to earn the respect of this tight-knit community.

Less than two years later, I would be on the national stage at the Canadian Festival of Spoken Word, hosted in Saskatoon, Saskatchewan. After immersing myself in the Hamilton arts scene, I became a contracted artist with the Hamilton Youth Poetry Slam team, a competitive slam poetry troupe that spent several hours a week moulding poets into skilled wordsmiths and performers. It proved to be a place of strength and healing for me that I hadn't expected I would need. Following an unsuccessful application cycle to medical school in my fourth year of undergrad, I'd taken a gap year to throw myself wholly into poetry—something that ultimately mended the heartbreak of medical school rejection. The feeling of failing not only myself but my mother (despite her reassurances that her love for me was never contingent on any prospective career) lingered with me as I competed and gigged in cities across the country.

Going exclusively as Chika Stacy, I performed a poem called "Letters" in the semifinal rounds of the national competition in Saskatoon. Unlike the first poem I performed at the Drake, it remains one of the best poems I have ever written. To me, it's playful yet merciless about my redemption in the wake of romantic heartache. It swept the round I entered, and the performance left me exhausted yet restored.

Losing myself in words allowed me to find peace in the uncertain journey of pursuing medicine in Canada, where less than 10 percent of applicants get admitted to medical school each cycle. I had been devastated by the rejections, but I firmly believed that becoming a better poet would make me a better doctor, as it allowed me to explore humanity in a transcendent way that connected me to others. It was also the most visceral way for me to express my lived experience, and it has blossomed into an outlet that I have repeatedly tapped into as an artist, physician, advocate and beyond.

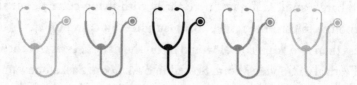

"I've had enough," said my patient, Maude, as her torso swayed back and forth, her middle-aged body threatening to collapse with every movement. She appeared to undulate as if her limbs were submerged in molasses, yet somehow she was besting gravity's attempts to pull her toward the floor of the psychiatric emergency room. The smell of liquor gripped me from the doorway, while she retched periodically and heaved her upper body toward the bucket that sat by her feet. The hand-sanitizer dispenser near the entrance was intentionally empty, given the history of some patients drinking whatever was available to get an effective and inexpensive buzz. I caught her glancing intermittently at the container and wondered what factors could erode a person's spirit to that degree of desperation. Of course, I understood theoretically that avoiding the painful and potentially fatal experience of withdrawal was a significant driver, but surely there was a tale of being dealt an unfair hand by life that long preceded this moment.

Wefts of matted hair were slicked to Maude's forehead by the thick evening heat. Dribbles of sweat beaded on her temples, slipping down her chin onto her shoulders. Some formed a stream that met like a confluence of rivers with her tears, which ran hot along her cheeks. A tartan of fresh and healed linear scars was etched down Maude's forearms, alluding to a tortured life beyond what I could glean in the electronic chart review and collateral (supplementary information provided by those with insight into the patient's life) that I had acquired before the assessment.

Some stories, I learned, could only be felt and not told.

We sat in the dimly lit enclave, a thick curtain separating us from the wails and groans of the packed psychiatric emergency department. Maude was one of many that night who were flagged for assessment of suicidal ideation. She sat among others experiencing manic episodes, substance withdrawal and an acute exacerbation of obsessive-compulsive disorder, to name just a few frequently observed psychiatric presentations. It was my first abbreviated call shift as a third-year medical student on my psychiatry rotation, one that had started shortly after a chaotic day on the inpatient psychiatry wards several floors above. This kind of call shift required me to work in the emergency room until close to midnight, before being relieved of my duties and summoned back to the wards in the morning. I felt exhausted, but not with the kind of existential exhaustion that resided within Maude.

At this stage in my life, which now included my stint in medical school as a clinical clerk, I thought I had seen almost every kind of person on the spectrum of inebriation, from tipsy teenagers in high school, to wasted friends during undergrad orientation, to wedding guests passed out on chairs, sapped by a night of dancing and disinhibition. But I had yet to encounter this unique mixture of intoxication and determination to end one's life.

"I'm ready to die," said Maude, as she laid bare her extensive plan for suicide, to see what awaited her on the other side of a life replete with suffering. Her plan was detailed, with directives on asset donations to charities and how to inform her estranged children of her passing. A stockpile of prescription medications was stashed under her mattress, waiting to be ingested while she soaked in a warm bath. All she ever wanted to do, she said, with a glazed stare and reddened eyes, was make the world a better place than she had found it. If she couldn't do it in life—a failure she deeply lamented—she would ensure that she did it in death.

She had started to run a bath, then fallen asleep in a drunken stupor in her subsidized apartment hours earlier. She, like so many others in the room that night, was brought in to the department by police, at her roommates' behest, when they found her on the bathroom floor as the tub overflowed. Maude didn't want an admission or assessment. She had a singular request for our team in the psychiatric emergency department: to be surrounded by calm, to listen to her favourite jazz record, and to ensure that her plan

was executed with precision. Most important, she stressed, was the dona-
tion of her grandfather's telescope. Maude hoped that the recipient, if
ever they felt the darkness closing in, would look through the telescope
into a starry night sky and capture all the light they could not see otherwise.
This practice had brought Maude solace in the bleakest of moments, and
when the sparkle of a distant celestial body no longer brightened her spirits,
she was convinced it was time to let go.

Our job as the psychiatry team, on the other hand, was to do all that we
could to extend and improve the quality of her life. To convince her that her
purpose on earth was greater than the pain that she was suffering. To let
her know that she wasn't alone, although every shred of evidence she had
convinced her that she was. To persuade her that the darkness that consumed her was likely escapable, if we could buy the time to find the right
combination of therapy, medication, addiction support and social stabilization. To give us an hour, a day, a week, a year. To make it to tomorrow. To
do what no doubt felt in the moment like the impossible.

"Please, I've had enough," she said, letting out a low whimper, followed
by a series of wails that accentuated her precarious swaying.

Maude's ability to recount the minutiae of her suicidal ideation struck
me as both deeply heartbreaking and perplexing. I learned that she had
been working toward this plan for years and was, in fact, a frequent visitor
to the bustling mental health crisis unit situated in the rougher underbelly
of our hospital. Her medical and psychiatric history revealed a sordid tale
of multiple psychiatric hospitalizations, failed trials of anti-depressants and
anti-psychotics, different psychiatrists and diagnostic labels, and innumerable presentations to the emergency department for either suicidal ideation
or a near attempt. She was never able to complete her plans, as her drive
toward the perfect death eclipsed her conviction to end an imperfect life.

After I collected a full psychiatric and medical history, intermittently jolt-
ing forward in the moments I thought gravity would prevail and she would
come crashing down like a tower of Jenga blocks, my senior psychiatry
resident took over the dialogue. She had been observing my interview

silently, waiting for me to finish so she could fill the gaps in my assessment.

"Would you be willing to stay here while we help you sober up?" asked Charlie, the skillful third-year doctor and chief psychiatry resident in the program. She wore blue-green hospital scrubs over a fitted turtleneck, black slacks and runners that carried her from room to room, patient to patient, and life to life that teetered on the edge.

"Fine, I guess," said Maude, as she rested her head on her arms and sipped slowly from the ice water provided by the nurse. Daybreak was only a few hours away, and so was the opportunity for Maude, likely with a clearer mind, to chat with another psychiatrist. She had been through this choreography before, and on the other side of the night waited a possible admission, a referral to an urgent care clinic, a rehabilitation service or other time-buying intervention.

I learned from Charlie, and others throughout my journey on my third-year psychiatry rotation, that sometimes when a patient cannot commit to the magnitude of staying on earth long term, they may commit to a smaller micro-decision. An overnight stay and the opportunity to chat with a staff physician. A new medication, one that might better suit their biological profile than others that barely made a dent in the drudgery of their existence, as many patients would lament after an ineffective trial. A chat with the social worker during their stay, to see if every avenue of government aid or housing had been exhausted. Or often, giving the patient space to commit to nothing at all and simply *be* for a while.

Several months after this shift, during one of my residency interviews for psychiatry, I was asked to write an essay on whether medical assistance in dying (MAiD) should be extended to patients with mental illness. All candidates had forty-five minutes to argue their point, writing on a clipboard.

To take a stance on either side seemed impossible, and that was exactly the moral quandary the residency admission committee hoped to conjure in the room full of nervous psychiatry resident hopefuls. How well did we tackle a debate that had been simmering in Canadian and global health policy for decades? Were we brave enough to put our position on paper, knowing that whoever reviewed the file might hold an entirely different perspective?

It took me several minutes of reflection before I poured my thoughts onto the page.

I thought of Maude, and every patient I had encountered in psychiatry and other medical specialties who was afflicted with mental illness. If we, as specialists in medicine, were convinced that mental illness was every bit as real and as debilitating as physical illness, were we not called upon to validate the suffering that could follow someone for decades even after exhausting every avenue of treatment? At what point is mental illness intractable? And if we denied patients the right to a humane end of life, what measures would they take on their own to seek liberation?

Is our goal as doctors to extend life, by any means necessary, or to maintain dignity and grace in end-of-life care?

I hurriedly jotted my thoughts on the back of one sheet and started to formulate my argument.

I left my seat uncertain, as candidates spilled into the lunchroom and swirled their thoughts in the air—some for and some against MAiD for patients with mental illness. The debate would rage on, over lunch, in health policy boardrooms and in my mind every time I thought of Maude.

Extending her life by even one day felt like a win that evening in the emergency department. But I sometimes wonder who the true victor was.

Chapter Three

My hands were clammy as I stood outside the interview door; they weren't perceptibly shaking but had a kind of pulsing flutter. After three years of performing my poetry before audiences and judges, I wasn't easily unnerved. In fact, I had grown to crave the competitive energy of slam poetry performances and had a bloodlust for a flawless execution; the high of a near-perfect slam round was ecstasy. I prided myself on having developed nerves of steel while on stage, a quality I was sure I could depend on during one of the most decisive days of my life. I needed to.

But this competition was different. There was no audience squeezed into a pub on the outskirts of Hamilton, no galvanized crowd of hundreds at the foot of a national competition stage, no eccentric host introducing my feature set as I waited on deck for my name to be called. There was no sacrificial poet who would whet the appetite of the audience before the slammers took the stage. I understood that I would be offered no do-overs or secondary rounds to make up the lost points from a potential blunder.

Instead, there was just me, a different series of evaluators determining a much more important fate, and a heavy metal door that divided us.

This was it. My time had come.

After achieving the MCAT scores required to be a strong medical school candidate, and dedicating months to curating my application package, I stood at the edge of the final frontier of the admissions journey: the medical school interview. I had received two invitations: one from the University of Toronto, and the other, approximately one week later, from the University of Ottawa.

I closed my eyes and thought of my mom, who was similarly skittish in anticipation several kilometres away in Brampton. She had gathered a group of African aunties to lead a prayer circle at the time of my interview at the University of Toronto, a mercilessly early 8:00 a.m. start. I giggled at the thought of one of them bursting into tongues, overcome by the Spirit of the Holy Ghost. The belief I invested in assiduous preparation she invested equally in the power of prayer. No mountain, she believed, was insurmountable through the application of pure faith.

"Make sure you pray before you enter the room, so you are anointed with the blood of Jesus during the interview," said my mom over the phone as I entered the looming doors of the Michener Institute, a school, embedded within Toronto's University Health Network, that was dedicated to health sciences research and education.

"Of course, Mommy," I said back, silently questioning whether Jesus would really anoint me in that moment. I wondered if He was anointing everyone who was arriving for a medical school interview that day, levelling the playing field and rendering my prayers pointless. Maybe He would unevenly dole His heavenly favours onto those who were more pious and observant of their faith, those unlike me whose commitment to religion hadn't faltered and nearly collapsed. After high school and into university, I came to question the religious doctrines that had been instilled in me. My dedication to science and social justice seemed incompatible with certain biblical teachings, so while I inched closer to a career in medicine and advocacy, I grew distant from God—or at least the version of Them that I was taught in church. Much like my relationships with the male figures in my life, this schism would take years to eventually heal as my spiritual journey evolved.

You can do this, I said to myself, putting thoughts of religion aside.

I thought instead of four-year-old Chika, playing with her fair-skinned, thin, blond Barbies that she imagined were doctors who looked like her, with kinky hair and cinnamon complexion. They donned white coats that I fashioned out of pieces of tissue paper taped together with childish imprecision. Teddy bears four times the size of the doctor dolls, with scraped knees and butterfly tummies, waited patiently to be seen.

You were made for this.

Admission to my top-choice medical school, the University of Toronto, Faculty of Medicine, was the golden ticket to the career of my dreams. It would be the actualization of a lifetime of effort. Blood. Sweat. Tears. So many tears.

I stood in front of the door, feeling my once hardened nerves give way in disappointment—years on the slam stage couldn't prepare me for the gravity of this moment and the pressures that came with it. My shoulders shivered in reflexive compensation, begging to shake loose the anxious energy from my bones. I fixed my gaze on the numbered page taped to the front of the door over a glazed window that blurred the visual of what lay ahead.

The air in the hallway felt thick, as if its very molecules were coated with the glistening sweat of the medical school hopefuls. It made me feel warmer than I wanted to be, already slowly broiling under the heavy threads of my newly purchased black suit. I wished for a blustery draft of January wind to sneak its way into the building and find me in that stuffy hall. Each breath felt laboured, as if we weren't just competing for a spot at the best medical school in the country but for precious particles of air. There was a palpable nervous energy, the kind that could swallow you whole if you weren't careful.

"Please remember that you will have twelve minutes at each station, with a bell chiming at the tenth minute to signal the final two minutes," said the invigilator, who had a raspy, unusually calming voice, on the overhead. She called for us to stand quietly outside our respective doors and place our fingers on the handles without turning them. We would be instructed when to enter.

You were made for this.

Upon direction, I turned the handle downwards, gently releasing my grip as I pushed the door open.

The interview room felt clinical, sanitized even. The air was less dense than in the hallway, entering my lungs with ease and oxygenating muscles that were tense and frenzied. I scanned the room with the same fight-or-flight drive that one would have when assessing a threat. I quickly softened my shoulders and curled my mouth into my best, most engaging smile. It felt unnatural—smiling when every instinct told me that this moment was critical, terrifying and necessitated an unprecedented seriousness. However, in my weeks of diligent preparation since receiving the interview invitation, I'd learned that first impressions could tarnish a perception or win over even the most intimidating evaluator.

So I smiled—the same gummy, full-mouthed smile that I inherited from my mother and maternal grandmother. I knew that although I entered the room alone, I carried the strength of the African women who came before me. The women who overcame, adapted and survived. The women who challenged, redefined and endured.

This moment was the next step in that legacy. I was made for this.

The walls were the kind of white that's blinding, a kind of white that made my heavily melanated skin seem ten shades deeper. I was always acutely aware of my Blackness in academic spaces, where people who looked like me were scarce. This moment was no different.

An empty chair sat tucked under an expansive grey table, across from an older white gentleman with thinly framed glasses and a crisp button-up shirt. A two-way mirror stretched across the wall behind him, suggesting that this room was normally used for clinical teaching and standardized assessments. I wondered how many medical trainees had left that room holding back tears or breathing a sigh of giddy relief.

I prayed to fall into the latter category.

The doctor stood when I entered and extended his hand; he was exceptionally tall and wore a cheerful grin. In almost military fashion, I stretched my hand to his for a firm, professional handshake. I had practised this introduction to an almost granular level: the intensity and duration of the shake, the warmth of my smile, the connection of our gazes in a way that was confident but not off-putting.

"Hi, I'm Chika!" I said, willing myself to ignore the sound of my heart pulsing in my ears. I calibrated the tone of my voice to land somewhere between the commanding confidence of taking the slam stage and the inviting humility of meeting a significant other's parents for the first time. I wanted to sound "doctorly" but accessible, like the kind of person who was self-assured but not arrogant. The kind of paradox my father had hoped to raise.

Our hands met, his nearly twice the size of mine. His handshake was surprisingly warmer and softer than I'd expected. He returned to his seat as I pulled out the chair and sat with the straightest posture I could muster. After I had spent years lazily slouching while reading, writing and studying, the muscles in my lower back felt taut and unforgiving, aching under the strain of perfection. A sub-clinical tremor resurfaced in my hands as I interwove my fingers to stifle my jitters.

"Hi there, I'm Dr. Galloway, an academic cardiologist at University Health Network, affiliated with U of T. I'll be your interviewer for this station, and we'll chat about your CV and some of the things you've done. Pretty easy!" he said, with an informality that was reminiscent of two old friends catching up over coffee. His eyes were a coral blue that seemed to have the ability to detect any insincerity. His smile was genuine, and it melted my residual terror.

As I willed away the strain in my lower back, he opened a chestnut brown folder that lay on the table between us, revealing a stack of papers with my name in bold lettering across the top. Immediately, I recognized my CV, and I savoured a moment of stillness as the feeling of surrealness lifted.

"Sounds amazing!" I said, feeling excitement and confidence begin to rise within me. The unique thrill of winning over an audience came back to me, like the experience I'd had performing guerrilla poetry to a group of half-interested teenagers. If I could win them over, I thought, maybe I had a chance here, too.

I quickly lifted my arms and placed my hands on the table, in his line of sight, as I had practised endlessly with my friends in the preceding weeks.

Executing a medical school interview was a calculated science of sorts. You needed to come polished and rehearsed, without sounding robotic and inorganic. Your hand gestures needed to be well-placed and frequent enough to demonstrate personality and interest without becoming distracting or appearing frantic. Your answers to the interviewer's questions needed to be detailed yet sufficiently brief to leave space for further questions, or you ran the risk of appearing disorganized. You needed to present the best version of yourself, not only in how you spoke and articulated your compatibility with a career in medicine but also in how you *looked*.

I tucked a loose lock of hair behind my left ear, then quickly placed my hands back on the table and tightened my smile, ready for his first question. The singular twist swiftly sprang back out, almost in retaliation, as though it was demanding to be seen.

My natural hair, having grown well past my shoulders in the three years since I shaved my head, was styled in mini twists that landed just above my shoulders. They had taken me approximately five hours to style, following the painstaking process of detangling, moisturizing and parting through my freshly washed afro, which in its unmanipulated state grew outwards and not downwards, seemingly defying gravity. I had taken extra care in smoothing my edges down with gel, sweeping the coily baby hairs into one of the tight twists and hiding the kinky, wild texture that was historically seen as "unkempt" and "unprofessional." By the next morning, my edges had already started to kink in defiance. I dug out a jar of Eco Styler gel and an old toothbrush, flattened the fraying hairs and begged them to behave for once.

I believed then, through both a visceral understanding and explicit warnings from others, that wearing my hair in its most natural state would not meet the standard of presentability in a medical school interview. There was not enough room for my afro to sprawl in the halls of the ivory tower, and so it needed to be hidden away, out of sight.

Although I had written and performed poetry on the topic of reclaiming the beauty and power of natural, afro-textured hair, challenging universally upheld Eurocentric standards, I felt then that my medical school interview might not be the best place to exercise a political leaning. Too much, I understood, was riding on this moment to let myself risk falling victim to unwelcome stereotypes.

"Why don't you straighten your hair?" my mother had asked a week prior to the interview, as she examined the afro that I'd thrown into a precarious pineapple bun. I combed my fingers through the densely knotted curls and tried to tease them apart. Quickly, I shook my head. I didn't want to incur heat damage on the tresses I had so carefully nurtured over the past three years. Silk presses—a style in which afro-textured hair is blow-dried, parted into small sections and pressed with a flat iron—are a beautiful style that represents the versatility of natural hair and Black beauty. But when done with too much heat or too frequently, they can lead to the destruction of one's natural hair pattern, leaving one with curls that don't revert on wash day. Every naturalista's nightmare.

I had invested too many evenings in watching YouTube tutorials by natural hair gurus on how to achieve waist-length 4c hair—my type, according to the Andre Walker Hair Typing System—to wash away my progress.

"I don't think so, Mommy. I have a better idea," I said, pulling a loose curl taut and watching it spring back into its firmly wound position.

I determined that mini twists would be the perfect middle ground; my hair would retain its natural curls while being styled in a way that would come across as less "imposing." I promised my coils, as I twisted them into singlets the evening before the interview, that if I got in, I would unapologetically embrace them once more. A small and temporary sacrifice of identity—or so it seemed.

As I entered the Michener Institute that fateful January morning, I realized that I was the only Black medical school interviewee in a crowd of dozens. I couldn't help but wonder whether the other candidates shared the burden of combatting their natural features. I questioned if they could feel the weight of their skin, heavy and conspicuous in its obvious hue and difference. I wondered if they even noticed that I was the only Black candidate, and if they questioned how this could be possible at an interview in Toronto, one of the most ethnically diverse cities in the world.

Even you? The voice of the border officer seemed to echo through the halls of the building, the memory pummelling my confidence as I prayed for another Black interviewee to push through the front doors and give me that reassuring glance to let me know that I wasn't alone. The same glance of solidarity that was shared moments after a racially insensitive comment was made or a derogatory stereotype uttered.

But they never came.

I pondered whether the other interviewees, and maybe even interviewers, would be silently asking the same reflexive question the officer asked that day. Maybe they, too, would think I was out of place, lost, had accidentally wandered into the wrong building at the wrong time. Sitting across from the older, white, male cardiologist, I wondered if he was questioning whether I fit the mould of what a physician *really* looks like.

While I was standing in that hallway and sitting in that chair, my skin felt like hot, smouldering coals. My Blackness had never felt heavier.

Dr. Galloway flipped through the first couple of pages of my CV and landed on the section about my extracurricular activities during university. His index finger slid down the page before landing on the second last line, and he tapped on a bolded section.

"I see you did some research in adolescent maternity and mental health. Tell me more about this," he said, with a tone of authentic interest.

Having built an arsenal of answers to every possible inquiry about my autobiographical sketch, I explained how my lived experience with my sister's teen pregnancy had inspired me to explore the unique challenges faced by teenage mothers and their children, and how to address them. As rehearsed, I linked this skill set to how it could be transferred to a career as a proficient, caring physician. He nodded, seemingly pleased with my answer. I felt my muscles soften and my pulse slow. *I can do this*, I thought to myself.

We spent the next five minutes combing through my resumé, dissecting areas of my past that piqued his interest. It felt like an archeological dig, unearthing the parts of myself that were hidden, yet invaluable, ready to be assessed under a microscope. He inquired about my stint as a barista at Starbucks for a year and a half and joked about how dealing with a pre-caffeinated lawyer at the crack of dawn was the best preparation for bedside medicine. I chuckled agreeably, withholding the darker stories of me crying in defeat while mopping the floors and scrubbing the toilets at work after my first round of medical school interview rejections the year prior. I remembered standing in the bathroom, staring at my puffy red eyes in the mirror, green apron stained with tears, and praying for this exact moment. I knew that the interview would be where I would shine; if I could just land an interview, I knew that I had a good shot of getting in.

Our time together was waning, and in a matter of minutes he had already learned an incredible amount about me. I had the opportunity to gush about my experience as a slam poetry coach at Westdale Secondary School, leading a group of novice poets to become regional slam poetry champions. I explained how I taught them to use poetry as a platform for self-expression and socio-political activism, transforming them from shy, uncertain teenagers to confident, boisterous performers. One of my favourite poets on the team, I recalled, was a teenager who was neurodivergent. They were reserved and rarely spoke during our after-school practices, but when they shared their brilliant poetry, our group was dazzled. The power of their voice, I shared, empowered me. Coaching and watching the evolution of my students through poetry was one of the accomplishments of which I was most proud.

Dr. Galloway studied me closely as I spoke, peering at me over the rim of his glasses, smiling gently. He continued to flip through the pages, looking at pre-circled headings and scribbles in the margins.

"Canadian Slam Poetry national finalist?" said Dr. Galloway, surprised, as he skimmed through the awards and accolades section.

I smiled and nodded. "Yes, I just competed in my second national spoken-word competition this past October in Saskatoon. My team and I placed second in the country."

"Ah! So, I'm in the company of a nationally ranked poet? Well, isn't that different!" he said, eyes widening as he returned the papers to the chestnut folder. I blushed, thankful that our conversation had rested mostly on the topic of my poetry, a landscape I felt most comfortable navigating.

There was only a matter of minutes left, and a premature feeling of victory crept into my consciousness. *Now for my questions*, I thought to myself, eager to put forward my carefully selected inquiries about the school and what unique opportunities it had for research and the intersection of humanities and medicine. Fifteen years after my parents told me I had to become a doctor *before* I could be an author, I still held close the aspiration to marry my two loves, medicine and writing. But Dr. Galloway spoke before I could begin.

"Why don't you perform some poetry for me? Maybe one of the pieces you shared at nationals?"

Time seemed to slow to a grinding halt and the air became denser, hotter.

Perform? I thought to myself.

I had *not* prepared for this.

In the three weeks leading up to the interview, I had examined every moment in my life, from birth to the present, that had primed me to become a physician. In the quiet section of the top-floor library at Ryerson University (now Toronto Metropolitan University), I had splayed out three notebooks, highlighters, pens and my laptop and mapped out the story of my life. Each day, I built a small colony of Starbucks decaffeinated oat lattes and half-eaten bagels that energized me while I developed a meticulous record of my history.

The timeline began with my origins as the middle daughter of African immigrants, moved on to my discovery of and fascination with medicine, covered my burgeoning love for advocacy throughout university and even how I sought to educate young Black women on how best to manage their natural, afro-textured hair. With a red pen and yellow highlighter, I jotted bullet points under each formative event in my development and found a compelling argument as to why it made me an exemplary candidate for medical school. No question, I believed, would come as a surprise. I felt like a high-ranking military officer preparing for battle, or a lawyer readying their client for cross-examination.

Of course, my love for writing and poetry was the recurring motif throughout my timeline, rearing its head through elementary school, high school, undergrad and my gap year. I established what I felt was a convincing narrative of how striving to be a better poet made me a better person and ultimately a better doctor.

At no point, however, did I think to prepare for a performance. In fact, it had been exactly four months since I had rehearsed any of my poetry or taken the stage. The gruelling preparation for nationals meant that I'd had to rehearse the same eight poetry performances hundreds of times, until my throat was hoarse and my body ached. We were even required to take to the streets of Hamilton, standing on public corners and performing for curious onlookers.

After nationals, I'd wanted a definitive break from competitions and performing so that I could not only focus on preparing for medical school interviews (should they come) but also write poetry that was just for me—not under the influence and critique of my manager and coach.

"Sure, of course!" I replied to Dr. Galloway, with enough enthusiasm to conceal my reticence. I knew that declining his request to perform could demonstrate a lack of confidence in myself and my abilities, ultimately casting doubt over my synergy with medicine—a field that invariably requires doctors to act quickly under pressure.

I consciously slowed my breathing as I rapidly scanned a mental catalogue of my poetry, wanting to select a piece that would serve as a window into my soul and yet be effortless for me to perform under this inimitably stressful circumstance.

What about "SKIN"? I immediately thought to myself. The choice was risky. It had been several months since I had rehearsed and performed this piece, and it was also a deep examination of racial politics and police brutality against unarmed Black civilians. It would be a powerful performance, I knew, but one that would also magnify the gap between me and my interviewer—a young, Black, politically charged woman appealing to the ethos of an older, white, male physician whose political leanings were unknown to me. Would it be worth the risk?

I hesitated before locking in my choice.

"SKIN," my favourite of all the poems that I have ever written and performed, was composed in my fourth year of university for a creative writing assignment in a course on leadership and effective professional communication. Our professor was a brilliant industrial and organizational psychologist who assigned us the task of creating a captivating piece that would serve as a call to action. Fresh off the heels of the 2014 murder of Mike Brown in Missouri, which was a heinous abuse of police force and a case of racially targeted violence, I was galvanized to write a poem about what it felt like to be Black. To be targeted. To live in perpetual fear of white violence and silence. Although the experiences and historical context of Black Canadians differ from those of Black Americans, we are often connected in our experiences of being marginalized, subjugated and brutalized through systemic racism. I knew I had to speak up.

I wrote the poem, start to finish, in a matter of hours.

I memorized it—gestures, cadence, speed and tonality—within a day. I stood at the front of my class, boldly, bravely. Black.

The only Black person in the room.

I wanted the audience to feel something—a visceral discomfort, the deep unease of the pain that comes with the Black experience. Beyond this, however, I wanted my classmates to deeply question what it felt like for me, as the only Black person in our year in Health Sci, to navigate the halls of the prestigious—and often othering—Health Sciences building. Would they leave the performance and recall the time that another student asked me during our anatomy lesson, in front of classmates, why Black people loved fried chicken and if the reason was related to slavery? Would they have felt the same smouldering embarrassment I did as our classmate chuckled and turned away?

I wondered if they would have remorse about the Health Sci Halloween party of 2013, when one of my classmates came painted in Blackface, with a fake gun, fake marijuana blunt, chest-length dreads and costume cup of "purple drink." Would they feel the need to atone, given how many people had openly encouraged this classmate in the days leading up to the party, while I confronted them about the inappropriateness of the idea? I wondered if one student would be eating his words after telling me that "it's not that big of a deal" and I should "get over it."

To be Black in my undergraduate program was to be painfully discernible and erased in the same moment. "SKIN" is a cathartic release, an in-your-face, no-looking-away exploration of racism, police brutality, Black trauma and non-Black apathy. It challenges the listener to step into Black skin, stand in the scope of the white gaze and public inaction, and question how they could change their behaviour, or at least their subconscious thoughts, to be a better ally.

As I took this poem from the classroom to the regional stage at the Hamilton Youth Poetry Slam, it became known as my most evocative, gut-wrenching, beautiful piece of poetry.

It was written to make people uncomfortable, since change rarely happens in spaces of comfort. It was written to make people think. People like Dr. Galloway.

I decided to perform "SKIN" during my medical school interview. Not because I was certain that it would earn me a spot in the 2016 matriculating class at U of T Medicine, but because it was the clearest path into my humanity as a Black woman—it was truly the window into my soul.

My Blackness, I thought, was already amplified from the moment I set foot in the Michener Institute. No amount of edge-controlling gel and tightly twisted singlets could hide the fact that I was a Black girl in a blindingly white space.

I decided to lean into my identity and my conviction that, should I be admitted to the University of Toronto, I would bring my whole self—my Black, feminine, feminist, outspoken self. The same girl who a year earlier had protested outside Hamilton's city hall against disproportionate police carding in Black communities. The same girl who made a personal goal of using poetry to teach little Black girls that they are beautiful—full lips, broad nose, coily hair, deep, glimmering melanin and all.

Dr. Galloway leaned against the table and folded his arms in anticipation of my performance. His head was slightly tilted, his eyes focused on me.

Every poet has their rituals before a performance. Some artists will get to the stage and warm up the crowd with silly banter and pleasantries. Others will silently take the mic, pause and dive head-first into their first stanza. I fall somewhere in between.

I smiled at Dr. Galloway before closing my eyes and drawing a slow, deep breath. As I had done hundreds of times before a performance, I interlocked my fingers, clasping my hands on my lap and mildly flexing my thumbs. I let my shoulders relax, slowly lengthening my neck and bringing my chin upwards and opening my eyes.

I pulled the first line of my poem from my mental catalogue and set off.

My skin is like
[*beat, hands outstretched before me, fingers widened*]
Dark ebony under the blazing sun, won't you tell me that I'm
   beautiful?
[*smiling widely, brightly at Dr. Galloway*]
But don't preface it by telling me the limiting conditions of
   my beauty.
My skin is like [*beat*]
Sunday mornings, sweaty pews. Uncomfortable shifting.
   Uncomfortable silence.
As the congregation waxes and wanes to the preacher's words,
Don't tell me that I'm sinful.
Don't judge me for being religious, our white God is the only
   thing you left for us.

I was stern, unwavering and serious. Our eyes were locked.

My skin is like, poisonous repellant.
You shift uneasily in my presence on the dusk of the horizon.
On street corners turned war zones.
Don't tell me you had no hand in this.
Don't follow me sanctimoniously through store aisles.
Look straight in my eyes and realize that you've stolen my
   innocence
And I've simply come back to look for it.

Our intense gaze broke as the buzzer rang out, mildly startling Dr. Galloway and me. There were two minutes left in our interview and five stanzas left to my poem. I was mid-gesture, my arms outstretched and curled into a semicircle in preparation for the next verse, which served as a mental cue so that I wouldn't forget my lines on stage—or during this impromptu performance. My body reverberated not only with the energy of accurately recalling my lines and poetic punches months after any rehearsal, but also with the anticipation of how my poem would be received. I was terrified.

Oh my God, I thought to myself instantly. *I just told this white doctor, who holds my medical school destiny in his hands, that white people left Africans with only a white God after taking everything else from us.*

Quickly recalibrating my mental setting from slam poet to medical school hopeful, I lowered my arms back to a gently folded position on the table and nervously smiled at Dr. Galloway. My heart thrummed.

The weight of my skin intensified as the room got impossibly warmer; the walls seemed to glow, becoming whiter and more incandescent. I felt as though I might suffocate.

He rested his chin in the nook between his left index finger and thumb before slowly parting his lips in a grin.

"That . . . was incredible." He opened his arms and lifted his palms in elation.

I was stunned. I started to giggle anxiously. *What, really?* I thought, gathering my scattered nerves to promptly say thank you. I clasped my hands into fists and bent my head in gratitude, as I normally did on stage after a performance. I couldn't believe I had taken that risk, especially within the walls of a crushingly conservative institution, and it had seemingly paid off. The gap between me and this physician, who seemed to come from the opposite end of the identity spectrum to my own, was closed through the transcendent power of words.

"Wow, I wish you could finish that poem. I'm dying to know how it ends," he said, leaning back in the chair and tapping his finger on the table between us. I desperately wanted to finish the piece, believing that if the first half of the poem had impressed him, the remainder would render him speechless, as it had done with crowds in the past.

"Hopefully one day I can perform the rest for you!" I said happily, the words nearly tumbling out of my mouth.

"I would love that," replied Dr. Galloway, seemingly digesting my stanzas in pensive thought.

Executing this performance was unlike any competition I had won. The rush of accomplishment and joy was unparalleled, though there were no fingers snapping or "Mmm, go off, sis!" hurled from the audience mid-routine. As a poet, I had reached a new high.

The temperature in the room seemed too cool now, though I could feel the nervous sweat continuing to pool under my black suit. There was less than a minute left, and we spent the remaining time discussing the questions I had about attending medical school at U of T. Feeling emotionally safer in the space, I spoke about the excitement of potentially joining the Black Medical Students' Association, and how U of T was one of just a few medical schools that had a safe haven such as this for Black students. It was, among many other reasons, one of the main attractions of U of T for me, after I had spent the past few years as the only Black student in my class at Mac.

The conversation ended just as it started, with the familiar rhythm of old friends at a café and the shared hope that we might bump into each other again sometime soon.

The final buzzer rang, signalling the end of the station and prompting the interviewees to exit the room and make their way to the adjacent door on the left, where another examiner awaited. I stood up from my chair, straightening my blazer and feeling the lower muscles in my back rejoice in sweet relief. With more ease than during our introduction, I shook Dr. Galloway's hand, offered him a warm, professional smile and thanked him for his time and consideration. He thanked me for my impromptu performance and shook my hand in return.

I pivoted to walk out of the room, my twists bouncing freely with each step. I abandoned any effort at repositioning them behind my ears and let them fall around my cheeks, framing my face and features. After closing the door behind me, I looked around at the other medical school

hopefuls exiting their first station. Some appeared confident and trium-
phant, others defeated and listless. All of us collectively tried to centre
ourselves in anticipation of the next three stations, knowing that our fate
was not yet sealed. I felt a measured sense of triumph, cognizant that I
may have won the battle, but that the war continued.

Even you? echoed the words of the border officer in my head as I
studied my competition, many of whom looked like younger versions of
Dr. Galloway. Many of whom fit the traditional mould of what a doctor
looks like. None of whom looked like me.

Even me, I thought to myself.

Especially me.

Chapter Four

It had been four months since I had sat across from Dr. Galloway in the Michener Institute, performing "SKIN" and gambling with my shot at admission; each hour that drew closer to the morning of medical school acceptances seemed to stretch out toward infinity. During the days in the weeks of waiting, my mind was preoccupied by the routine tasks of a Starbucks barista: crafting expensive lattes and Americanos for skittish lawyers and investment bankers in downtown Toronto, brewing caffeinated and decaffeinated coffee on a regimented rotation, filling the dishwasher with blenders that dripped with the remnants of mocha Frappuccinos, and refilling the napkin dispenser before the final napkin was pulled out. The days passed with a welcome predictability, set to the soundtrack of repartee with our regulars—the soft-spoken banker who ordered a quad-shot Americano four times a day and the cloak-donning judge who could never remember my name but always appreciated that I never forgot his order.

I would often hope that one of my favourite customers, a pediatric neurology resident at U of T, would enter and get her usual tall latte with a warm blueberry scone. Surreptitiously, I would observe her scribbling notes in an intimidatingly dense fundamentals of neurology textbook while periodically reaching for her cup and taking a swift sip. She seemed to possess a razor-sharp focus and was unbothered by the deafening sound of coffee beans being ground and blenders turned up to the highest speed. I admired her from afar and daydreamed that I myself would one day be in her shoes, sitting in a café, studying for an exam in medical school, undisturbed by the chaos that surrounded me. I would be preparing to become a doctor, and there was no greater calling for me than that; nothing, not even the frenzy of what felt like the busiest Starbucks in the city, could distract me from this goal.

One day, I gathered enough courage to abandon my duties (refilling the syrup basins), and I asked her about what it was like to be a medical resident. We spent the next hour chatting about what had led her to medicine and, ultimately, to neurology. We enthusiastically discussed our shared love of science and the thrilling mystery of the brain—the final frontier of medicine, begging to be demystified. Over time, she would share interesting clinical anecdotes, and she'd ask how I was faring in the weeks before my fate was to be revealed. Our conversations kept my hope afloat as I drifted through the time-warped weeks that stretched between my interviews and admissions day.

As the final minutes of my shifts crawled across the clock, I would often prepare a venti half-caffeinated latte to restore my energy before taking the subway across the city to the rich suburbs of Toronto. A few evenings a week during my gap year, and eventually into my first year of medical school, I worked as a part-time private tutor for wealthy children at astonishingly expensive private elementary and high schools. As I approached the gated communities where I would assist the kids of doctors, lawyers and business executives with their homework, I wondered how differently my story would have unfolded if I had been afforded the same privileges at their age.

While I walked my students through introductory calculus and reviewed their English essays, I couldn't help but think of a few of my classmates in Health Sci who'd had the opportunity to scrub into the operating room in the eleventh grade and were published in medical research journals before they had earned their high school diplomas. I learned that many were able to gain these invaluable experiences through family connections. In contrast, I would be halfway through university before I even had an opportunity to do research, or realize just how behind I was compared to other medical school hopefuls who had inherited opportunities from their networks, while all I had inherited were the hopes and dreams of my parents.

When I started to realize that my tutoring agency rarely connected me with racialized children, who were scarce in private schools and in these illustrious gated communities, I started to piece together the puzzle of the factors that had led me to being the only Black interviewee just months prior. Privilege, often inherited, is a powerful ingredient in the recipe of success in the medical school admissions process.

As I sipped the last few grainy, cold drops of my latte while descending the stairwell of the subway, I could feel my body give in to the exhaustion of consecutive shifts and a racing, anxious mind. I would often return to my apartment in the Annex and climb the winding stairs to the third-floor landing, pausing with defeat before I nudged the creaking door open. I was greeted by the cramped, three-bedroom, one-bathroom space that housed five twenty-somethings trying to find our place in the world. My boyfriend and I shared a room, and also the understanding that our two-year love story was nearing its final chapter.

Most nights I collapsed into a pool of fatigue. Like a sponge, my hair and skin soaked up the scent of ground coffee beans, aromatizing my pillows and clinging to me despite long, extra-hot showers. Although my muscles cried out for rest, my brain obeyed the siren call of checking the online forums for pre-medical students on PreMed 101, which hosted hundreds if not thousands of medical school hopefuls across the country waiting for that fateful May morning. There was an endless stream of detailed, heart-attack-inducing stories of envied admissions and unexpected rejections from all-star candidates, spanning nearly a decade, on the forum. I had invested years analyzing their trajectory, alternating between taking a mental health hiatus from the website and scrolling through dated posts and comments until my vision blurred and my forehead throbbed with a migraine.

When I wasn't preoccupied by tutoring or mopping the café floors, I replayed every second of my U of T interview down to a microscopic level. Over time, in my sleep-deprived haze, my recollection of the details became distorted.

Did Dr. Galloway *actually* like my piece, or was that performance a fatal miscalculation of judgment? Maybe I was too brazen in my choice; I should have done a piece that was apolitical, like a love poem. *Everyone* can relate to heartbreak, I thought, and not everybody can relate to the experience of Blackness, its intricacies and uncomfortable humanity. Its constant examination of itself. Its juxtaposition to whiteness. Its ability to polarize, whether undue or justified. In my mind, I begged for another chance, a do-over, an opportunity to hide the things that made me painfully different. Painfully other.

Despite my mental acrobatics, examining my interviews from every angle, I understood that there was nothing I could do but wait for the result to be revealed. Like patients who awaited a diagnosis, I figured that it was better to know than not know; having an answer would be better than the purgatory of uncertainty.

Pebbles raced toward the front lawn, dragging me in tow down my parents' suburban driveway. Only an hour stood between me and the release of the medical school admissions, and I reasoned that there was no better place to receive the news than the comforting familiarity of my childhood home.

We paced the sidewalk that curled around the interior of the cul-de-sac, flanked by freshly cut grass and gardens tended by attentive neighbours. As a child, I would colour these same sidewalks with chalk and build snowmen that stood guard at the edge of our driveway. Eventually, we turned in to the field behind my parents' house. Pebbles, with an encyclopedic knowledge of the route, pulled me toward the alleyway beside my elementary school that brought us to the main street in our block.

The roads were still subdued at this hour, with the traffic lights cycling from red, to green, to yellow, but no traffic. We dashed to the other side of the street, which brought us to the foot of a Presbyterian church, before we made our way into the three soccer fields that lay behind it. I could let Pebbles off the leash here to freely roam through the bushes, as my mind roamed through the possibilities of how the day might unfold.

"We're going to get through this morning together, Pebs," I whispered to her, though we were completely alone in the misty fields. She looked up at me and offered a gentle, comforting lick of my wrists, sensing the disquiet that no doubt emanated from my core.

Suddenly, at 7:53 a.m., my phone vibrated with an email notification. The heading was: "Offer of Admission—Faculty of Medicine—University of Ottawa."

Pebbles sniffed the grass by my feet before zeroing her focus in on the squirrel under the bench and sprinting off to chase it up the nearest tree. Usually, I would beckon her back immediately, but I could barely feel the ground beneath me.

I began to tremble, my eyes widening in disbelief, almost afraid to blink and have the message disappear.

It had finally happened. Nineteen years after I'd declared as a toddler that I wanted to be a doctor, my dream of being admitted into medical school was happening. Though my goal was to be admitted into U of T, and that decision was still pending, I was endlessly grateful to simply have the opportunity to study medicine, especially in Canada.

Shaking, I immediately opened the email and read through the first line.

"Congratulations! I am pleased to inform you that we wish to offer you admission to the Doctor of Medicine program of studies for Fall 2016 at the Faculty of Medicine of the University of Ottawa."

Doctor, I thought to myself, tears slowly rolling down my cheeks. *I'm going to be a doctor.*

Right away, I called my mother, who was driving home from work.

"Mommy! Mommy! Where are you?" I said through tears, gripping Pebbles's leash and falling to my knees in the empty field.

"What is it? What is it? Did you get in?"

"I GOT IN! I GOT IN! TO OTTAWA! I'M GOING TO BE A DOCTOR!"

I broke down in sobs as Pebbles—satisfied with having successfully terrorized the squirrel in the tree—came running back to my side.

Immediately, my mother began to shriek with excitement and begged me to make my way home, where she would be arriving in just a few minutes. "Okay, okay, I'm running," I replied, as Pebbles jumped around me in a frenzy of excitement.

At home, my mother embraced me and cried out, "Doctor Chika Stacy Oriuwa! Doctor! My baby is going to be a doctor!"

When my admission offer from the University of Toronto, my top-choice medical school, arrived by email almost an hour later, my home swelled with the tears and pride of intergenerational progress. In true Nigerian fashion, my father began calling all our relatives, along with his friends and colleagues, eager to spread the good news of success. It was the purest joy I had ever seen him express, and it confirmed in me—despite the years of uncertainty—that his love for me was real and profound.

I immediately thought of my grandmother, thirteen years after her death, and the many tears that my mother had shed in its aftermath. I thought of her hands, soft and delicate, extending from her frail body, which lay lifeless in her bed.

I wish I could have been part of the medical team that might have saved her life, or helped to ease her passing. That was all in the future for me. But I had promised her that I would become a doctor and make her proud. As my mother held me, jumping from side to side with glee, I felt the unique warmth of my grandmother's touch envelop me as well.

A hard-won battle. A collective, ancestral effort. A dream realized.

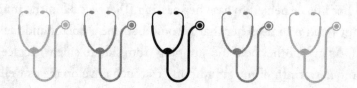

Cecil was the first patient I ever assessed on a twenty-six-hour internal medicine call shift as a third-year medical school clerk. When I arrived at his bedside at 2:30 in the morning, he was more chipper than his grim situation seemed to allow.

"My partner, Dewin, brought me in tonight because he's worried about my weight loss. I am too, but he is a bit of a worrywart," chuckled Cecil, who was visibly emaciated, with wrinkles that placed him somewhere in his mid-sixties or early seventies. Cecil seemed more interested in learning about me and my training in medicine than answering the questions I volleyed regarding his medical history and presentation to the hospital.

"Were you born here, sweetheart?" he asked genially, after I collected the long list of his medications.

"I was, in Ottawa," I stated matter-of-factly, most concerned with trying to remember the elaborate sequence of an internal medicine consultation. I started with collecting the history of his presenting illness ("What brings you to the hospital? What symptoms do you have? How long ago did they start? What makes it worse or better? Have you seen someone for something similar?" etc.). Next, I inquired into his history of preceding illnesses, medications, social situation and lifestyle, and ended with a thorough physical examination.

My body was still adjusting to having a pleasant conversation in the dead of night when my circadian rhythms had set my "sleepy hormones" in motion for rest. It seemed purely unnatural for anyone to function under these conditions, after nearly twenty hours of being awake, let alone to take responsibility for the care of someone else's life. Yet when I read through Cecil's chart, the constellation of his clinical symptoms shook any residual fatigue from my mind.

Cecil had lost an appalling amount of weight in a relatively short period of time, leaving him looking gaunter and frailer than his elderly body would have naturally allowed. He had been experiencing increasingly painful lower back discomfort that kept him up at night and nagged at him throughout the day.

"I dunno, Doc, I feel more tired than usual, I guess," he reflected, running his nimble fingers through wispy grey-white hair. A faint shake emerged when his arms were tested by gravity, a clinical condition known as a postural tremor; this could have been clinically significant, or just another byproduct of aging. I jotted my observation down as I encouraged him to continue.

"I normally love gardening and watching musicals, but now I don't have the energy to stand in the yard or go to the theatre. Maybe it's just these old bones getting more tired."

Maybe, I thought to myself. *Hopefully—but unlikely.*

"Dewin thinks I've been forgetful, too, which I've kind of noticed, but not really."

That's the paradoxical cruelty of cognitive decline: the person who experiences it almost never recognizes its full brutality—when it is painfully obvious to everyone else.

"Let's get you admitted and run some tests, Cecil," I said, as he hummed and smiled, his gaze directed off into the distance. "I'll call Dewin in the morning."

Given my patient's age, decades-long history of tanning bed use, protracted vacations to the tropics, and a remote history of treatment-responsive melanoma, I pieced his clinical symptoms together like a hor-ror-themed jigsaw puzzle.

"I think we should get a pan-CT scan," I said to my senior resident on call, as I ran through my clinical impressions and plan. He agreed, and we understood that what the findings would reveal could upend this person's life forever.

I input the order for the tests, prompting the co-sign from the senior resident. Then I dragged my weary body back to my call room as the clock neared 6:00 a.m. Even in the minutes that I was able to squeeze in a nap on call, I could never let my body melt into the unfamiliar lumpiness of a call-shift bed. The rooms were often windowless and lit at night by the glow of a computer screen or landline telephone. Even in the depths of exhaustion, I could never achieve real rest, afraid of sleeping through a critical page or code blue; I never wanted to be the clerk who showed up late to resuscitations and scrambled to be brought up to speed. I learned to rest in a semi-conscious state, tossing from side to side on an uncomfortable mattress and pulling the thin linens over my scrubs.

Some nights, I would simply lie atop the perfectly made bed, runners still snuggly tied on my feet, and rest the pager beside my head on the pillowcase. I often wondered how long the human body could endure this state, and how we as a profession allowed this to continue for decades into our career. I abandoned rest for the remainder of the early morning, and instead spent the time rehearsing and editing my presentation for rounds to the backdrop of dawn.

Only two hours and rigorous clinical questioning by my attending stood between me and the softness of my bed at home. The rest of my post-call day would pass by in an indistinguishable haze, where I somehow managed to shower, sleep, eat and prepare for the next day on the wards.

The morning after my post-call shift, when I was back in the hospital after a night of adrenaline-disrupted sleep, I pulled Cecil's chart up on the computer screen. A tiny red flag pinged beside his results, calling for my immediate attention to his radiologic findings.

The hyperechoic lesion lit up on the CT scan of his brain. It possessed the pathognomonic findings of a cerebral tumour: increased vasculature, striations and clearly circumscribed borders causing regional compression to the surrounding structures. In correlation with the clinical findings of drastic weight loss, back pain, fatigue and cognitive difficulties, it didn't take our team long to deduce what was at play. The diagnosis was as certain as it

could be without a definitive pathology report: a recurrence of his melanoma, metastasized to his brain.

I went with my attending, Dr. Hannah Grindle, to break the news to my
patient and his family. There is never an easy way to give someone a devastating diagnosis, even when following the formulaic structure provided
to medical students during small-group learning. How do you infuse hope
into a patient and their loved ones when the diagnosis is almost as grim
as it gets in medicine? I learned, through observation, to infuse hope into
uncertainty when giving the details of a result pending pathology report:
"This *could* mean a recurrence, which *may* mean it could be responsive to
treatment / we can't make any confident guesses at prognosis at this time,
but we've seen these cases go in *xyz* direction."

"*Brain tumour?*" said the patient. His shoulders slacked and his eyes widened as he gradually processed the news. We gave Cecil and Dewin a
beat to let the news sink in. Dewin took it harder, immediately weeping,
then racing to wonder what treatment options were available. Surgery?
Chemotherapy? Radiation?

"There's got to be something we can do," he pleaded, with the kind of
desperation you'd only find within the walls of a hospital or hospice home.

"We will know more once there is a biopsy available from the central
lesion," Dr. Grindle replied, referring to the primary lesion that was found on
his back, where his original cancer had surfaced years prior.

Cecil seemed to absorb the news quickly, shifting through the emotional stages to land on acceptance in a way that made me question
if this was how he truly felt. I wondered how I would have responded in
Cecil's shoes: would it have been easier to fast-forward to acceptance of
fate when presented with my own mortality, or rail against the universe for
the cruelty of life?

"We'll start with steroids to reduce the inflammation around the tumour
in his brain and hopefully alleviate some of the accompanying symptoms
from that," we explained. "Radiation may also help with the compressive

symptoms of the tumour." The rest of the immediate management plan would emerge when the pathology results returned. Dewin thanked us for the care we were providing, and Cecil assumed his natural role of adding levity to the situation.

"I'm in the best hands," said Cecil. He tossed a sweet grin to his love, who stood like a sentry by his bedside.

"I'll be checking in on you every day," I said, placing a hand over his spindly fingers. They reminded me of my grandmother in the days immediately preceding her death. The tangle of IVs from her arms, the thinned skin and violet bruises, the signs of a soul ready to shed its mortal coil. The resemblance was haunting and comforting at once.

The following morning, and every morning thereafter for the remainder of his admission on our unit, I returned to Cecil's room to complete my daily rounds and do an assessment on his interval state. Most days, his disposition matched the rays of sunshine that shone through his window facing the east side of the city.

"There's my girl!" he would exclaim as I entered, ever excited to tell me the happenings from the hospital wards the night before. It's astonishing what you can overhear as a patient or silent roamer of the ward halls. I always strove to redirect the conversation to how he was feeling, whether he was nauseous or had a headache. "Oh, I'm fine! Just get me better food and maybe I'll eat," he chuckled with a wink.

Cecil often would regale me with tales about the visitors from the night before who came to see him, and he always had a joke in his back pocket to share. Our morning banter became my favourite part of the day, like stopping by the front porch of an elderly neighbour on the way to school or work.

It didn't take long, however, for an unsettling pattern of inquiry to emerge in our daily exchanges.

"So, Doc, have they figured out yet why I'm here?" he would ask, partway through our routine conversation.

The first time it happened, I stumbled over a potential response, confused.

Had he simply misunderstood the initial discussion with Dr. Grindle and me? Or was he expecting the diagnosis to evolve during his admission?

"It's just a diet thing, right? Maybe something to do with what I was eating at home? Maybe I picked up a bug from gardening?"

Cecil wore a look of genuine curiosity and anticipation, almost as if he wondered why the process of figuring out a diagnosis was taking so long.

"Mr. Cecil, I apologize if our explanation the other day was unclear or misleading. I'm happy to explain again." I started slowly, working my way through each word with the trepidation of a medical clerk who hasn't quite mastered the art of giving a potentially terminal diagnosis. Is there ever a perfect way to tell someone that they're dying?

"Based on the radiology and symptoms that you have presented with, it appears that there has been a recurrence of your melanoma skin cancer which has, unfortunately, spread to your brain. We are awaiting the pathology reports and determining the best course of treatment for the malignancy moving forward. The radiation and steroids are being used to help reduce the severity of symptoms from the tumour in your brain."

"*Brain tumour?*" said Cecil, with the same degree of astonishment as the first time we broke the news to him with Dewin at the bedside.

"Oh God, well, that's horrible," he continued, as his breathing got slightly more laboured with the shock.

"Are you going to take it out?" he questioned. The location and size made it relatively inoperable, I explained, as his expression shuffled through fear, anxiety, disbelief and finally acceptance once more. Within an hour, he was back to his jovial position, wisecracking and painting silver linings.

When it happened again the following day, and in the remaining days of his admission, the full cruelty of his condition declared itself. Cecil's cognitive decline made him forget his diagnosis, again and again, leading to repeated delivery of the worst possible news. Some days he would chuckle. Some days he would cry. Most days he would try to find the simple joys in being alive for another day. Every day my heart would break a little more for him.

When the pathology results returned and his terminal diagnosis was confirmed, we prepared him for discharge for outpatient care and palliative treatment. On the day he was discharged, I arrived at his room with the printed summary of his visit and found Dewin standing at the bedside ready to take him home.

"Thank you for looking after me, Doc!" said Cecil, before expressing his joy at being able to return home. He didn't ask about the reason for his stay or what diagnosis he was given.

The hole in my morning when I would stop by my favourite patient's room was filled immediately by another sick patient newly admitted to the wards, a young transgender woman with pancreatitis and a complex psychiatric history. As medical students and doctors on the internal medicine wards, we learn to attach just enough to our patients to be empathetic and compassionate, yet detach quickly enough to preserve our ability to provide care to the next patient who needs us most.

But there will always be the stories that stick with me—the patients I think about on the subway ride home after work, or between sips of tea on quiet Saturday afternoons. The ones whose spirits stay behind in their rooms long after they leave.

I think of Cecil often, wondering how the rest of his story unfolded. Did he ever get to plant another gardenia or take Dewin's restored motorcycle for a final spin around the block? Did he ever lose his optimism and sense of humour? I surely hope not, and still feel his warmth when I walk past the room that housed his resilient spirit.

Chapter Five

The mid-August 2016 heat scorched the cobblestones that lined the alleyway between two lofty downtown Toronto condos, mirroring each other in their design and intimidation. A purplish-pink sky hosted the setting sun as the humidity in the air settled and started to dissipate, mercifully, giving my lungs a chance to breathe with ease. My ruby red shoulder bag, given to me by my father the morning of my interview at the University of Ottawa medical school, was swaying at my hip as I wobbled in my heels over the grooves between the stones. I held my arms out for balance and prayed not to fall.

I knew I should have worn flats, I thought to myself as I calculated my next few steps, leaning my weight onto my toes and skipping like a child playing hopscotch. I lifted the gold-dipped latch of the bag and fished for my phone in the side pocket, resting a moment to give my calves a break.

My phone blinked with the notification of a few unread messages: one a lengthy prayer from my mom, wishing me good luck this evening at the soirée for incoming Black U of T medical students, and another from my sister Chizoba, asking me to send a picture of what I'd finally decided to wear, after a long period of deliberation.

Promise I'll show you later, I texted her back, nervous of being caught mid-selfie by another Black medical student. Like in the medical school interview with Dr. Galloway just seven months prior, first impressions here were critical, and I had dreamed of this night for weeks. It would be the night I would finally meet the other Black medical students in my class—the people who I dreamed would eventually become friends turned family.

With childlike giddiness, I imagined walking into the soirée that evening and becoming fast friends with the other Black girls in my class. I dreamed of us studying for mastery exams together, rotating among the Gerstein Library beside the Medical Sciences Building, popular hipster cafés in Kensington Market, and quiet gems we had discovered while exploring the outskirts of the city on our weekends off. During study breaks, I pictured us sharing a kiki over the latest posts on The Shade Room and swapping secrets about our wash day routines or DIY deep conditioners. They would tell me, under hushed breath, that the *real tea* was strained rice water as a co-wash and a three-hour clay mask before twisting my hair into Bantu knots for a quick, cute, cost-effective style. We would have night-long study dates, committing the fundamentals of cardiac electrophysiology to memory, as our hair sat deep-conditioning under tightly tied grocery bags; we would be free from judgment and safe in the Eden of our sisterhood.

Maybe, I fantasized, we would share the stories from our undergrad that scarred us, such as when a classmate told me to "go sassy Black girl" on our anatomy professor, who refused to give us extra marks on an unfair exam. The others would groan in response, detailing moments in the preceding years when their Blackness had left them feeling othered as well. But the future was more promising, we would say, because we would have each other.

At the very least, I thought to myself before entering the first BMSA soirée, even if we didn't become the best of friends—because friendship takes more than just having similar lived experience—we could at least feel safer simply by having each other in the same space.

We would enter a room full of our non-Black classmates and share *that* knowing look, the look that says, "I can't believe there aren't more Black people here, but that's cool, because I got your back, and you got mine, if anything goes down." The look that would make our classmates think twice before saying something cringe-worthy and trite. The same look I wanted to see on the day of my interview at U of T but didn't.

I shuffled through my iPhone's home screen, looking for the details of the directions to the event, hoping that another guest would come along and lead me to the condo room like a shepherd herding lambs. When it became clear that I was on my own, and I was going to be late to the party, I mustered the strength in my calves and continued my journey, finally reaching my destination.

The condo's lobby was palatial and glimmered with large windows, majestic chandeliers and mirrors that flanked the elevator doors. As the elevator was making its descent to the ground floor, I inspected the network of bobby pins carefully tucked into my coils, ensuring that its structural integrity had withstood the journey from my new apartment in the Annex to the concrete jungle of the Bay-Bloor intersection. August heat and humidity are the Achilles heel of any Black girl's curl definition, so in the moments before such an important evening, I handled my kinks with extra care.

My hairstyling, like my outfit choice for my upcoming stethoscope ceremony, was methodical. My edges, kinky and lining the perimeter of my hairline, were left unsmoothed—the moisture in the air and the sweat I accrued on the walk from the subway to the condo would have humbled me quickly anyway. My hair was cornrowed into tight braids that lay flat against my scalp, winding from the crown of my head to my nape in an intricate circular design, letting the ends of the braids sprawl out and hang suspended over my shoulders—like magic. The delicately woven plaits bound me to ancestral spirits who, I was sure, would be smiling in elation at their daughter entering a profession where women like her were seldom seen.

Historically, cornrows date back to 3,000 BCE, first worn by Africans in the West Coast and Horn of Africa. During the trans-Atlantic slave trade, when millions of Africans were brutally kidnapped and murdered or forced onto plantations (including those from the Igbo tribe), cornrows were used by enslaved peoples as a method of communication—braids fashioned to resemble directions to freedom to escape enslavers. Over time, and into the modern era, cornrows (also known colloquially as cane rows and plaits) were given a negative connotation and unfairly seen as unprofessional or unkempt for the workplace. Some institutions have even gone as far as to ban their employees from wearing the style. En masse, this reflects the ways in which the natural beauty of Black people has been systematically denigrated, forcing Black women and children (such as me and my sisters in our childhood) to straighten, chemically relax and find alternative ways of changing their natural afro texture. The internalized anti-Blackness lingers for most of us like perfume in a poorly ventilated space; it stifles and congests.

Wearing my hair in cornrows at my first event for medical school was symbolic of the impulse I felt to usher in a new beginning for myself, one where the narrative of being the only Black person in my class would no longer follow me. One where the border officer would be chewing his words for breakfast. My cornrows were the road map to an academic space where my Blackness would be seen not as a threat but as an opportunity for inclusion and celebration.

I tapped on the touch-screen panel in the elevator as it made its swift ascent to the top floor. I checked my hair a final time in the mirror before stepping out into the hallway, where a sign with an arrow pointed toward the party room.

This is it, I thought to myself. *This is happening.*

I stood outside Party Room A, as I'd stood at the first interview door at the Michener Institute, my hands once again with an imperceptible tremor. I smoothed the wrinkles in my dress, placed my hand on the knob and pulled the door open.

"Hey! Welcome!" said Salem, a second-year Black medical student and the co-president of the BMSA. Her hair, the first thing I noticed about her, was styled in a large, curly afro, nearly twice the size of my own. It was mesmerizing and seemed to levitate; I could feel my curls bounce in solidarity.

Her curl pattern was closer to 3c/4a, a looser texture than mine on the Andre Walker Hair Typing System. I was instantly in awe of her confidence and elated at the sight of another Black girl embracing her natural hair.

She placed a handful of forks and napkins down on the table, next to the jerk chicken, coleslaw, and rice and peas that sat cooling in the centre. The scents were powerfully familiar, reminding me of family barbecues. Cupcakes and other enticing delicacies were there, ready to be feasted upon. The room was beautifully decorated, and the smell was divine, exactly what I had expected from the soirée.

"Hi! I'm Chika, one of the first-year medical students! So happy to meet you."

I had rehearsed this introduction several times in the mirror in the hours leading up to the event, miming an extended hand, not as firm as the one I used in interviews, but one that was softer and more inviting. I'd practised how I would sum up my journey to medicine thus far: "I grew up in Brampton, did Health Sci at Mac, took a gap year for performance poetry, and I'm beyond excited to be here at U of T, and especially to be a part of the BMSA."

Instead of a firm handshake, however, Salem and I shared a warm hug as she introduced herself and ushered me to the nearest table, where two men—Yusuuf and Jonathon—stood up as I approached.

"We do hugs here, fam," said Jonathon, as we shared a friendly embrace. "We're family."

I sat at the table with the boys as I peeled away the lining under a vanilla cupcake, quietly approximating how to eat it without leaving an embarrassing moustache of pink icing on my face. Jonathon and Yusuuf, whose bromance was obvious from the outset, introduced themselves as second-year medical students. They reminded me of my guy friends from high school, goofy and lighthearted.

"Chika? You must be Igbo. Kedu!" said Jonathon, using the Igbo word for "hello." I quickly learned he was a fellow Igbo descendant. He had spent his early years in Nigeria and moved to Canada as a small boy, eventually finding his way to medicine with dreams of becoming a pediatrician, before he pivoted to child and adolescent psychiatry. His speech had an unmistakable Nigerian lilt that was devilishly charming. He wore dreads that stopped just short of his shoulders and were adorned with jewels that hugged a few strands, and his stylish glasses gave him an inquisitive look. His fashion was reflective of Nigerian contemporary streetwear, a refreshingly unique coolness that created an air of mystique around him. Jonathon (whom I would later affectionately call JoJo) embodied what I would have pictured a budding psychiatrist to be like: curious and quirky, with an unmatched ability to make you feel safe and at home in any setting. His presence could soften even the most intimidating figure, and his gaze compelled you to spill your deepest secrets. I felt instantly drawn toward his brotherly warmth and energy.

Yusuuf, similarly, was a compassionate and captivating force. He was born and raised in Ontario, with roots deepened in Somalia. He was tall, with a bright smile and deep, dark, glimmering skin. Yusuuf (whom I quickly referred to as Yuzzy) had a commanding genius and conviction when he spoke that was both daring and endearing. Like Jonathon, he had long, full, natural hair, and his was thrown into a ponytail with a sprawling puff at the back. Being in a room full of Black medical students who unapologetically embraced their features was a liberating moment, one I had yearned for over the years. I felt an instant familial tie to them, like a younger sister ready to be shown the ropes of how to survive medical school—*especially* as a Black girl.

"I guess you're the first one here from your year," said Salem, as she joined Yusuuf, Jonathon and me at our table.

"I didn't see another RSVP from your class, but you know people can forget to respond to the invite and just show up anyway," she said, reassuringly.

Salem was right, there was no one else yet from my year at the soirée. I looked around the room, which was mostly empty aside from the four of us, and realized that my future Black classmates were nowhere in sight, my imaginary besties included.

"Yeah, it's the summer! Maybe they'll show up. Or maybe they're on vacation, salvaging the last few days of normalcy before we get thrown into the chaos of med school." I chuckled nervously. I was trying to convince both them and myself that I surely wouldn't be alone. Not at U of T, in a city that boasts the highest population of Black people in the country, and certainly not in 2016.

"Melin and Zeke should be on their way. They're the two other Black medical students in our year. You'll love them, too, they're mad chill!" said Jonathon, as he took a swig of his fruit punch.

I was ecstatic for them to arrive and fill the room with more Black excellence.

"Wow, so there's five of you in second year? That's amazing!" I said, filling myself with the hope that, at the very least, my class would have as many Black students, too. The numbers should only go up year after year, I reasoned, believing that the reverse would be implausible.

As we dug into more cupcakes and steadily filled our plates with heaps of rice and perfectly seared jerk chicken, I sadly learned that the number of Black students in their year was somewhat of an anomaly. In the year ahead of them, the class of third-year medical students, there was only one Black student, named Naoira.

I'd had the privilege of meeting Naoira in mid-January that year, a week after I had received an invitation to interview at U of T and happened to come across a link to the Community of Support (COS) on its webpage. Through the COS, an initiative within the faculty that was aimed at supporting historically under-represented students on their journey toward a health care profession, I was connected to Naoira for an interview preparation session. When I learned, only two weeks before my interview, that the COS also provided resources such as free MCAT prep sessions, medical school application support, conferences and research opportunities for historically marginalized high school students with an interest in health care, I was dismayed to consider the help I could have received in the years of readying myself for medical school, if only I'd known it existed. However, my disbelief was washed away by my gratitude for having the chance to pick the brain of a Black medical student and further manicure my rehearsed interview answers. I promised myself that if I got in, I would support other Black medical school hopefuls, as Naoira had supported me.

We'd met in a Starbucks and chatted over steaming lattes. I learned about Naoira's dreams of becoming a pediatrician, and she listened attentively to my answers to prospective interview questions. Her first question was a simple one: "Why do you want to be a doctor?" I wanted greatly to impress Naoira, who stood as the personification of my wildest dreams, but how does a person passionately articulate a lifetime of working toward a singular goal in under three and a half minutes, during the most critical moment of their life? After I'd responded—pivoting from stories of my childhood as a daughter of immigrant parents to how my unexpected love of writing and poetry led to a career in medicine—a young woman approached our table.

"Excuse me, I don't know you, and I didn't mean to eavesdrop, but I couldn't help but listen to your story. It moved me to tears, and I just want to let you know that you are meant to be a doctor. I really, really hope that you become one."

I sat in shock, once again straddling the line of humility and gratitude, and thanked the kind stranger as she made her way back to her seat.

"I agree with her," said Naoira, as shivers ascended my spine. "That was beautiful. It needs to be tightened a little for time, but the narrative was compelling. They will believe, I'm sure, that you truly are meant to be a doctor."

The following week, I also met with Zeke, the second-year Black medical student, and I rehearsed my "Why do you want to be a doctor?" spiel. He nodded in slow, silent approval before continuing with an onslaught of difficult ethical questions and dissections of my interests and endeavours before medicine. He was relentless in his appraisal, opting for critical feedback over commendation. I was humbled immensely and even grew slightly concerned for my performance at the real interview.

"You know I'm being harder on you than the actual interviewer for a reason," he said, with a tone reminiscent of a father or an older brother. "You are an excellent candidate, and I'm sure you'll impress them. But you're also Black, and you can't forget that we have to operate in a different gear. We need to work twice as hard, as you know. In moments like these, we need to be perfect."

Zeke and Naoira had provided me with exactly what I needed before my U of T interview: equal doses of measured tenacity and optimism, with the painful reality of being Black in medicine.

As I sat now between Jonathon and Yusuuf, seven months later, I was eager to see Naoira and Zeke again, excited to let them know that they'd been right about my chances of a successful admission.

"Naoira is the *only* one in her year?" I asked Yusuuf, with an amazed look I couldn't stifle, even if I tried.

"Yup," he responded, with a look that said *"Ain't that wild?"*

I learned that Naoira was not alone in her position as the only Black person in her class. In fact, only approximately 1 percent of U of T's incoming medical classes between the years of 2010 and 2015 identified as being from African ancestry. Though there is a dearth of data to capture the diversity (or lack thereof) in the decades preceding these studies, it was understood anecdotally that Black students matriculated through the medical school at noticeably lower rates. The fourth-year class of medicine, known colloquially as CC4 (clinical clerkship 4), had two Black medical students, which seemed like an unbelievably low number, but at least they were not *completely* alone.

The second-year medical cohort, in which there were five Black medical students, was bested in size only by the medical class of 2007, which had ten students. These two cohorts, as one might imagine, were more like family than peers, and they defined the sisterhood and brotherhood solidarity often seen in Black friendships. The kind of solidarity I craved and had anticipated that night.

As the evening went on, filled with boisterous laughter, dope music and delicious food, more people—ranging from medical students to residents to fellows and staff—filtered in. Zeke and Naoira joined, followed by the fourth-year medical students, and even alumni from the original cohort of the BMSA. Dr. Sean Wharton, a clinical pharmacist turned obesity medicine physician specialist, showed up with dreads that reached down his back and a sense of Black pride that brimmed from his lips. When he'd started the BMSA in 1999, there were only a few Black medical students within the entire faculty. He told me that watching the group blossom over the years, the family tree of Black excellence sprawling, filled his heart with pride and joy.

I had never been surrounded by this much Black beauty—varying in depth of melanin and kink of hair, sophistication and full-out badassery. After years of waiting, I had found a safe shore—Black doctors that existed beyond the imaginations of Shonda Rhimes or Bill Lawrence. Yet I continued to silently pray for another student in my class to enter the room, sit at my table and joke about how they were running on *African* or *Caribbean time.*

I lifted a forkful of rice and peas to my mouth as I quietly eyed the food table. There was enough nourishment left to feed the crowd, but it was certainly dwindling. It had been years since I'd recovered from my first bout of disordered eating, and the days when food would sit on my plate untouched were far behind me. As I strategized how to coyly return to the table for seconds, a petite woman with bouncing ringlet curls sat down at the table next to mine. After I gave my poised introduction, abandoning my attempt for another cupcake and more jerk chicken to a later moment, I shook the woman's hand and pushed my plate to the side.

"Hi there! I'm Lisa, a doctor here at the university and a member of the faculty. Pleased to meet you," she said, with a soft smile and gentle handshake. Immediately, I felt as though I was sitting with my mom at our dinner table; she had the same tranquil, protective presence. Over our conversation, I learned that Lisa, known formally as Dr. Lisa Robinson, was a pediatric nephrologist and clinician scientist at the Hospital for Sick Children and chief diversity officer within the faculty. She, like Dr. Wharton, was an alumnus from the University of Toronto Medical School, graduating in 1991, twenty-five years before I was set to start. I learned that she, like the fourth-year medical students in attendance that evening, had been one of only two Black medical students in her year. The experience, she divulged, was difficult—dealing with racial dynamics layered unfairly on top of the challenging demands of medical school. She expressed her delight in seeing the room full of Black medical trainees and commented on how things were finally starting to slowly shift in terms of demographics and progress.

"Last year was promising," she said, sensing my growing unease at the absence of other attendees from my year. "We are hopeful that your year will be similar, maybe even bigger."

"I hope so," I said, quietly willing my future classmates to cut the prank, walk through the doors and transition from figments of my imagination to reality. "I guess we'll find out at the stethoscope ceremony in a week and a half, right?" I said, looking at my watch, realizing that the evening was nearing its end.

"Yes, you're right," said Lisa, her eyes full of hope.

I felt my mood of desperation lift, in spite of myself.

Chapter Six

The Winter Garden Theatre boasted cathedral-like ceilings draped with dried beech leaves and lanterns, rows of velvet seats angled toward an illuminated stage and curtains lifted to an imposing height. On the night of my stethoscope ceremony, in late August 2016, a row of faculty physicians sat regally at centre stage, commanding respect and sending intimidation into the hearts of the incoming class of medical students at the University of Toronto. Dr. Lisa Robinson was the only Black physician in the group, reflecting the reality she had faced in medical school nearly twenty-five years prior. As I found my seat, clutching a freshly printed copy of the Hippocratic Oath, I wondered if I'd discover by the end of the night that this was something we would share.

The host of the evening, Dr. Patricia Houston, Vice Dean of the Faculty of Medicine, provided a welcome address that segued into the main event: the draping of the stethoscope onto each incoming future doc. In 2010, U of T had replaced the traditional white coat ceremony—in which new medical students were initiated by having the iconic white coat of the medical profession placed on their shoulders—with this new version. Believing that the most fundamental skill of a physician is to listen to our patients, the U of T medical school chose the stethoscope, with its bell and earpieces, as a symbolic icon. I laid the Littmann's case housing my newly purchased stethoscope, in classic black, across the hem of my Ankara skirt. I had chosen, quite intentionally, to wear an outfit made of West African lace, head to toe, on the evening that celebrated my induction into the medical career. It was an unapologetic, open embrace of my Nigerian roots in a space where Black students were admitted and trained in chronically low numbers. More nuanced, however, was the hope that another future Black classmate might see me boldly embracing my Blackness and feel the intrinsic safety that I had desired for the past several years.

My anxiety suddenly peaked, both from knowing that my name would be called in the middle of the pack of students—259 to be exact—and also in anticipation of watching each student cross the stage, finally discovering whether my future Black classmates were at another interview date, on vacation during the soirée, running late to the stethoscope ceremony, or simply didn't exist.

When the usher reached our row, we stood and made our way down the aisle, shuffling past the collapsed theatre seats, moving to the sound of names being announced and congratulatory applause. My legs trembled, threatening to give way, while my heart thumped in excitement as we approached the curtained enclave. I handed my stethoscope to the faculty member waiting by the stairs in the wings and interwove my hands in anticipation of my name being called—my sacred routine before taking any stage.

I had already earned my place; I had already won the golden ticket.

The little girl within me twirled with excitement, clutching her teddy-bear patients.

This is it, I thought to myself. *This is happening.*

The stage lights were powerful, nearly blinding me as I investigated the crowd, unable to see my friends or family. The doctors, dressed impeccably, seemed more frightening up close, almost larger than life. I caught Lisa's eye, and she smiled proudly from the middle of the row. I wondered if she was doing the same silent calculations, questioning if we would be the only two Black people on stage that night. There was still a good chunk of the alphabet after me. There was still hope.

"Chika Stacy Oriuwa," announced Dr. Houston, slowly enunciating each syllable, executing the phonetic pronunciation that was written at the bottom of the card. I breathed a sigh of relief as I walked toward Dr. Houston and the physician who held my stethoscope.

There was an instantaneous roar that was unmistakably my loved ones. It carried the same energy as the cheers we make during any celebration, when we shamelessly proclaim "Igbo Kwenu" (meaning "Igbo Unity"), followed by an uproarious "Eyy!" A celebratory Biafran can be heard from a mile away.

I walked proudly across the stage, carefully taking each step in the same heels I'd worn for my graduation from McMaster University. I vividly remembered the desire to shrink in shame before ascending the stage to get my honours degree after failing to gain admission into medical school while most of my class was preparing to matriculate through that fall. I stood in those heels heartbroken, eager to avoid overhearing conversations about white coat ceremonies and summer vacations, while I was readying myself to rewrite the MCAT and work at Starbucks. The feeling of failure had been overwhelming, but my determination to enter medicine had been just as strong.

I bowed gently before a tall male physician who reached behind my Marley twists and placed the stethoscope onto my shoulders. Then I turned to beam a proud smile into the crowd and posed for an official photo. I waved in the direction of the loudest cheers, savouring this moment as a historic win for not only me, but also my mom and my family. As I made my way back to the crowd, following another usher on the opposite wing of the stage, I ducked back to my seat and fixed the stethoscope around my neck.

The rows behind me slowly filtered down the aisles as the remaining surnames in the alphabet were announced. I fiddled nervously with the diaphragm of the stethoscope, running my fingers over the rubber rim and closely studying the flow of my classmates.

Clearly, there won't be five, I thought to myself, realizing the statistical improbability given how late we were in the alphabet, *but maybe there will at least be another one.* When the deck of cards clutched in Dr. Houston's hands thinned down to only a few, and the last incoming first-year student crossed the stage, my heart sank with an undeniable truth.

In the matriculating class of 2020 at the University of Toronto, Faculty of Medicine, the largest and most prestigious medical school in the country, in one of the most ethnically diverse cities in the world, I was the only Black student.

One of 259. In 2016.

As I inched closer to my dream of earning a medical degree, my hopes of doing so with the inherent solidarity of fellow Black classmates (and the imagined sisterhood) crashed under the weight of crippling disillusionment.

Later that week, when Lisa reached out to me to express her shock and offer support, I realized that there weren't any clear explanations.

"I'm sorry," she said.

I was, too.

"Easier?" I replied to a fellow classmate, as we waited in line to receive our coveted teal-coloured medical school backpacks during orientation week. I wanted to ensure I had heard them correctly before weighing my indignation against a measured response on my mental scale. I've learned that even when my upset is justified, I still need to repackage it in a way that is palatable for the receiver—taking the ingredients of my rage and baking them into a pie of Black respectability.

"Yeah, like, did they make it easier for you to get in? Did they lower the criteria for you or something? Like, is there a separate stream for

Black students since there aren't that many of you here, I don't think?" they replied, confident in their assessment of the demographics of the class, oblivious to the pain and insecurity they were coaxing within me.

"No" was all I managed to say, as the anger quietly seethed. "I applied through the general stream," I continued through a strained smile. "I had to get the same MCAT scores and high GPA cut-off as everyone else, write the same essays and go through the same interviews. Nothing was made easier for me." The reply was quickly accepted before the conversation shifted to the specifications of our backpacks and when we would get our locker combinations for the anatomy labs. It was clear that the moment was inconsequential for them. However, their question settled into the corner of my mind, making itself at home, leaving the door open and the lights on so that self-doubt could lead the way.

Even you? echoed through the halls of the Medical Sciences Building, the main hub for medical students' education on U of T's central campus. The words grew louder and louder as they neared, like a freight train careening toward my composure.

I returned home that evening and crawled into my bed, atop a mess of throws and pillows, and felt a rush of anxiety course through me. I felt foolish for convincing myself that no one would notice I was the only Black girl, and that if they did, it wouldn't be fodder for critique of my merits. *What else do they think?* I asked myself. If they presumed the path into medicine was easier for me, did they think I didn't deserve to be there? Maybe they weren't the only ones who saw me, an ink blot in the middle of a historic painting, and wondered how and why I'd managed to finesse my way into the school.

Maybe they thought I wasn't as intelligent, that I didn't have the chops to compete against the best and the brightest. I wish I could have shown them my transcript from undergrad, my MCAT scores and my autobiographical sketch for U of T. I wish I could have told them that my grades were hard-won, and that I'd never had anything handed to me in my life.

But I couldn't do that. I couldn't walk back up to that classmate with a stack of my credentials to prove that I was worthy of the spot, that I hadn't taken it away from someone who was more deserving, that there was no easier path carved for me.

I deserve to be here, I thought, equal parts trying to convince them and myself.

I determined that, instead, I would be the best medical student I could be and get the best grades I could muster. The numbers wouldn't lie, and I would prove that I deserved to train at one of the best medical institutions in Canada.

Even if it killed me.

Leaning against a coffee table in the middle of the student centre, I placed my backpack on the floor, giving my shoulders respite. As I massaged the knots in my neck, worsened by a night of sub-optimal sleep, I waved to my friend Nayantara, whom I knew from undergrad. She was a year below me in Health Sci, yet our friendship grew when we were both Welcome Week reps at the start of my second year at Mac. A steadfast pediatrics resident hopeful, she was sunshine in human form and a familiar comfort in the unknown sea of med students. We chatted about our excitement for the camping trip, supposedly the most exciting part of U of T's orientation week (O-week), and how we loved the powerful feminine energy in the class. I wanted greatly to tell her about the question posed to me a couple of days prior and ask her whether she had noticed that I was the only Black incoming first-year.

But I didn't. I was worried that someone might overhear me, and I didn't want to rain on our feminist parade. It was a position I was used to: Black women become accustomed to repressing discourse on racism in predominantly white female spaces and on feminism in predominantly Black male spaces. Rarely is there an intersecting space where we feel comfortable to discuss both. Rarely is our humanity fully explored without reservation.

I was thankful, at the very least, to have a few friends and acquaintances I knew from Mac. I noticed quickly that distinct social groups were already beginning to form, some drawn together by what appeared to be cultural ties. It made sense to me that other minority groups (especially those historically marginalized) would find comfort and solidarity among those with whom they identified—something I also would have sought if the opportunity had presented itself. Instead, I knew I had to push myself past the awkwardness of meeting new people, but do so while Black and ostensibly different.

"I'll catch up with you later, Cheeks!" said Nayantara, before she was pulled into a nearby conversation with another set of girlfriends. The silence of my solitude was then broken by the chatter of a small group of male medical students a stone's throw away.

"You know, there are more women than men in this class. Like, 60 percent or something," said one of my classmates as another rolled his eyes.

"It's like they're discriminating against male applicants, trying to make it more diverse or whatever. It's disgusting, like reverse sexism," he concluded, as the other men nodded in agreement. I immediately pivoted and gathered my belongings to return to the main group, in shock.

Efforts to increase the number of female doctors have been long standing in Canadian medical institutions, a hard-fought battle that invariably improved patient care over time. Still, it was clear in that moment that there were those who resisted change and felt that a sacred male space was being encroached upon. I wondered if they would have felt the same if more Indigenous, Latinx or Black students were admitted; I wondered if their tempers would have flared then as well.

It did not take me very long to find out.

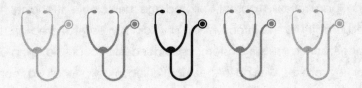

The neurological examination is one of the most comprehensive physical exams that we as physicians conduct with our patients. It is one that, as a first-year resident doctor and aspiring neuropsychiatrist, I still strove in earnest to master during my four-week block in consultation neurology. Through a series of quick manoeuvres assessing cranial nerves, movement, balance, coordination, strength and reflexes, the exam provides invaluable insight into the functioning of the central (brain/spinal cord) and peripheral nervous systems. A perfectly angled tap on the knee with a reflex hammer should elicit the patellar reflex, sending the lower leg kicking out in a swift upward arc. A pinprick on any of the extremities should elicit a pain-withdrawal response, suggesting that the nerves carrying painful stimuli back to the brain are in working order. A light shone in the patient's eyes, swung back and forth between each eye, should provoke pupillary constriction (shrinking of the pupil), suggesting appropriate functioning of the brainstem—the most primitive part of our brain that keeps us alive.

Maxine's eyes, when exposed to the bright yellow light shone from our penlight, did not constrict; it remained fixed at exactly four millimetres. When our consult-neurology team irrigated fifty millilitres of cold water into her external ear canals, her pupils failed to deviate toward either side and elicit the caloric reflex. Upon stroking the right corneum (the transparent structural barrier of the eye) with a cotton swab, there was no blinking or tearing of the eye nor consensual blinking in the opposite eye. Further, no facial movement was provoked in response to a painful stimulus applied by our team.

The residents watched from the bedside as the staff physicians continued the neurological examination. Maxine's family stood outside the door of her room in the intensive care unit, clinging to hope.

"The gag reflex is absent," stated the neurology attending, under hushed breath, to the intensivist. All physicians present shared an understanding that Maxine's brainstem, as evidenced through the failed elicitation of key reflexes, was no longer functioning in a way that was compatible with life. These critical diagnostics, in tandem with the patient being irreversibly comatose, pointed toward a grim diagnosis of brain death. The outstanding feature needed to confirm the diagnosis was an established proximate cause, which was supported by Maxine's neurological imaging. Heartbreakingly, in her case, it was a hypoxic-ischemic brain injury (tissue death due to a lack of oxygen) secondary to severe complications from COVID-19 infection. She had been admitted to the ICU for almost two months battling the disease, with her family waiting in the wings, praying for a miracle. Unfortunately, that miracle would never come.

Maxine's eyes remained fixed toward the ceiling as tubes and wires roped around her. Get-well-soon cards were scattered across her bedside table, and bouquets of sun-deprived lilies were wilting in the corner. Rosary beads were draped over a nearby Bible, untouched by Maxine since they were blessed by the priest and laid at the bedside by her sister. A small teddy bear with a locket was perched on the nightstand, seemingly observing the final hours of Maxine's life. The beeping of her vital signs monitor was punctuated by weeping from across the unit, ushering me back to when I was just ten years old at my grandmother's bedside. It was the guttural sound of a broken heart emerging from deep within one's core, a sound I had only ever heard, before entering medicine, in the aftermath of my grandmother's death. In my days as a doctor coursing my way through residency training, I would hear that uniquely arresting sound more and more often.

A closer murmur of muffled sobbing penetrated the glass doors of Maxine's room, coming from just outside, where her family stood, holding one another. They had been urgently called to the hospital to say their final goodbyes, as Maxine's clinical status had become unstable and the determination of brain death was imminent.

The sobs gave way to wailing, coming from Maxine's children—her eight-year-old son and thirteen-year-old daughter. Their father hugged them tightly, holding a composure and bravery that no parent wants to possess—but must, for their children. Maxine's loved ones, like many of us, couldn't comprehend how some people managed to contract the virus and rebound relatively quickly, while others went on to develop severe, life-threatening disease or lifelong complications. I bristled at the cruelty of their final goodbye with their mother, whom they had rarely seen in the prior two months due to visitor restrictions in place at the height of the pandemic. No child should have to witness a parent in that state; no person should be left with that memory.

The neurology attending placed the syringe used for irrigation back onto the procedural tray and turned toward our group for further discussion. The criteria for brain death had been met, and the family would be informed. The determination of when to withdraw care would ensue. We, the residents, would be excused from the room as Maxine's family was told of the results of the examination—one that meant their mother, wife, sister and friend would not be returning home. Tragically, the delivery of this worst possible news was a scene that played out repeatedly, like a broken record, during the pandemic.

Paola, the senior neurology resident, and I stood by the nursing station as Maxine's loved ones were invited into the room. Once the news was broken, the staff physicians excused themselves and left Maxine with her family to say their parting words. The portrait of palpable grief is etched forever into my mind: her children on either side of her bed, holding her hands while they wept, their father kissing her forehead as tears streamed down his face. A once vibrant life extinguished. Another family devastated by the coronavirus, stitching another scrap to the patchwork of sorrow within the halls of the intensive care unit.

When I arrived home that night, I sat for nearly an hour in my parked car in the darkness. The glowing icons of a near-empty gas tank, speedometer and timestamp dimly illuminated the space around me. The gentle hum of nearby cicadas was harmonized by the pitter-patter of neighbour-hood critters coming alive after sunset. I turned off the engine and let Taylor Swift's *Folklore* steer me through the night.

"Are you coming inside?" texted Dale, my partner, whose thoughtfully cooked meal was slowly going cold.

"Soon," I replied. He offered to bring out a plate, but I didn't have an appetite.

The image of Maxine's lifeless body, with the relics of her life surrounding her, haunted me as I sat unmoving in my car. My body felt heavy with the weight of the day, my legs felt leaden, my mind was stalled. I badly wanted to go inside, be embraced in Dale's warmth and scarf down a homemade meal. I wanted a hot shower, with candles, and a facial mask—but these things seemed indulgent, almost selfish, in the wake of what I had witnessed that day. Instead, I wished to be completely alone with my thoughts, away from the world, in a moment of silence for Maxine. I held vigil in my car, let further text messages and notifications go unanswered, as I stared into the twinkling night sky and wondered how many souls had found their new home in the stars.

Usually, in moments like these, I would reach for a journal and pour my heart onto the page. I always kept a small pocketbook in my purse, so I pulled it out and placed the ballpoint to the lined sheet.

But my hand wouldn't move.

The sheet stared blankly back at me, my mind toiling with the questions that doctors, scientists and philosophers couldn't answer with certainty.

Why is there such suffering in life, and why is it doled out unevenly? Where do we go when this life ends? Is there anything after? When does the soul leave the body?

I wondered if Maxine's soul was still present in the room when her children cried out for her. I pondered if it remained until life-sustaining care was with-drawn, or if it was gone the moment the brainstem ceased to function. When, I wondered, does someone truly die? Is it when the last breath is released from the lungs—or when the last person who held our memory perishes?

I said a quiet prayer for Maxine's family, hoping that, though the pain of her loss would be imprinted for an eternity, they would somehow arrive at a place of peace and acceptance.

Realizing I would have only a few hours of rest, I finally decided to retire inside. I gathered my belongings, stuffing my stethoscope into my purse, and swung my badge around my neck. Pausing for a moment outside my back door, my eye caught the glimmer of a glowing neon heart on my neighbour's windowsill—a popular show of gratitude for frontline workers during the pandemic. The term "health care hero" was similarly popularized during this time, as doctors and other staff were recognized as icons of bravery.

However, the metaphorical cape of a health care hero seemed ill-suited and impossibly heavy on me, when I simply felt like a human who was also lost in the complexities of our collective new normal. I, too, was scared and uncertain. I was fallible, and struggled to shake the emotions from one case as I pushed through to the next. I carried the loss of my patients with me through the doors of the hospital, into the parking lot, and all the way to the corridors of my home.

When I finally made it inside, Dale was asleep on the couch, sports highlights playing on the television. I hung my keys, took a few bites of my cold dinner and headed to the shower.

The remnants of the day would be washed clean, and the halls of the hospital would beckon me forward in the morning.

Chapter Seven

I spotted Melin—one of the second-year medical students in the BMSA, an orientation-week coordinator and co-president of the class of 2019—chatting with another incoming first-year student on the opposite side of the dance floor in The Ballroom night club. Pulsing multicoloured lights shone from the ceiling, cutting through the dark atmosphere of the club and painting our faces in streams of blue, green and gold. There was an ocean of first-years between us, swaying to the tunes by Orbital Groove, a band made up of U of T medical students. Melin and I were the only Black women in the room, and she was the first BMSA member I had seen since the painful revelation at the stethoscope ceremony. I drafted a strategy of how to efficiently manoeuvre through the crowd to catch her attention and pull her aside to chat; I sought her presence like water in a desert.

A collective inebriation loosened whatever residual inhibitions remained among my classmates as we bounced to the sound of "Closer" by The Chainsmokers, the unofficial song of O-week. As the band took a break to grab drinks and socialize, the DJ took over the mic and started playing more popular tunes, including my favourite genre, hip hop. I lost sight of Melin, who was busy in her role of ensuring the first-years were having a good time while still behaving like responsible adults representing the faculty.

I resolved to find her later and instead joined my first real friend in medical school, Victoria, whom I called Vic, on the dance floor.

Vic was a striking, tall, blue-eyed girl with dusty blond hair and a warm disposition. Her sophistication and intelligence were clear from the start; it wouldn't take me long to learn that she was one of those whip-smart girls who never really had to study for anything yet managed to always ace an exam. We had met during the orientation camping trip in the field behind the Hart House Farm, both suffocated by the crowd of intoxicated first-years and tired of the blaring music ("Closer" had been played nearly ten times a day at that point). She had noticed me standing uncomfortably, still trying to figure out how to blend into a friend group, and introduced herself with her signature tight hug. Our friendship was instantaneous; we shared a love for outspoken feminism, discussing politics, mental health, exploring tough topics like sexuality, racism and vulnerability, and dissecting our list of favourite authors and orators. Vic would not only become my first friend in medical school, listening to me cry about a recent failed relationship and the current predicament with my isolating identity, but also become my closest ally and fiercest protector in med school.

In true Toronto fashion, Drake boomed from the speakers flanking the stage as Vic and I bopped gleefully to the soca-pop fusion of "One Dance." As the DJ blended the end of the song with the start of another popular rap single, I momentarily abandoned any discomfort and rapped the lyrics along with the rest of my class. While I sang out every word, with my hand in the air punctuating the beats, I slowly realized that the upcoming chorus had an unmistakable N-word sandwiched into the middle, as most rap songs do. I kept dancing along, but quietly observed whether my classmates would be brazen enough to bellow out a racial epithet (albeit ending in an *a* and not the hard *er*) in the presence of Melin and me.

Sure enough, while most people didn't, there were a few who did—and did so loudly. I chuckled, feeling once again paradoxically invisible yet painfully conspicuous at the same time. I looked around for Melin, who was no longer in the room, and wished I had even one other Black classmate with whom I could share that glare that silently said "Oh hell, no, they didn't" with a raised eyebrow, and a smirk that responded "Mm-hmm, girl. They did."

I tapped on Vic's shoulder and motioned that I was going to head toward the bathroom, taking the opportunity for stillness amidst the chaos. The weight of code-switching, a practice whereby someone alters their speech, dress and behaviour to optimize the comfort of the domi-nant group, was beginning to weigh on me. Though I had subconsciously code-switched throughout university, abandoning my Brampton slang and occasional Naija (Nigerian) pidgin for my most eloquent English, the toll of suppressing my natural disposition became apparent only when I expected there to be someone in the space with whom I could share it. Being the only member of the BMSA in my year, I knew I needed to lean into the familial bond I could find in the upper-year classes; within this space, around Jonathon or Salem, I could relax into a Nigerian lilt with ease and reference a topic that gripped the Black zeitgeist without explanation. I knew I needed to have a space where I didn't need to code-switch. I needed someone who would just *get it*.

I knew I needed to find Melin.

I left the bathroom and walked past the dance floor toward a cocktail table, where I pulled out my phone and texted my sisters that I wished they were here. Though I had the friendship of Vic, I still felt deeply alone watching the groups of friends form around me.

Suddenly, I felt a hand on the crest of my shoulder, and I whisked around to see Melin. Her hair was styled into Senegalese twists down to her waist, mirroring my similarly fashioned kinky, ginger-coloured Marley twists. She stood a couple of inches above me, tall, with a deep, flawless brown complexion and perfect posture. I was instantly awestruck and relieved to be by her side.

"Oh my God! Hi! I'm Chika! I've been meaning to track you down all night!" I said, feeling the words start to choke in my throat while I leaned in for a hug. I felt compelled to immediately ask her if she had noticed that I was the only one, if the word had spread to the upper years, if there was something that could be done. More than anything, I just wanted her to tell me it would be okay.

"Same! I'm Melin. Sorry I missed the BMSA soirée. I was busy planning O-week with the team. I've wanted to take a moment to chat with you since I saw you at the stethoscope ceremony," she replied, her words and facial expression communicating *I know. I've noticed. We all did.*

Against the backdrop of blaring house music, and eventually the instrumental of Orbital Groove, Melin and I began to lay the foundation of our budding sisterhood. I learned that she had been class co-president since the first year of medical school, and that she was a more mature medical student, having had a career in public health before going into medicine. She was destined to be an OB/GYN, a goal that I shared with her at the infancy of my journey; standing before her felt like standing in front of a mirror into the future. Melin embodied fierceness; she was bold, confident and oozed sophistication, everything I wanted to be as a senior medical student and eventual physician.

We gushed about our similar hairstyles, and the ease of protective styles year-round, before joking about how we were itching to take the braids out immediately after styled to see how long our hair had grown, a common Black girl affliction. Our conversation started off light, before the reality of my plight demanded discussion.

"I can't believe it," she lamented. "I'm sorry that you're the only one in your year. We were all hopeful that with our class having five, you would at least have two or more. It's shocking," she concluded, as I sombrely gazed onto the dance floor. I wished in that moment that I'd been admitted a year sooner, right out of Health Sci, so that I could have been in their class. I would have been the sixth BMSA member. I would have been home.

Melin promised that the second-year Black medical students would welcome me into the fold, and that although I was alone in my year, I would never *truly* be alone, because I would have them. The BMSA organized many community events throughout the year and would also have frequent family dinners and study dates; I wouldn't be left behind, she promised. I was reassured that I could message them day or night, and whenever anything happened (which we understood would be an inevitable racially insensitive comment, at the least), they would be there for me to vent, cry and debrief. We discussed the distinctive pressures that Black people, especially Black women, face within medicine—how we are held to a different standard, how we need to perform at a higher level just to be seen as adequate. Her words provided validation of what I already knew was at play within the illustrious walls of medicine, and reaffirmed my determination to bring excellence (and *only* excellence) to the table.

It was harder for us, we lamented, and we needed one another to tough through it.

I saved her number in my phone, while she promised to check in on me when the crushing pressures of second year gave her a moment to breathe. I knew that though the upper-year BMSA students hoped to be there for me, our worlds would rarely collide on the day-to-day; they were still learning under the old four-block curriculum, while my year was the first cohort to learn under the novel "Foundations" curriculum. The result of this shift, dividing our years and our training styles, meant that our schedules were vastly different; my cohort would be doing exams every two weeks, a much more intense and frequent style of examination. U of T Medicine was also divided into academies, akin to a Hogwarts-style division of students, which allocated us to specific training hospitals and teaching sites—further widening the chasm between me and the upper years.

"I can only imagine how hard it is, but I'll be seeing you soon, promise. Stay strong, sis," she said, before sharing a parting hug and goodbye.

I turned back to the dance floor, my body and mind begging to go home to the comfort of my bed. I felt momentarily restored by my conversation with Melin, but I still couldn't shake the fear that had settled just beneath the surface.

Excellence, I thought to myself. *I have to be excellent.*

No room for error.

Chapter Eight

The barista placed my venti mint tea with a splash of almond milk onto the speckled marble counter before zipping around to grab my warmed pumpkin scone. "Thanks!" I offered, with the kind of vivacity that is hard to conjure in the early hours of the dawn but can make a small difference in the humdrum days of a barista.

The morning rush of pre-caffeinated physicians and medical students pulsed through the café, each of them eager to grab their routine beverages before rounds, surgery and clinical teaching at the nearby hospital. It was my third week of medical school classes, a crisp Wednesday morning in September when all first-year students had case-based learning sessions (CBLs) at their respective academies. Such sessions were meant to consolidate our learning through application-based questions and clinical situations, taken up discussion-style with a small group of peers and a staff physician assigned as our preceptor. At our first, intimidating CBL session, we'd learned that each query needed to be not only answered in advance of our seminar but well researched, with academic sources ready to be cited when we were quizzed by the tutor. The pressure to impress our preceptor was rivalled only by our fear of embarrassment should we not come prepared with the most comprehensive answers.

We were in the middle of our first block, Introduction to Medicine—a grab bag of medical topics that served to lay the foundation of our first year of medical training. We had just finished a week on medical genetics, embryology and the origins of cancer, followed by a week on acute dermatological presentations. That morning, the CBL questions examined skin cancers and burns, how they present and how they are treated. I swam in the tsunami of medical information with enthusiasm, ready to soak it all in.

"Hey, guys," I said to my classmates as I rested my mint tea on the communal table and scanned the room for a free chair. There was one spot left near the end of the table, beside where our preceptor would eventually sit. I tucked into the available seat and pulled out my MacBook, and soon I was perusing the Word document housing my CBL case study and answers, addended with potential queries I could pose to my group and preceptor. The ever-ready keener, fresh with the reminder that I had something to prove—to them and to myself.

Our group—roughly nine first-year medical students—broke into small talk as we awaited the arrival of our staff physician. We briefly exchanged ideas about potential answers and discussed the already heightened intensity of medical school. The new Foundations curriculum was structured under the premise that material frequently examined would be better consolidated into the minds of medical learners, as opposed to being tested every few months in hefty blocks. We were taught medical topics in modules with weekly online quizzes (leading to many suspenseful Sunday evenings spent flipping through our notes and texting our friends before submission) and mastery exams that occurred roughly every two to three weeks. These exams were about ninety minutes, forty or so questions, and were taken by all 259 students in person in the Medical Sciences Building (MSB); one could nearly smell the anxiety that wafted through the room on the mornings of these tests. Our medical school, though pass-fail, had a minimum pass rate of 70 percent, and students were allowed to fall below this percentage only a few times before they would need to repeat an entire section, spanning a couple of months. Notably, only a couple of sections could be repeated before the student was flagged for remediation and faced being placed on mandatory leave or repeating the entire year. The result of this structure was what felt like non-stop exams and relentless studying, with only a few days of rest every couple of weeks, lest we risk failure—and failure, as Type A U of T med students, would be our undoing.

Feeling the pressure to prove that I had merited my spot in medical school, I placed an expectation upon myself that I would score at least 90 percent on each exam. Though I wasn't one to share my grades, I wanted the confidence that would come from knowing that I could walk into a room and prove I belonged, *if* necessary.

I revised the burns module quickly as our staff physician entered and the side conversations fell into a hush. She sat and straightened her well-worn white coat and freshly pressed pencil skirt, which stopped short of her knees.

"Let's get started." Her voice boomed. "Would someone like to volunteer to read the first clinical anecdote?"

A hand shot up in my periphery, followed by an eager voice that animated the first sentence of our clinical scenario. "Keith, a thirty-three-year-old male with an unremarkable past medical history, presents to the emergency department following a firepit accident . . ."

As we posited our preliminary thoughts, readying ourselves for the first question in the case study, she interjected with her own queries, which caught us off guard and tested our real understanding of the material. My heart thrummed in my chest, and I was equal parts fearful of being called upon and giving the wrong answer and staying silent and looking unknowledgeable or meek.

As the hour raced by, with each student periodically stating their responses to questions and seeking clarification on the material, I studied the criteria for identifying the stages of burns in a patient presenting to the emergency department. The lecturer from the week before had used textbook photos of fair-skinned patients with different degrees of burns and clinical points as to how we could quickly spot them. Immediately, I wondered why these photos, and all the pictures used in the preceding weeks, were only of fair-skinned patients. *How*, I thought to myself, *would someone like me or my family members with darker skin be identified?*

When we were through approximately two thirds of the case, I raised my hand during an opportune break in discussion.

"In question five, we talk about how to appropriately identify a second-degree burn on our patients, but I noticed that the picture provided in the lecture material shows it only on a fair-skinned patient," I stated. It was obvious where my question was headed. "How would you go about applying these criteria to a Black patient, or really any patient who has darker skin?"

The other students fell silent and looked toward the staff physician, who puzzled over my question, twirling her hospital lanyard pensively. I wondered if my classmates shared my concern, because they surely would be responsible for taking care of non-white patients, too, especially in downtown Toronto.

Our staff physician looked up at me with a raised eyebrow and chuckled. "Well, that's your problem, not mine."

I instantly took a small gasp, my jaw slacking in response.

There is a moment, seconds into encountering blatant racial insensitivity, that's characterized by bewilderment and a quick assessment of the situation. It's like being the victim of an armed robbery when you're defenceless. Do you fight, fly, or freeze?

I froze, confused by the dismissal of my question, which seemed not only valid but critical to our learning. I looked around at my classmates, whose eyes also widened in disbelief before they turned away to their computers.

"I'm just joking, I'm just joking," said the staff physician, recognizing the cascade of discomfort that had washed over the room. "But really, I don't know. I suggest you look it up and let us know in the next class."

I nodded in agreement, chuckling quietly as my skin became hot to the touch, broiling like a coal held in an inferno of rage. The corners of my mouth were pinned to the apples of my cheeks in a forced smile. I was fully aware that I was an infant in the life cycle of my medical career, offended by a Goliath in the medical community; I dared not provoke an issue, only three weeks into medical school.

I thanked the physician for her response and turned my head toward my laptop screen for the remainder of the session, letting the discussion around me fade into a detached murmur. Beneath my stoic repose, I felt dejected, embarrassed and foolish for even asking the question in the first place. Her words found a welcoming home next to "Did they make it easier for you to get in?" and "Even *you*?"

Your problem, I thought, as the rest of the group continued with the remaining questions. *What does she mean by that? Would I be the only person taking care of Black patients? Or if I were a Black patient, would it be my responsibility to navigate my own care in an emergency?* I felt a knot settle into the grooves of my throat.

It was just a joke, I thought, desperately, to calm myself as the session drew to a close. I packed my belongings while the others broke into conversations and dispersed from the room, without mentioning the painful interaction that had occurred mere moments ago. The silence from my other classmates made me wonder if they, like me, were deeply uncomfortable in confronting a staff physician at the start of medical school, or whether they had overlooked her reply as a simple quip, a funny joke.

Maybe I was taking things too seriously.

I felt the angry heat dissipate from my core as I bathed my mind in reassurance.

It was just a joke. Try not to be too sensitive.

Still, embers of doubt remained.

▼

The glass walls of the medical student lounge in MSB stretched from the stippled, white-tiled floors up to the outdated ceilings, curling along the corners that elbowed into the main hallway. A mural, painted by medical students of yore, graced the back wall, with caricatured clerks lingering on campus in scrubs and stethoscopes; they seemed happier than most of the clerks I had seen in real life: demoralized, drained by twenty-six-hour call shifts, and wearing a look of defeat. Though the first two years of medical school would be marred by constant studying punctuated with biweekly exams, I was not in a rush to start clerkship, which was touted as the hardest part of medical school.

I studied the mural as I stood at the centre island, my laptop perched open and showing the notes for that morning's mandatory in-person lectures, as a steady flow of first-year students trickled in in droves. *How will I ever learn enough in the next two years to become a proficient clerk like those depicted in the mural?* The responsibility of caring for patients as a senior medical student felt like a lofty goal, achieved only through fervent studying, asking the right questions and seeking the right answers.

After the exchange with the staff physician earlier that week, I had investigated the ways in which dermatologic conditions presented on darker skin, forcing my mind to skip over her insensitivity and instead focus on what would make me the best possible doctor. I was satisfied with what I had started to learn independently online, and I reminded myself to bring it up at the following CBL session and fill the gap in our collective knowledge. I still struggled, however, with the pattern I was noticing as the days progressed and medical topics shifted: fair-skinned patients were often the default in our learning, and there was a scarcity of Black professors teaching us the material. What impact, I pondered, would this have on how we, as the next generation of physicians, would provide care?

The smacking of billiard balls, exploding in opposite directions by the kinetic force of the cue ball, startled me from my contemplations as another student cheered in victory at his lucky shot. I pulled my pink noise-cancelling headphones from the bottom of my backpack, plugged them into my iPhone and played Chance the Rapper's album *Coloring Book*, while I narrowed my focus back to the lecture PowerPoint on the screen. By the time I got to "Blessings," knee-deep in the sweet vocal serenade of Jamila Woods, silently mouthing the words as Chance rapped through the hook, I'd noticed another student sitting on the opposite side of the island. I grinned cordially at him, while he wrestled a thermos from his teal bag and waved in my direction.

I noticed his name embroidered on the side of his hoodie.

Pilot Adam Shehata.

The conversation-starter seemed obvious, tempting me away from my notes.

"You were a pilot before medical school?" I asked as I pulled off my headphones, my interest piqued by the potential backstory.

Adam chuckled humbly, sharing that he had attended Osgoode Hall Law School prior to starting at U of T med, and he was a pilot and aviation instructor before he became a lawyer.

"Pilot, lawyer *and* now doctor?" I laughed. It was hard to believe that he had the stamina to survive all those years of school, let alone embark on a medical journey that would span at least another six or seven years.

"Yup! And father. My daughter is four years old," he said, showing me a precious photo of his daughter in pigtails. I melted at the sight, and we went on to share how we had been finding the first few weeks of medical school.

At this point, beyond a few trusted friends in the BMSA and mentors in the faculty, I had disclosed my concerns about being the only Black medical student only to Vic, who shared my surprise and disappointment. No other student had yet ventured into the waters of that discussion, though I had felt a growing urge to voice my concerns at the top of my lungs, cutting through the silence. Each time I wanted to tell a fellow first-year and unburden myself of the discomfort and frustration, I pulled back out of fear of being seen as someone creating racial tension, especially within the conservative halls of medicine. The sheen of my "unapologetically Black" armour was starting to dull as I crawled beneath my melanated skin looking for a way out.

Sitting across from Adam, however, I felt an instinctive emotional safety in his presence; maybe it was his legal background guiding me to the belief that raising a semi-political issue, such as classroom demographics, would be welcome. I decided to take my chances.

In a furtive hush, I leaned against the table, narrowing the gap between us, and whispered, "Did you notice that there are no other Black students in our class? I am the only one." I looked around the room, which had started to empty, with only a few students left relaxing on the couch, chatting and unaware of the secret I'd finally let spill out of me. I felt a rush of relief that their ears had not perked up at the sound of "Black"; I had previously learned that in mostly white academic circles, some people believe racism exists only because we keep talking about race—colour-blindness was surely the antidote to our racial divide, and simply saying "Black" could spur a furrowed brow.

Adam's eyes widened in shock as his mouth flew open.

"You're the ONLY Black student?" he exclaimed, clearly not sharing my reluctance to draw our classmates' attention. Heads jolted in our direction as my heart hammered against my rib cage and sweat pooled under my arms. Eyes narrowed on me, as if I were a double agent, exposed for infiltrating a sacred space.

"Are you kidding me? You're really the *only* Black student?" Adam continued, unconstrained by the glances and growing unease of the other students.

"Yeah . . . I am," I sputtered, still in a whisper, embarrassment hot on my skin.

"I didn't even realize. I can't believe I didn't notice. This is a real problem," he said, in a tone of remorse. It was clear that the other students, some looking on in similar shock, had also not noticed the lack of other Black students in the space. Our absence had been normalized to the point where my presence was either completely overlooked or an utter surprise when identified: a Black, female Waldo.

Adam, spirited with the belief that something should be done to address the disparity, gave me the space to share how difficult the situation was for me. I told him about how dissimilar I felt from the rest of the class, dealing with the microaggressions that arose unexpectedly, like lightning bolts in an otherwise crystal blue sky. I became acutely aware of how I dressed and spoke. I regulated my tone and the things I discussed, as a new friend in the class had already joked that I was "so ghetto" and another had told me that I looked "intimidating for some reason" that she couldn't *quite* put her finger on. I just "scared" her. Sadly, she wasn't the first and would not be the last person to tell me that I looked intimidating at first impression. The byproduct of these experiences left me feeling dejected and apprehensive, longing for a place and space that was more inviting, warm—safe for me to *be me*. How, I often wondered, had my dream medical school become fertile ground for my nightmares? As I would come to describe it in keynote speeches years later, I viewed these microaggressions as "death by a thousand cuts"—repeated moments of racial slights that chip away at one's spirit and humanity. Despite my best efforts, I could slowly feel the anxiety and sadness creeping in, as they had in the months before I wrote my first MCAT.

Adam shook his head in astonishment and mutual frustration.

"I really hope they do something about this. I'm sorry," he said, as we packed our belongings and prepared to head out.

I, too, shared that wish that something would be done.

It would be only a couple of weeks before I'd learn that *something* would be done and that I would be part of it.

Chapter Nine

Tears pooled in the corners of my eyes, blurring the fine details of my email draft to Ike Okafor, the Senior Officer of Service Learning and Diversity Outreach within the Faculty of Medicine.

"*Hi Ike,*" I began typing, recalling the first time we met, in his office after orientation week, when he promised to be available when needed and to support me through this unusual medical school journey. His disappointment in the precariousness of my situation as the only Black student in my year was shared among those in the faculty, especially other Black faculty members, who had seen the year above me as potentially indicating an upward trend in the number of Black trainees. Little did I know, they were already in the midst of ushering in an initiative that would ensure a definitive change in the years to come. Too late, however, for me.

"I am really struggling to feel welcome in this space. I am having a lot of regrets about choosing this medical school and beginning to struggle with the isolation and anxiety."

It was September 21, 2016, not even a full month into my training, and I was already grasping for a lifebuoy in what felt like choppy waters.

"I've tried to spend more time with the upper-year BMSA members, but it's only making a marginal difference on my experience, as it's clear to me that they have one another in their year and I don't."

I began to type more urgently.

"I would like to meet as soon as possible, as I can feel myself becoming more withdrawn. Thanks, Chika."

After hitting send and exiting my mailbox, I sat in my solitude, staring blankly at the paused lecture recording from that morning. This library on the southern end of campus hosted a hurricane of undergraduate students who swirled around me, bursting into occasional eruptions of laughter and giddiness that juxtaposed uncomfortably with my own innermost feelings.

Yes, I was making new friends in my class, swapping numbers, and had even found a couple of study buddies. Vic and I would meet often for lunch; Adam and I would catch up between lectures in the student lounge. But there is a singular pain that comes with feeling lonely when you're not alone, among friends whose realities are so different from your own that you feel like the only option is to dilute who you truly are. Worse yet was the way in which I gaslighted myself by questioning whether racial slights toward me were real or imagined, mild or severe, afraid to check in with my peers only to have them play the role of devil's advocate. Even when they didn't, and extended comfort, there was the lingering feeling of sympathy in lieu of empathy that made me feel even more alone. Years later, I would come to explain this feeling to my husband as "having a front row seat to my pain, but never being able to step on the stage with me."

Ike, in contrast to my few friends in medical school, understood.

"We're here for you" he said the next day in his office, as I sat on the opposite side of his desk, despondent.

"There are a few people I can connect you to within the faculty who could also provide support outside of our in-house therapist," he continued, pushing forward a box of Kleenex as I sniffled into my shirtsleeves.

"Lisa Robinson and Onye Nnorom, Black female docs in the faculty whom I believe you know," he continued. I nodded slowly. "And Pier—a psychiatrist and an incredible ally."

▼

Pier Bryden, the Vice Chair of Education in Psychiatry and Director of Program Integration within the faculty, was a child and adolescent psychiatrist at SickKids hospital, a published author, and a friend and mentor to many within the institution. At the start of October, a couple of short weeks after being connected by way of Ike, I found myself sitting across from Pier in her brightly lit MSB office. An assortment of books with polychromatic spines adorned the wall behind her, enticing curious onlookers to sift through their pages at an opportune moment.

"Pleasure to meet you, Chika," she chimed, with a gentle voice that commanded both respect and wonder—exactly what would be needed in the field of pediatric mental health. She was a petite woman, no more than five-foot four, with soft eyes and short-cut grey hair swept behind her ears. I felt an immediate ease in her presence that, admittedly, took me by surprise.

When I first entered Pier's office, I carried a mild trepidation. As two women, and self-proclaimed feminists, Pier and I were inherently con-nected in the fight for gender equality. Conversations around sexism in medicine, the challenges of balancing the demands of life as a working mother, and the push for equal pay would surely flow with ease. What remained uncertain, however, was whether I could be truly candid about my experiences of anti-Blackness with a white faculty member. Would she try to placate my concerns with skillful reframing of perspective (which sometimes happened with white girlfriends) or sit with me in the discomfort of my lived experience? The former threatened pushing me further into the corners of my own isolation, and the latter was critical to my persistence.

Opening up to Pier was one of the many calculated risks I would take at U of T.

Nonetheless, I was hungry for support and a community to hold me in the earliest days of medical school. Lisa Robinson had assured me that Pier was a fantastic ally to the Black community and would be sympathetic to my circumstances. During a recent coffee date, Lisa had apologized for my predicament, almost as if she had promised herself twenty-five years ago that she wouldn't let another Black woman pass through the halls of U of T Medicine alone, as she had. Lisa was like a homing beacon, representing the "other side," when I would be a staff physician and somewhat immune to the racism; surely an MD designate would be enough to combat judgment and doubt from skeptical patients, peers and strangers.

When Lisa shared with me that recently she had been mistaken for a ward clerk by a fellow staff doctor, I became sullen.

"Sadly, it never goes completely away, especially as a woman of colour," said Lisa, solemnly, knowing that the road ahead of me might be paved with similar misfortune. She promised me that, like Melin and the other BMSA members, she would always be there to protect me during this journey; whatever adversity lay ahead would be confronted collectively. Building a coalition of allies within the faculty was of paramount importance, Lisa stressed, and (as Ike had mentioned) Pier would be the best place to start.

I placed my lips on the edge of a piping hot mug that Pier had extended to me, with lemon ginger tea steeping inside, its steam rising to the ceiling. I pressed my fingers against the sides for warmth and began to unpack the heaviness of the past several weeks, starting with my revelation at the stethoscope ceremony and working my way through the microaggressions and racial slights that followed.

"I'm so sorry that this is happening," she said, conveying the resounding disappointment shared by other equity-focused leaders in the faculty.

When Pier offered to anonymously report to the faculty about the staff physician's comment, on my behalf, I immediately shivered at the charade of anonymity. I imagined the prominent doctor reading the complaint about "making a racially insensitive comment regarding Black patients" and being easily identified as the only Black person in my class—blacklisting would invariably ensue, bleeding from the one department into other specialties that tendrilled from the core faculty. My years of painstaking effort to enter medicine would be reduced to dust, I surmised, and I quickly declined her offer while explaining my reasoning. Pier understood, listening intently as I went on to express frustration toward the institution for leaving me in this precarious situation. Like a seasoned psychiatrist, she validated my experiences and sat with me in the mire of my emotions.

She, like Lisa, assured me that she would be available whenever I needed someone for support, guidance navigating the institution or just a listening ear.

I believed her, and in the years that followed, Pier would prove to be one of the most consistent, loyal and strongest allies in my corner.

We brainstormed names of who else I could tap for support, especially other Black physicians within the faculty and in networks of Black medical trainees across the province and country.

I inherently trusted Pier and grew to feel safer in her office than I did within the walls of our clinical teaching quarters or the MSB classroom.

She stood, turning to her in-house library, and fingered through the collection of literature. I carefully sipped from the mug and studied the rest of the office; a shaggy rug in the middle of the room and eclectic prints on the wall completed the space with a homey feel.

"I would love for you to have this," she said, sliding a paperback book across the desk, its orange spine facing me. "It's a book I wrote with another psychiatrist, Dr. David Goldbloom, about a week in the life of a psychiatrist. It demystifies what we do in our specialty and might be a good read, since you mentioned that you're a bookworm, like me."

I marvelled at Pier—the embodiment of my greatest goal to be a writer, doctor and mother. I packed the book into the front pocket of my bag and thanked her for her generosity, with both her art and her time. It would be the first of many books that Pier and I would exchange over the ensuing eight years, as our intergenerational mentorship deepened into friendship.

"I'm here for you, just an email away," she said, as I stood to leave her office. I carried her warmth with me as I pushed through the heavy faculty doors and turned toward the aged stairwell, heading for the MSB exit.

Chapter Ten

The pre-lecture buzz in the MSB auditorium was a hodgepodge of side conversations ranging from exam answer comparisons, sports news, workout routines and clinical shadowing opportunities. Sound bites would often break through the white noise of dialogue and snag my attention.

"Guys, I know it's last minute, but I'm down to go to Paris this weekend if you are!" said a classmate to a few others, who excitedly agreed without hesitation.

Maybe, I thought to myself, they were eating into a handsome line of credit provided by their bank, most of which offered anywhere between $100,000 and $400,000 in loans to future docs. Practising physicians, the banks understood, are usually well situated to pay back the investment on their education—plus the healthy interest that accrues. As someone who was not in a position to receive financial support from my parents and had been accumulating student loans since the start of undergrad, I'd had no choice but to take one of these loans. After all, medical school tuition at U of T can cost a student well over a hundred grand, plus the cost of living in Toronto, one of the most expensive cities in the country.

Or maybe my Paris-bound classmates were among the many who had the familial financial support to help them cover some, or all, of their med school expenses. When I learned that several of my classmates were educated at private schools, entered medical school without pre-existing debt, and could graduate with minimal debt as well, I knew I was operating within an arena of privilege that was entirely foreign to my reality.

But sitting there, daydreaming of eating baguettes on the cobblestones of the Champs-Élysées, funded through my line of credit . . . that wasn't a savvy financial move. Nor would it get me any closer to financial liberation. Instead, I allotted myself a couple of modest vacations over the course of medical school and hoped to offset the financial burden by continuing my private tutoring gig—which never failed to show me the differences between the haves and have-nots.

After an afternoon studying at the library, I arrived at the door of a sprawling mansion in one of the city's gated communities and rang the bell. While waiting, I studied the agenda cradled in the crook of my elbow. Each date in the calendar for October was illuminated in lime green, pink and yellow highlighter, colour-coded for times allocated to studying, assignment completion, BMSA meetings and tutoring. Every minute of every day was accounted for, just as it had been in undergrad, high school and the final years of elementary school—some habits are hard to shake.

I had debated giving up my private tutoring gig at the start of medical school, but after the financial seminar provided during orientation week, where stories were shared of graduates racking up over a quarter of a million dollars in debt, I decided that I should use every possible opportunity to lessen the financial load of studying medicine in Toronto.

Atlas poked his head out from behind the chestnut door, his shaggy black hair fencing his deep-set eyes, and welcomed me inside. I had been tutoring him for nearly four months, every other week (or more often, as needed), during the evenings, in his family's spacious study. He was one of a few tutees I had carried over from my gap year. His father, Rupert, had hired me through the private tutoring agency, with the goal of supporting his son as he matriculated through one of the most prestigious private schools, just north of the city.

Over the course of two hours, I would walk Atlas through grade eleven calculus and English assignments until his focus and affability eventually petered out. The final thirty minutes of our sessions were marked by his increasingly audible sighs and glances at the clock, with me wrangling his attention back to the schoolwork.

Amazed, I had a front-row seat to the world of private high schools, a world that had hosted many of my Health Sci and medical school peers; one that I, and other racialized children like me, entered at noticeably lower rates than our non-Black peers. Atlas, like other students, was required to learn with a laptop; every class lecture note was available on their school's portal. They had access to incredible resources, academic and athletic opportunities, as well as a social network of prestigious professionals to guide them toward the career of their dreams. Every time I sat beside Atlas, who was a sweet kid somewhat oblivious to the privilege he was afforded, I would silently lament the opportunities that, as a child, I didn't even know I was being barred from. I wanted nothing more than to level the socio-economic playing field for all the children like me, though the systems at play seemed vast and immutable.

Rupert placed a bottle of sparkling water onto a crocheted placemat in the middle of the table as he implored Atlas to focus as best he could on the lesson. Atlas understood that if he wished to continue playing competitive golf, he couldn't let his grades slip under his father's watchful eye. Still, Rupert's hovering was beginning to wear on him. While we worked through his calculus questions first, Atlas groaned and asked his father to cut the session short, as he was tired and didn't feel like studying. Rupert quickly nixed the idea as, apparently, Atlas's grades were starting to slip below the 92 percent minimum average he had put in place for his son; Rupert had always dreamed that his only child would follow in his footsteps into the field of law, so he held Atlas to a high standard of academic excellence. The two of them began to bicker as I sat awkwardly between them, a semi-neutral third party who just wanted to get through the session, make enough money to do some grocery shopping the next day, and return to my own studies.

"If you don't appreciate being at one of the best private schools, I'll pull you out, and then you'll have to attend a public high school, *without* a golf team *or* the high acceptance rates to the best universities," said Rupert, as Atlas scoffed at the suggestion. "And, trust me, you don't want to go to a public school and throw your future away."

My stomach tensed into a familiar knot, the same ghoulish presence that choked the air from my lungs. I found it ironic that Rupert counted on the tutelage of a medical student who was educated in the publicly funded school system, without any private tutors or other support, to help his child. I was never in any special stream within the public system, either, no International Baccalaureate Program or anything that would suppos-edly make me stand out from the crowd of university applicants. I was just a young girl in a Brampton-based Catholic school, with big dreams of becoming a doctor, unaware that private schools like Atlas's even existed.

"Well, not that I think you should drop out of private school, but I went to a very good non-private school in Brampton, and as you know, I'm now at U of T Med, one of the best programs in the country," I inter-jected, with a thinly veiled annoyance colouring each word.

Rupert sneered. "Well, that's *rare*, isn't it?" he said, before using more labels like "poor quality" to further describe public schools and etch an indelible mark of fear into his son's mind. I shrugged off his comments, praying for an early release from their home. As I watched Rupert, I wondered how he spoke about the people who were educated through these schools when I wasn't around.

"I have to take a call with a client," said Rupert, as he picked up his briefcase and strode out of the study. I bit my tongue so hard I thought I would draw blood.

The following week, while I sat in my usual spot in the study waiting for Atlas to arrive from school, Rupert sparked a conversation while he poured me a cup of water.

After I'd spent four months frequenting his home, guiding his son through coursework and the occasional affliction of high school (private schools are not immune to the relational drama of teenagers, and I remembered that all too well), Rupert seemed grateful for my influence on Atlas's academics. I folded his words from last week onto my mental shelf for things to unpack later, and I indulged him in small talk.

"Medicine, like law, is a brutal and self-sacrificing career, I bet," Rupert bantered. "Just like how we tend to fretful clients at all hours of the day and night, you guys have to be ready to go at a moment's notice."

I nodded. "It's like it resets the hard-wiring in your brain. But it's worth it, and I'm loving it so far," I responded, answering automatically to fill time until Atlas arrived. Finally, he popped through the door with a golf club in hand and wandered through the study, buying himself more time before feigning interest in his schoolwork.

"You're quite bright, to make it into U of T Med. I'm sure your parents are proud," said Rupert, as my guard slowly fell. I was grateful that there was respect between us, despite his problematic views on public education. Maybe he thought I was different. Or maybe I could gradually shift his perspective. Either way, I needed the extra hundred dollars a week, so I let the heat of our last interaction dissipate.

I continued to chat about medical school, and we lauded the rising numbers of women graduating as doctors. He was pleased with this improvement, praising the field for how far it had come, openly embracing the title of a "proud male feminist." He commented that he went out of his way to sponsor promising female lawyers at his firm—unlike many of his predecessors, who turned a blind eye to the issue.

"It's pretty great," I said, carefully weighing what I wanted to say next. Something about his alignment with radical feminism and deep investment in his female colleagues made me believe that he might be upset by the lack of Black students at U of T; after all, a rebellious male feminist should commiserate with the plight of racialized people, right? Maybe his shaky views on class didn't muddy the rest of his social justice waters. I hedged my bets.

"Except that I'm the only Black student in my year, which is a real problem," I shared. I quickly felt the atmosphere in the room shift. Rupert's sickly-sweet grin chilled as his teeth disappeared behind tightly pursed lips.

"Nope, I'm certain that didn't matter at all," he retorted, waving my words out of the air like a cheap cologne that had drifted into the room. "They don't care about your race, and neither should you. Everyone had an equal opportunity to get in."

Atlas's eyes shifted between us, reading the adult discord and my growing unease.

"Well, I do think race is an important component of this, actually. I think it's a big issue. In one of the most diverse cities in the world, at one of the most prestigious medical schools in the country, in a class of 259, to have only *one* Black medical student? Toronto has the highest population of Black people in the country . . . I think that should be considered."

My heart galloped. My muscles tensed.

"You were clearly the only one who tried, made the best of a bad situation," he rebutted, confidently, comforted by the luxurious threads of meritocracy.

His words hung between us, nearly knocking me off my feet, pulverizing the part of me that felt foolish enough to engage in an equity-related discourse concerning higher education. I gaped at how calmly he denigrated an entire community to which I belonged.

Black, educated in the public school system. Unfit for medical school, it seemed, in his eyes.

A collective *bad situation* that I'd managed to escape, by some stroke of luck.

I retreated from the conversation, immediately pivoting toward Atlas. My dignity crumbled to a pile of dirt on the ground, to be swept into the dustbin after my departure.

I emailed my boss the next day to resign from private tutoring, citing how busy medical school was getting, leaving out that I was simply tired of being invalidated. I had been worn down. Any pay came at the too-high cost of having my humanity consistently called into question, or having to grit my teeth through racially insensitive comments. When my old manager had told me to "go home and fix your nappy hair," I didn't quit, because I needed the minimum-wage pay for survival. This time, I was on a clear path to financial security through a medical career and could forfeit this gig, even if it meant accruing more debt in the interim.

Balancing tutoring with studying for mastery exams was proving too strenuous anyhow, so I welcomed the extra couple of hours a week that I could invest in myself.

"Are you sure?" my boss replied immediately, no doubt understanding the market value of a medical student as a private tutor.

"I'm sure," I emailed back, thanking her for two years of part-time employment.

Realizing I would be dipping more frequently into my line of credit, I made peace with my decision to leave and viewed my debt as an investment. I felt the chasm of difference between me and my classmates—the ones who didn't rely on loans—grow. My dedication to reaching the other side—where financial freedom and inherent respect for my merits awaited—grew as well.

The halls of the first floor of MSB wound through the building like a labyrinth, becoming more intricate and confusing in the area cordoned off for the science labs. Our class was split into several small sections, by alphabetical order, for our longitudinal Medicine and Ethics seminar throughout the year, hosted in labs where the scent of formaldehyde lingered and sank into the clothing of those who entered. Returning from our respective academies over the lunch hour, we scurried through the halls looking for our rooms, latching onto a familiar face for guidance.

The sound of rusty hinges squeaking as lab doors were opened, and shoes hitting the floor in a nervous effort to not be late, echoed through the hallways.

At the end of a lengthy stretch of weathered blue lockers was my lab room, where my classmates were settling into the orange chairs arranged around thick black tables. Erlenmeyer flasks were left drying beside stainless-steel sinks in the middle of lab benches; stools were tucked underneath. Partially erased organic chemistry equations were chalked onto the board, written by the undergraduate science students with whom we shared the corridors of MSB.

Yuzzy, who volunteered his time to co-facilitate the afternoon's seminar with another clinician within the faculty, stood up for a hug as I entered the room. It was one of the first times I had shared a space in medical school with another Black person, since we had yet to have a Black lecturer or preceptor teaching us—even though there were roughly two to three new lecturers every week and we were days into November. His presence was inherently calming, without words or action.

I leaned into Yuzzy's hug and whispered that I was *so happy* he was there. Though the BMSA members were a haven for me in medical school, a small family I cherished when I felt unlike the rest, I didn't often get to see them around, as our schedules just didn't align. Sometimes, Yuzzy, Jonathon and I would meet in Robarts Library for study dates, where they would cradle me in their protective bubble of brotherhood. Together, they were irresistibly hilarious, breaking my streak of concentration with an off-the-cuff joke or giving me their best tips on how to approach exams. There was no need to pre-calculate my words or actions, no fear of using Black slang or Naija pidgin and being called "ratchet" or having my intelligence silently questioned. With them around, I felt at ease. I became myself, and not the manicured version of Chika that left her Blackness at home.

Yuzzy handed out pieces of crumpled paper as the room filled and attendance was taken. He randomly selected a few medical students to stand closer to the garbage can, while the rest of us were placed through-out the room with our bunched papers in hand.

"All right, folks, I ask that you try to shoot your paper into the garbage bin, one by one," he said, as the people in the farthest corner snickered at the sheer improbability of a successful shot. Over the next five minutes, balls of bunched paper flew across the room, many landing just shy of the bin, while those closest cheered as their makeshift ball clunked at the bottom of the can. We took our seats at the end of the exercise, before unpacking the allegory of the game.

"Some of you, by luck of the draw, were positioned closer to the goal than others, who were far away and less likely to achieve the task," said the clinician. "This game is a metaphor for privilege, and how some of our patients—due to socio-economic, political and cultural factors—are unfairly disadvantaged in life, and health care," he continued, while heads slowly nodded. "Some people are born into privilege, making it much easier for them to achieve their dreams, have good health and good for-tune, while others are not."

They segued into the first seminar question, where we unpacked how privilege and bias can affect our patients, especially those disadvantaged by race and class. The conversation remained focused on the patients, as if physicians weren't susceptible to the same plight.

While the discussion developed, my participation grew, and the con-versation became spirited. The clinician, who shared how few women had been in his medical school class decades prior, heaped approbation on the faculty for the impressive number of women in our first-year class. He, like Rupert, regarded himself as a champion of women's rights, and he was thrilled to see more female doctors in the field.

"Your class is pretty diverse," he told us. "U of T has come a long way," he concluded, as I bristled at the schism of our views.

Diverse? I thought to myself, the urge to challenge his assertion rush-ing to the forefront of my thoughts. Yes, there were many non-white individuals in my class, particularly those of Asian or Middle Eastern descent, but historically under-represented groups in medicine, such as Black, Indigenous and Filipino students, matriculated in chronically low numbers. A quick risk calculation lapped through my mind: Yuzzy was here (safety in numbers), and this was a seminar on diversity and inclusion—so if not now, then when? More than anything, I was simply tired of my situation being overlooked, the utter normalization of the paucity of Black students in medical school—as if it were to be expected, as if the status quo should be upheld.

I raised my hand quietly, catching the attention of the clinician co-facilitator and the rest of my group.

"I agree with you that strides have been made for educational and gender diversity, but I wonder if that's the only benchmark that should be used as a metric for success? Our class is not only quite wealthy, but many of the students are children of physicians, and there are hardly any Black, Indigenous or Latinx people in the class—those who make up historically under-represented groups in medicine … and this is Toronto, where we are treating diverse patients," I stated, an unexpected urgency to get my point across underscoring my statement.

I continued, "I just wouldn't describe our class as diverse, at least not yet. I think there is a longer way to go to increase representation from traditionally marginalized groups. For example, I am the only Black person in our class." When I concluded, the room fell quiet.

It was the first time I had openly stated my predicament, and a vulnerability hangover instantly overcame me. I felt awkward and uncomfortable.

The clinician cleared his throat. "I don't know if I fully agree with that statement, actually. I think your class is more diverse than most medical schools in this country," he stated, boldly, as the space shifted into a courtroom.

My peers looked on like jurors, ready to assess our opening statements. I readied myself for a rebuttal, as though I were gearing up to go tête-à-tête with a seasoned cross-examiner.

"I believe that in a place like Toronto, where the Black citizens make up nearly 10 percent of the population, the future class of doctors should reflect this diversity."

"But do we *really need* a medical class that is reflective of the diversity, in terms of percentage, to be diverse?" he retorted.

Another student hummed in agreement. I felt heat radiate from my skin as she chimed in, "I agree with the professor. I would say our class is quite diverse, and I don't think that 10 percent of our class *has* to be Black."

"Maybe not exactly 10 percent," I stated, my voice shaking with frustration, "but certainly more than whatever negligible percentage it is now. Until there are more racialized and historically marginalized people in this school, I'm wary about calling it diverse. There is real harm to our patients in not being able to identify with their doctors."

As my discussion with the clinician got increasingly heated, with statements and rebuttals flying between us, more students began to side with him. Yuzzy tried to mediate the discussion, cognizant of his role as arbitrator. He suggested we try to finish the rest of the questions in the remaining time, throwing a life raft over to me before I was fully submerged in the dissent.

I felt the heavy hand of invalidation crush me, the past few months of emotional turmoil being reduced to nothing. I wanted to tell them about the disquiet that sweltered within me every time I walked into a room, how acutely aware I was of my race in any space I entered. I wanted to ask them if they felt the need to calibrate every measure of their existence, afraid of being pigeonholed into a stereotype. How deeply unfair it was to be put into this position; how deeply alone I felt, daily; how unsafe I was made to feel in that room.

I closed my laptop quickly as the clock struck 4:00 p.m., while Yuzzy placed a hand on my shoulder and gave me a look of understanding. "You held it down, don't worry," he said, as I turned toward the door.

Tears welled in my eyes as I descended the front steps of MSB, blending into the rush-hour underground crowd in the St. George subway station.

Chapter Eleven

Vic kicked her winter boots against the doorsill as she entered my home, leaving condensed gritty snow behind with the imprint of the sole's architecture. She slumped her bag onto the hardwood slats, unwrapped the wool scarf securely bundled around her neck, and pulled off her damp, knitted blue mittens. Freshly fallen snowflakes lined her eyelashes, thawing in the warmth of the apartment.

She found me curled up on the couch under my fluffiest throw blanket, my coziness contrasting with the chilly December weather outside. Cuddling beside me, she leaned her head into the nook of my shoulder, which had become more noticeably angular in the past few weeks. After four months in medical school, the anxiety, isolation and feverish perfectionism had caused me to slip into old, comforting and dangerous habits; from late October to early December, I had lost nearly thirty pounds from restrictive eating and skipping meals. Vic, who had noticed some weeks ago and gently probed with concern, shelved any present worries to prioritize the matter at hand.

Ike had reached out to me with a proposal to be a part of the campaign to launch a new initiative within the faculty: the Black Student Application Program, abbreviated to BSAP. The administration had given this project the green light, and now it needed the hard work and energy of supporters to carry it forward. BSAP would create a separate application stream for Black pre-medical candidates at U of T, with the aim of enhancing equity in admissions processes that had historically led to only a few Black students matriculating through the medical school each year.

Unlike many equity initiatives of medical schools in the United States (which, in my opinion, can serve a role in addressing the systemic barriers that limit Black/minority success in medicine), BSAP would not be quota based, and it would require candidates to achieve the exact same criteria as applicants in the general stream. Applicants through BSAP would also need to write an extra essay to describe why they were applying through the stream, and how their identity as a Black individual would influence their medical career, if at all. Moreover, the file review and interviewing process would integrate members from the Black community—a far cry from my experience at U of T the previous year.

Contrary to the idea that the program unfairly privileges Black applicants over others (as some may fear, and as some have even vocalized to me in the years following BSAP's launch), the program establishes a system that sidesteps the racial bias to level the playing field. This playing field, ironically, has historically benefited those who have already been gifted the most privilege, both socially and financially. Of utmost importance, the program makes clear to Black applicants that they are not only accepted into the medical community, but actively sought after and welcomed.

The importance of this new program, and how critically it was needed within the faculty, could not be overstated. Research had demonstrated that subconscious racial/anti-Black bias may permeate medical school admissions committees, potentially contributing to the paucity of successful Black medical school candidates over time. This understanding underscored my reticence to discuss my involvement in advocacy for Black women through natural hair tutorials and poetry within my essays, despite them being a significant part of my personhood. A friend whom I had asked to review my essays for U of T even cautioned me against stating my identity as a second-generation Nigerian Canadian, out of fear that I could be seen as race-baiting or attempting to leverage sympathy by "playing the Black card." The explanation of my identity stayed, as taking it out seemed like an affront to my humanity, and the school would know I was Black once we got to the interview, anyway.

I heard this narrative again, a couple of months into medical school, expressed by a well-intentioned friend after an interview to be one of the following year's orientation week leaders: "You don't need to *tell* them you're Black, they can already see that, and it could be seen as trying to gain sympathy." I learned that my skin needed to be worn with caution, like a concealed weapon or heavily thorned rose.

Ike had already reached out to the upper-year BMSA members in an attempt to recruit support for BSAP, whose creation had been the culmination of a hard-fought battle spearheaded by Black faculty physicians and allies within the institution (namely, Drs. Onye Nnorom, Renée Beach, Mark Hanson and Lisa Robinson, and Mr. Ike Okafor). We were asked to participate in an interview about the necessity of the initiative, which would be published on the medical school's website to be used in perpetuity. Additionally, this material would be used for a general announcement to the public and made available within a syndicated media circuit.

"We politely declined," said a couple of BMSA members, who confirmed that a few others had similarly declined the invitation to participate. Some, understandably, had cited a demanding study, extracurriculars and clinical research schedule leaving little room for much else. Like many BMSA members, they were already doing incredible advocacy work within the Black community, and they offered to lend their moral support to BSAP in different ways.

Others, however, had reservations of a different nature. Although they supported and believed in the importance of BSAP, some BMSA members worried that taking such a public stance would cast a spotlight on them that could derail their medical careers. It was understood that there might be people within the medical institution who dissented with the idea of the program, and such individuals could wield real power over how careers evolved—including residency program admissions, staff appointments, promotions and beyond.

I had already heard whispers from a few classmates within my cohort who viewed the program as an unfair advantage doled out to prospective Black students who might otherwise not have been competitive enough to earn a spot at our school—which was a radical misunderstanding of how the initiative functioned. What was missing from this analysis, however, was the ways in which many equity-seeking groups, not just Black students, have been historically under-represented in medicine due to a myriad of interconnecting socio-economic factors and oppressive systemic and educational barriers. Additionally, many brilliant Black Canadian students are regularly recruited to Ivy League medical schools in the States, with built-in networks of cultural supports and tantalizing scholarships. As someone who was similarly positioned and who heard of many others also given this opportunity, I believed the Black Canadian "brain drain" to the States was a real factor in why under-representation persisted.

Nevertheless, among a few of those asked to participate, me included, the fear only grew.

A close friend warned me of the risk of being tokenized by the faculty for presenting myself as the face of the new initiative for Black students, or even being seen as a "troublemaker" who challenged the status quo. "You worked too hard to get into medical school just to be blacklisted during the residency matching process," one of my friends concluded. We were already dealing with respectability politics and knee-jerk stereotyping, navigating racial microaggressions and working twice as hard to dispel any untoward assumptions about our capabilities. It was clear that adding to this burden by championing an inherently controversial, albeit crucial, initiative would be unwise. I was advised, not only by my peers but also by friends and family, to be methodical and prudent, safeguarding the future of my medical career.

Once Ike had finished his pitch on the BSAP campaign involvement to me, I paused while my mind tussled with uncertainty. The words of advice from other BMSA members, driven equally by concern and rationality, swirled within my thoughts as he waited for my response. From the time I broke down in his office in September, Ike had an intimate understanding of my struggle as my year's only Black medical student, and he had kept in close touch with me thereafter. He presumed, correctly, that this program would strike a sympathetic chord in my consciousness, hitting the core of my desire to effect change for other Black medical students.

But I couldn't shake the counsel of my friends and family. I not only trusted their assessment of the political climate within the culture of U of T, but I also understood that they had a grasp of the inner workings of medical school to which I was not yet privy. I told Ike I would think about my decision and give him an answer the following day.

The next morning, during clinical teaching and well into the afternoon, the divide between what my heart was leaning toward and the fear in my mind only ballooned. Finally, Ike called me, asking for my decision.

"It seems that you're the only one left in BMSA who would be willing to speak up for this campaign, and I understand why the other members are reluctant," he said, sombrely. "But I think that your voice would be especially important, as you're the only one in your class and you can speak to the hazards of having no other Black classmates. You're the only one who can give this unique insight into the dire need for BSAP."

Ike continued to share a thoughtful plea with me, reminding me of the future students who would hear my story, feel compelled to apply, and avoid my current predicament. His sentiments, he shared, were grounded in more than simply a desire to have representation in the campaign. As a founding member of the Black Students' Association during his post-secondary studies, and with his lived experience as a Black student leader, he understood that our voice and action were necessary in any initiative focused on the advancement of Black students.

The initial rollout of the initiative needed to be executed properly, or it could jeopardize the program's successful implementation.

I stayed silent on the phone, stymied by uncertainty.

"I'm so sorry, Ike," I said, finally. "I know I said I would think about it, but it just seems too risky. I'm worried about becoming the face of a program that the doctors who gatekeep residencies view as problematic."

Ike digested and respected my decision. He asked me to reach out if I changed my mind. But I told him I was certain in my choice, while my stomach twisted in disagreement. I believed in BSAP, and every cell in my body, as well as my moral compass, was urging me to do what I believed was right, even if it meant risking it all.

But I couldn't.

As I ended the call, shame and devastation settled in. The once-confident Chika, who had worn her Blackness unapologetically before medical school, assured in her identity and purpose, was now lost in the new version of herself, someone who wore her skin like an itchy woollen sweater, too hot, too heavy and ill-suited to the environment.

I sent a text to Vic, appealing for emotional support, and then cried on my living room couch, lost in the remorse that swallowed me whole, waiting for her to arrive.

Now she sat quietly with me, and we began to unpack the potential scenarios that could ripple out from either decision: stay silent, out of the scorching limelight of public-facing advocacy, or step into my truth, preventing another Black medical student from experiencing what I was facing. But at what cost? she asked. How bad could it be?

Very bad, I assured her, sharing the words of caution given to me. Even if I didn't face any direct initial scorn, there were people behind closed doors who pulled the strings on residency admissions. And some areas of medicine—surgical fields, for example—were more conservative than others. What if I decided during my clerkship that I wanted to become a neurosurgeon? How would my actions from first year affect my chances?

Over the next couple of hours, we lifted every stone of my doubt and fear, as I fluctuated through spells of intense remorse and calm confidence in my decision. Sharing my story would be a vulnerable exposure of what I was struggling with as the only Black student in my class; it was inviting a harsh spotlight on my internal world and allowing every part of what could be seen to be shared with the public. How could I possibly do this, when I was already fraught with fear over simply letting other people in my class know I was the only Black student?

I thought of Rupert, his immediate dismissal of my predicament with a scoff and the assertion that matters of race and racism don't permeate the illustrious walls of medicine. I thought of the awkward glances from students in the lounge that day when Adam repeated in shock that I was the only Black student in my class. I thought of the classmate who asked me whether my path to medicine was easier because I was Black. What would they—let alone strangers in the public and physicians on residency admissions committees—think if I were to tell the world how I *really* felt about being the only one?

But then I thought of the border officer, how his "Even you?" implied that I, and other Black women and men like me, didn't belong in medicine. I thought of the next Black student, full of hope for a more diverse class before the disillusionment crashed over them at their stethoscope ceremony, as it did for me, while I held the Hippocratic Oath in my hands.

First, do no harm.

Was the school itself failing to live up to the standards of the oath? Was falling short in the effort to create a more diverse, equitable cohort itself a violation of a principle I had now sworn to uphold?

And what about me? Obviously, many people I respected would not have called my refusal to offer myself as a public face for the program a "harmful" position. But my battered mind and bruised spirit could not rest easy with it.

I broke down in more tears, while Vic comforted me. I knew what I wanted to do, what I *needed* to do, but I was scared.

Terrified.

When Vic left that evening, her parting words were reassurance that, come what may, she would be there to support my decision.

"Bravery isn't the absence of fear, it's the courage to move forward in the face of it," she texted me shortly after reaching her condo.

I lay in bed that night, emotionally and physically depleted, but sleep eluded me as I wrestled further with the decision.

As the morning sun speared through the slits of my window blinds, I woke with a calm spirit and reached for my phone.

"I've had a change of heart," I said to Ike, after he picked up my unexpected call. "I want to be a part of the BSAP campaign. I hope it's not too late," I said, pangs of uncertainty rising from my core like solar flares.

"Oh my gosh, thank you, Chika!" exclaimed Ike, gleefully. His relief was palpable. "I can appreciate that it's a scary move, and you're being incredibly brave. But for every Black student that comes after you, I promise, it'll be worth it," he continued. His reassuring words had a soothing effect on my racing heart.

"Your story is important and deserves to be shared," he concluded. I thanked him for his patience through the turbulence of my commitment.

After hanging up the phone, I drew a deep breath and texted Vic that I had done it.

"So proud of you," she responded, extending a virtual hug.

I pictured fourth-grade Chika, poring over an anatomy textbook, playing doctor. I wondered if she would share that pride or clench her body in dread.

The risk of taking on the responsibility, threatening my medical career after a lifetime of dedication, seemed foolhardy and excessive.

But the risk of staying silent seemed greater.

Chapter Twelve

The shutter of the Canon DSLR professional-grade camera clicked as a bright flash stung my eyes. I relaxed my almost painfully fixed smile as the *Toronto Star* photographer brought the lens down from eye-view and stared at the series of pictures before adjusting the exposure.

"These are great, but we'll probably want to get a couple inside," he said, collapsing the portable tripod and other gadgets necessary for the newspaper's photo shoot.

I pictured my parents picking up the tightly wound bundle of their daily paper and unfurling it to reveal a salacious title and unflattering photo of their daughter, my father's greatest fears about my decision to speak up coming true. When I first ran the idea of being part of the BSAP campaign past my parents, my dad shared the concerns of some of the BMSA members and a couple of my mentors, cautioning that staying silent about racism and being affable among his white colleagues had saved his career. One of my closest friends, years later, told me that after my decision to advocate for BSAP had become public, they told others that it was a "stupid, foolish choice" that would cost me my dreams.

As I proceeded to fulfill my promises to Ike and the faculty, unease bobbed in my gut, rising to the surface every time the camera lens shuttered.

During a meeting to prepare for my interview, a faculty media rep had provided me with a list of potential questions and carefully coached me on how to answer in a way that was authentic without casting a potentially negative light on the faculty. "Be honest," they said, "but be careful."

I learned, from this experience and many others throughout the ensuing years, that journalists—in print media as well as radio and television—are often seeking the most gripping story, one that could shake up the dutifully manicured reputation of prestigious institutions like the University of Toronto.

When the reporter called me a few days before the photo shoot, not a minute past our scheduled time, she sounded professional and journalistic. Her questions were direct, succinct, each of my answers followed by a perfectly placed "Mmm, let's explore that further" and a skilled interrogation of my truest sentiments about my experiences. By the end of the interview, I had spilled my heart into a vulnerable pool in the virtual ether between us.

Before we began, I understood and agreed that I wouldn't be able to amend any statements in the article or have any foreknowledge of what was to be published. I, like the rest of the country, would be seeing the article and the accompanying photo for the first time in a few days. The pressure to ensure that my story was carefully crafted in the hands of the journalist, and not twisted into fodder for public scandal, was impossibly high.

The photographer took note of an imposing photograph that spanned the MSB lobby from wall to wall, documenting white male U of T medical students of yore.

"This is the shot," he whispered under his breath. The juxtaposition of a young, Black, female medical student against the black-and-white glimpse into the history of the school served to underscore the desperate need for change, and just how far the needle of diversity still needed to shift, even in 2016.

He shot several frames as the camera whirred excitedly, capturing my bravest smile hiding my innermost conflict.

"We got it," he said, flipping the camera around to show me the carousel of frames. "This would look great on the centrefold."

He smiled as I thanked him for his time, and the wet cement of my decision solidified, holding me still as the new, official face of BSAP, offering a cautionary tale of the many Black students who every year fall through the medical admissions cracks.

"You made the front page!" exclaimed my mom on the other end of the phone, peppering her excitement with a giddy squeal. She had awoken that morning, March 9, 2017, to go to the nearest Shoppers Drug Mart and purchase the day's copy of the *Toronto Star*.

"I got some for your dad and your aunties, but he also bought some for himself, his colleagues, and your uncles in the community," she blurted out as I chuckled, realizing that they had unlocked a new level of African parent humble-bragging. I wondered how long it would take for grainy, unfocused pictures of the article to make their way through the WhatsApp grapevine. Within just an hour, my father had created a chain message with a link to the article that was circulating through my relatives across the United States, Nigeria and even Europe.

"U of T aims to attract more Black med students," my mom read slowly, letting each word marinate on her tongue with pride, revelling in her daughter's accomplishment and newfound public profile.

"I'm so proud of you, Nnem," she proclaimed, before returning to the front page to reread the headline and captions, as if fearful that the ink would have evaporated and it all would have been a dream.

There, it's done, I thought to myself. *The worst is over.*

I finished the call with my mom, promising that I would call her back after my mandatory in-person lecture.

While I settled into my spot in the top left corner of the classroom, hundreds of my classmates were slowly filing into their seats, and Vic sprinted up the centre aisle in my direction. "The article was amazing!" she exclaimed, adding her signature tight hug in solidarity. "And you look like a total badass!" We chuckled, as feelings of pride began to stamp out my ambivalence. Adam, who was seated a few rows over, shot me two thumbs up in support and gestured that he would come and chat after class.

As we waited for our lecturer to arrive, my phone buzzed to the tune of Facebook notifications from friends, family and old acquaintances tagging me in the article on the *Toronto Star*'s Facebook page.

My jackrabbit heart began to beat rapidly as I scrolled through the dozens of comments that had already accrued under the post. The ones in which I was tagged, by people I knew, were overwhelmingly supportive. There were more from kind strangers, who commended my bravery and success in earning a spot at U of T Med; others thanked me for being a role model for Black and racialized youth who wanted to pursue medicine. Many people were shocked that there was only one Black person in my class. Others didn't care at all—and did not hesitate to let their indifference be known. A faceless commenter asked, "Why is this news?" and "Why should we care?"

And then there were comments that caused my heart to rip through my chest.

"I wouldn't let her touch me or treat my children," said a commenter, without any further explanation or reason. The thought, the mental image of someone turning away in disgust from my clinical care, caused me to freeze in dismay, breathing frantically. It didn't matter that I was studying medicine at U of T, a medical school notoriously difficult to enter and ranked as one of the best in the world. It didn't matter that I was concurrently earning my master's degree in health systems leadership and innovation, with the goal of going on to do leadership work within medicine. My ability to provide care was being immediately denied by this commenter, simply because I fought to have more Black doctors in the field.

The fears of my friends in BMSA were being realized, and in more ways than we had anticipated.

A chorus of faceless trolls quickly found their pitch and harmonized with the initial assailant.

"What are they teaching over at the University of Toronto, African bush medicine?"

"Nobody cares that she's the only Black student, if they worked harder, then they would get in."

An avalanche of shame, fright and worry crashed over me as I sent the link to Vic so she could see what was unfolding before my eyes. Social media, as I should have anticipated, was a battleground for public opinion, a place where strangers could openly bully and harass others without fear of reprimand. I watched as dozens of Likes popped up under the hateful comments that beat into my spirit with a powerful force. The air felt strangled from my lungs as I tried to stifle my sobs at the back of the classroom, silently wiping tears from my eyes and praying not to draw attention.

I knew that rushing to my own defence online would be futile, but Vic and Adam immediately replied to every inflammatory comment under the post. In response to someone who stated "She's clearly failing medical school, and did this as a favour so that they would pass her," they let them know that I was, in fact, doing well academically and was incredibly studious—something that they had witnessed time and time again throughout the academic year. To the other commenters, Vic rebutted that I would be an excellent clinician and their children would be lucky to have me as their future doctor. Her fingers rapped furiously over her keyboard as she repeatedly came to my defence, fighting every person whose opinions were blatantly false or intentionally hurtful. When the online bullies retreated to their corners of the internet, remaining dormant for their next target, Vic and Adam consoled me and reminded me of the importance of the work I was undertaking.

"Focus on the positive comments, Cheeks," Vic said, pointing to the innumerable strangers who had also started to come to my defence, sharing words of kindness and strength. Soon, they would spill into my inbox and send direct messages of encouragement. The article, quickly shared on Facebook, started to reach the corners of the country, and before long people in other provinces were reaching out for mentorship to get into medicine, for support, and just to send love. Vic was right; going forward, I couched my fears in the cushions of positivity and warmth instead of feeding the trolls and letting them win.

I logged out of my Facebook, fingers trembling.

"Remember, don't touch the cups on the set, they're just props, there's nothing in them," whispered the production manager, as Lisa Robinson and I waited behind the curtains of the wings leading to the CTV *Your Morning* studio. I nodded obediently as the makeup artist did a quick touch-up and fixed my twists in the mirror. It was just before seven o'clock in the morning, almost a week after the *Toronto Star* article launched, and we were inside the guarded CTV building on Yonge Street in downtown Toronto. It was the same building I would pass each morning on my way to work as a Starbucks barista several blocks down the street. Never in my wildest dreams could I have believed I would enter the building as a CTV News guest, just a year after I served my final latte.

I had never been in a television studio before, let alone in front of a camera and on live television. There was an intricate hierarchy among the show segment's staff; everyone I passed had a job that needed to be executed properly lest a live, on-air blunder ensue. The *Your Morning* hosts, who had only ever existed in megapixels on my television screen, were just a stone's throw from me, getting ready in their designated chairs. They were real, and seemed normal, with voices that weren't yet dramatic in the way that was needed to deliver breaking news and top stories.

Their makeup was immaculate. Not a hair was out of place.

It all felt surreal, as though if I were to extend my hand in a greeting, they would disappear like a mirage. I stood nervously beside Lisa, mentally pinching myself.

The segment, which spanned just under six minutes, went by impossibly fast. I remembered not to touch the cups, not to wriggle too much in my seat, and not to look directly into the camera but only at the interviewer. I tried to suppress the jitters that peaked moments before we went live, and I prayed not to sweat through my soft-pink dress.

The interviewer started with me, after stressing to the at-home audience, in shock, that I was the only Black student in my class of 259. She asked if I was "surprised by the numbers."

"Yes," I replied, calling upon my years of public speaking to steady me through the interview. "As you mentioned, it is 2017, and so you would expect the medical class to be reflective of the population that we serve," I said confidently, as I had practised that weekend with Adam.

"The lack of Black students does not reflect our general intelligence or tenacity," I concluded, thinking of Rupert.

Thinking of the trolls.

I went on to discuss how this issue spoke to greater systemic forces, not just at the admissions level, and cited how I had also been the only Black student in my Health Sci class during my undergrad.

After successfully answering the first questions, the words coming out of my mouth in an intelligible, articulate manner, I relaxed into my seat while the interviewer pivoted to Lisa.

A few minutes later, after we'd shared more words of wisdom and encouragement for Black students to apply through BSAP, the segment host thanked us for our visit, and we were quickly ushered off set.

Once I got home, the adrenaline of being on live television and somehow remaining poised and confident, while my gut backflipped with fret, still surged through me. My mom and dad sent me the same WhatsApp video that they had recorded of my television interview, from different angles of the living room, with my mom's cheers of "Go, Nnem! Go!" every time the camera panned in my direction. She called me, her pride booming through my phone's speaker, and praised my performance.

"Your English was excellent," my father said in the background. "You sounded like a real doctor, an expert on TV."

Within hours, the segment was available on the CTV News official site and uploaded to its YouTube page. It did not take me long to realize that, like the Facebook trolls, the dissenters on YouTube could be merciless.

"Why would you assume this is a 'systemic issue' rather than a reasonable representation of the average IQ and desire to be a doctor of the group involved?"

Again, the reflexive, long-standing racist notion that Black people are less intelligent was brought up in the comment section.

"This initiative will help UNDERACHIEVING BLACKS . . . Sorry Kevan Chang, you should have been Black and not as smart, then you might have gotten into Harvard. Sad to see Toronto is going this way. Obviously as a Black she just wants to help her own. Typical."

Black and not as smart.

Even though I knew the words were intentionally inflammatory and untrue, they punched through my confidence with unyielding cruelty. It was clear that the anger and vitriol stemmed from a place of ignorance, a place where seeing Black women with access to power ignites an inexplicable rage that drives people into social media comment sections.

I wanted desperately to reply through my YouTube account, but I had been instructed by the faculty, after my first encounter with trolls the week prior, not to engage in online tête-à-têtes with dissenters. I was cautioned that they would drag me into the mud, and no one would win.

Instead, the faculty arranged for a bouquet of flowers and a thank-you letter to arrive at my home that afternoon, a note of appreciation for my intangible sacrifices. A gesture that soothed the gnawing idea that I was being minority-taxed but didn't quell it entirely. An offering

I accepted, with gratitude resting on my lips and doubt weighing on my tongue.

The remnants of late winter thawed on the Romanesque towers that adorned King's College Circle on U of T's St. George campus. Spring broke through the frozen earth as my first year of medical school drew to a close and enticed me toward the summer respite.

I sat on my therapist's couch, leaning against the knitted cushions that begged my tired eyes to rest. As med students, we had just finished our final string of exams and were entering a three-month, exam-free stretch across June, July and August. Months earlier, I had relieved myself of the burden of attaining a minimum 90 percent on each exam, recognizing that I tied this numeric value to my self-worth and desire to prove to any doubters that I belonged at U of T Med. This cognitive reframe was driven partly by therapy-guided introspection, and partly by my mind and body struggling to keep up with an exhausting and untenable study schedule. My ability to skip meals, attend extracurriculars, advocate for BSAP, confront racism online and study with minimal rest proved to be a harmful combination. I needed, more than anything, to save myself from destruction.

As I would come to learn from one of the foremost contemporary anti-racism educators, Layla Saad, "Rest in the face of oppression is a form of resistance and liberation."

I couldn't do the advocacy work that fuelled me, or become the doctor I was destined to be, if my spirit was corroded through the systems that are meant to exhaust Black women.

"I'm really proud of how far I'm coming," I reflected to Lucy, my therapist, unconsciously rubbing the angles of my elbows and thighs hidden under baggy sweats. I no longer had ready access to my friend Vanessa's cozy closet, so I'd pulled from my old Mac sweaters and aged track pants to hide my thinner form. My family doctor had instituted weekly appointments in the early winter where I would get weighed and discuss my progress back to a healthy weight. I had become diligent with my meals and established a more robust diet, cataloguing what I ate and reviewing it with my doctor at each appointment. It was slow work, but I was steadily reclaiming my wellness.

"I feel like I've found purpose, through advocacy," I explained to my therapist.

Lucy sat with me as we unpacked the past few months, and my goals for the summer ahead. After the CTV News segment, where I'd been thrust into the public spotlight, and both praised and harassed online, I had felt a sense of clarity that had evaded me throughout the start of medical school. I had come to understand that helping others aided my own healing; empowering other Black students to enter medicine was not only liberating but empowering for me as well.

In the past few weeks, Ike had asked me to speak, alongside other BMSA members, at the inaugural IGNITE conference for Community of Support (COS) members. It would be the first of several speaking engagements that I would take on in the years to come.

"Seeing the auditorium full of Black pre-medical students was enchanting, and stepping back into public speaking made me feel alive again," I gushed, as Lucy listened attentively, legs crossed and hands interwoven on her lap. I wondered how she managed to remember the details of our session without scrawling notes into a journal. That was how I conceptualized therapists: Freudian and pensive, writing and questioning as the session progressed. Lucy was different: calm and collected, approachable in our session, making it like a conversation between roommates.

"I also have this really cool opportunity," I continued, perking up on the couch, like a child daring to spill a juicy secret.

Shortly after the CTV News *Your Morning* segment aired, I was contacted by the office of Michael Coteau, minister of Children and Youth Social Services in the Ontario government. The minister wondered if I would join him at Queen's Park, in the Legislative Building, for an afternoon in the Legislature. He wanted me to get a first-hand look at how policies could be enacted to help support local Black community members, a passion that we shared.

The world of politics was entirely foreign to me, as science, medicine and art had consumed my world since I was a child. In awe, I watched the elaborate interplay between political parties, which involved much less shouting and interjection from opposite sides of the floor than I had anticipated and secretly hoped to witness up close. Nonetheless, I was still enthralled.

"I've been invited by the minister to sit on the External Implementation Steering Committee for the Ontario Black Youth Action Plan," I shared. I explained that the External Implementation Steering Committee (EISC) oversaw how the program would allocate funds to community organizations dedicated to the advancement of Black youth in major cities in the province—Toronto, Hamilton, Windsor and Ottawa included.

"I'll be travelling with the committee this summer to lead community engagement sessions, listening to and learning from the Black community about the unique, youth-focused needs in their cities," I said to Lucy, with a hopeful grin that had been surfacing more frequently in our recent sessions.

I had spent many evenings on her couch, disillusioned, scared and angry.

Remorseful. Repentant. Confused.

Demoralized.

This session was a welcome change of pace.

"You have a busy schedule ahead," she chuckled, alluding to my upcoming master's courses and practicum that had already laid full-time claim over my summer schedule.

"I know, I know. I promise to build in protected time for meals and for self-care," I said reassuringly. Food was no longer my enemy, but I still spent a concerning amount of time determining *which* foods I could and should eat. I continued to step on the scale in my family doctor's office on a weekly basis, holding my breath until the numbers tabulated my weight. Past visits with my GP had been laden with disappointment; I was trying in earnest to put on weight, but my body was reluctant to shift from its set point. Yet I was getting better, slowly, cognizant that progress was more important than perfection.

"One more thing I'm doing this summer," I added, as our session was slowly winding down and the sun was beginning to set in the tiny window behind her. "I submitted a successful application to be a co-writer for the U of T *Daffydil* musical, so I'll be spending the summer writing the script."

Lucy gasped in amazement, partly at me stretching my already-packed summer more thinly and partly at me throwing myself back into the creative world.

"I know it's a lot on my plate, but I can't wait to get back to writing. I feel like I'll have the chance to reconnect with myself and share a compelling story that will be impactful and make people think. *Really think*," I shared excitedly.

"I think dipping back into art will be good for you," she replied.

I agreed with her, and right then I made up my mind to commit the whole evening ahead to hanging out on the "Button Poetry" YouTube channel and letting myself be carried into sleep by the melodic cadence of Sarah Kay's poetry.

I grabbed my bag and parted with the assurance that I would see her at the same time, same place, next week, feeling uncharacteristically buoyant in the fading spring light.

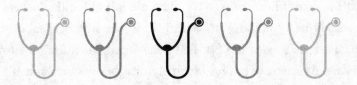

Finding the right café in downtown Toronto is, in many respects, like finding the right romantic partner. When I nuzzle into a corner seat in a shop, organizing my laptop, journal and latte atop a round oak table, I can determine by a gut feeling whether the atmosphere will be a good match—much like the spark instantly felt by soulmates when they lock eyes for the first time.

Usually, I can discern whether that spark is present within a matter of minutes; I feel for the comfort in seating, the volume of background chatter and overhead melodies, the dips and spikes in clientele, the aroma of freshly baked muffins drifting toward a vaulted ceiling, and the overall aesthetic that provides that perfect *je ne sais quoi*. This connection operates in a duality—to both catalyze productivity and transport me to a mental oasis where I can journal through the jumble of my life or reread chapters from *The Color Purple*.

Over seven years, I found myself falling in and out of love with cafés all over the city, pulled by the magnetism that each one possesses, until my creative eye would start to wander and look for a new home, a new romance.

Mere months after welcoming home my newborn son during the second year of residency, I began searching for the pieces of myself that felt lost in the upheaval of first-time motherhood; I yearned for a moment to write, to sit in the sun and steady my breath, to hold myself still in the turbulence of caring for a tiny, fragile life, and especially to grab some quiet at a local café. So when I happened upon an unassuming coffee shop planted just steps from my front door, I felt that familiar kindling set ablaze.

"Mama will be home soon, my love," I said to my then eight-month-old son, Eze, before handing him off to my husband and heading out the door. As Dale was finally on parental leave, we were intentional about carving protected time out of the day where I could sneak away to the coffee shop and write, edit my keynotes for upcoming conferences, catch up with girlfriends, or simply be still.

The barista placed my oat latte down on the wooden counter as I secured my favourite seat by the fireplace, beside the club chairs with deep-set cushions and the self-serve bar with cream carafes and stir sticks. I had exactly two hours before Eze needed to be fed again, and a 1,500 daily word count to meet for an upcoming manuscript deadline. I put in my earphones, tuned out the world and got to work.

"So sorry to bother ya," said an unfamiliar middle-aged man. He plunked himself down in the vacant seat at the opposite end of my table. He was clearly bested by the August heat that laboured his breathing, and he sat clutching a half-full coffee cup. As I was closing in on my word count for the day, I wasn't overly thrilled at the idea of breaking my writing stride or letting anyone barge in on my sacred self-care time.

He introduced himself as Peter, and I responded with my name—glancing at the time I had left before Eze would awake from his nap.

"I overheard you say that you're a resident doctor in psychiatry," he went on. I nodded politely, recalling that another regular-turned-acquaintance had just asked me what I usually did when not on maternity leave.

"I just gotta tell you, I hope you stay in this profession," he said, clearing his throat and meeting my eyes under the curved brim of his hat, as if we were covert agents exchanging concealed information. "I know you're busy, but can I tell you a story?"

I felt compelled to pause my productivity and listen despite the dwindling time I had left. Clearly, my maternity leave had left me feeling nostalgic for my encounters with patients.

Peter's tale swept me up from the outset. His mother, I learned, had struggled with severe clinical depression for many of her adult years—well into Peter's childhood. When Peter was an adolescent, his mom was found unconscious at home after a near-lethal suicide attempt that fractured the spirit of the family.

"After my mom left the hospital, she would go and meet this guy a couple times a week, for many years, but I never knew who it was or what he did for her. All I knew is that over time, slowly, my mom started to seem happier."

Peter revealed that it was only after his mother's death a few years prior, from natural causes, that he'd learned that she had in fact been under the care of a psychiatrist for nearly three decades following the suicide attempt.

"This doctor," he said as tears began to brim in his eyes, "saved my mom's life, and gave her the opportunity to become the best mother and grandmother we could have ever asked for."

Peter swiftly lowered his head and wiped away a tear with his beefy, tanned hand. "The doctor gave us back my mom," he said. Through the right combination of anti-depressants and therapy, I learned, his mother's clinical depression had gone into remission. She'd been able to return to her career and became a vibrant component of the family structure.

I sat silently, laptop closed and eyes softened and fixed on Peter, ready to engage with his gaze in a display of active, intentional listening. When he lifted his head, cheeks hot pink with emotion, he choked back the remaining tears before they fell.

I thanked Peter for his vulnerability and shared my gratitude that his mother was able to find clinical stability and extend her life by several decades—a gift that Peter and his family treasured.

"You guys are heroes, I hope you know that," Peter went on, promising that he was almost done sharing his story and butting into my time. I assured him it wasn't a bother—and meant it.

"You probably don't get a lot of thank-yous in your field, so I'm going to thank you now. You never know when you're giving a son back their mother or a parent back their child. You really are saving lives, and I wish there were more psychiatrists out in the world," he ended, before shaking my hand and grabbing his tepid coffee to go.

I sat in the thick August heat for several more minutes, leaving my laptop closed and letting the last ten minutes soak in.

Truthfully, unbeknownst to Peter, I was struggling with the decision of whether to stay in my psychiatry residency after maternity leave.

When I was in medical school, my clinical interests were piqued in the same fashion as my adoration for niche cafés; I explored the varying specialties like coffee shops, trying each one on for size and feel, falling in love over and over again until I was dizzied. The specialty of obstetrics and gynecology felt like a high school sweetheart; I came into medical school certain I would pursue that field, as I loved nothing more than immersing myself in women's health and brightened at the idea of bringing newborns into the world. But, like all time-tested loves, I began to question whether the specialty was really for me—did I love it because it was all I knew to love? Was there something out there more compatible?

Alas, much like my creative eye, my medical eye wandered. Each of my clinical rotations in clerkship was like a short-story romance: I loved the feel of a scalpel in my palm in the operating theatre, the ability to unveil the body through the eyes in ophthalmology, the Sherlock Holmes detective work in internal medicine, and the childlike wonder of pediatrics. When I landed on my last clinical rotation in clerkship, psychiatry, it felt like two star-crossed lovers meeting at a college bar. I fell hard and fast, pulled into the mysterious intersection of mind and medicine that I'd always found intriguing but never imagined could be "the one." Like a runaway bride, I left behind the other clinical interests that I'd been enamoured with for years.

Yet, unlike the ease of slipping in and out of a café at my discretion, I had to commit to a specialty by the end of medical school—even if I didn't feel like it moulded to all the contours of my life. When I spoke with mentors and friends in medicine, they told me that no one specialty, like a friend or spouse, will perfectly meet all that we want or need; there will always be something in the field that we have to tolerate, like relatively lower compensation, gruelling residencies, frequent call shifts or copious documentation.

"You just have to pick what you love most," said Pier during one of our catch-ups, "what you can see yourself doing at 3:00 a.m. without resenting the lost sleep or time away from your family."

Thus, like a marriage, I picked psychiatry and hoped to tough it out, for better or for worse. I placed my feelings for other specialties on the back burner and moved forward in faith.

At first, the flames burned wildly during my residency—I adored working in the psychiatric emergency department, pulling patients back from the brink of extinction, and doing clinical research electives in functional neurology. I came alive when discussing traumatic brain injuries in young women and devoured the newest research in psychopharmacology (the scientific study of the effects of medication on the brain, mind and behaviour). I learned to appreciate the parts that I didn't immediately love, like intensive psychotherapy education, and came to value how to translate this skill to everyday interactions. I promised myself, above all, that I would create a clinical niche that fit just right—most likely neuropsychiatry—but also let my curiosity wander into reproductive psychiatry and sleep medicine.

Still, I couldn't quite extinguish the embers from past clinical romances. When I dawdled in the hospital hallways and saw surgeons scrubbing in to the operating room, pregnant mothers in the labour wards, or physicians running toward a code blue, I wondered if I'd truly made the right career choice.

What if I had matched to obstetrics? What about family medicine or public health? Pediatric neurology? Would I be happier or more fulfilled if I were still using my stethoscope, physical examination or surgical skills? Would the longing stop?

These queries would sprout into frightful moments where I would spiral into thinking I had settled for a lesser love, and my true soulmate was still out there, wishing they had stopped the nuptials at the altar. Gradually, especially over my maternity leave, I started to lament the forgone opportunities and the vision of the doctor I had thought I would grow to be.

After Peter left that day, however, leaving behind a vacant chair and a story that riveted my heart, I felt a moment of assuredness in my journey. Like remembering our partner's quirks that charmed us in the throes of puppy love, I reflected fondly on the beauty and privilege with psychiatry to be present for someone as they travelled through the experiences that both scarred and defined them. I thought of my patients on the in-patient child and adolescent psychiatry unit, who held more hurt than any child should know, but had the wisdom and resilience to tough out their lengthy admissions and beyond. I thought of the young pregnant mother with bipolar illness whom I had supported through my consult-liaison psychiatry rotation, fighting for additional resources and clinical support to ensure her baby was delivered healthy and at term. I reflected further on my patients experiencing withdrawal in the emergency department, who needed not only the right medications to alleviate their symptoms, but also a compassionate, judgment-free milieu to inspire their sobriety and path toward wellness.

I thought of all the quiet ways in which we as psychiatrists make an impact in our patients' lives, doing the work that many shy away from, advocating for those left on the margins, and—most importantly—saving lives.

With only minutes left to my writing day at the café, I reopened my laptop and punched out a few more lines of my story. I do not know where this romance with psychiatry will take me or how the chapter will unfold, but for all the imperfections of this love, I've grown to realize that, maybe, it is perfect for me.

Chapter Thirteen

The nurses' station on the mother and baby unit chimed with the sounds of fetal heart monitors and murmured with the voices of obstetrical nurses receiving handover at the top of their shifts. Dr. Ridley, the attending OB/GYN whom I was observing that evening on a shadowing opportunity in my second year of med school, was salvaging a rare quiet moment to eat a late dinner as an unusual calm settled over the wards. We had just finished assessing the exposed abdominal cavity of a freshly postpartum mother whose Caesarean section stitches had separated shortly after delivery, leaving her with an open wound that needed to heal through secondary intentions (left open for tissue to close naturally). The visual was jarring, as fatty tissue and muscle sat exposed, while the patient winced in pain as Dr. Ridley debrided the necrotic tissue, carefully removing the dead tissue with a scalpel and forceps. We quickly offered her more anesthetic before continuing the debridement, which she accepted with gratitude.

Dr. Ridley was both surgical and clinical in her approach, explaining how to approach debridement in post-surgical patients, while also pausing repeatedly to reassure the patient and provide needed comfort.

Marlee Ridley was the first Black woman I'd had the opportunity of shadowing in medical school, and with a Stanford-trained expertise in medicine, she was the person I looked to as the pinnacle of Black female medical excellence. As an aspiring obstetrician at this point in my training, I wanted to soak up her knowledge about the field and use her journey as the roadmap for my own dreams. From the day we were introduced through a connection within the faculty, she generously assumed the role of one of my cherished medical mentors.

Between bites of quinoa and chickpea salad, we chatted about her experiences at Stanford, how she landed on obstetrics and gynecology, and how she juggled motherhood, advocacy, clinical research and a demanding surgical specialty. I wanted to emulate her in every fashion, right down to being a mommy to two little girls. She slid her phone across the desk and showed me a picture of the littles on Halloween— one was a chubby-cheeked dinosaur and the other a wand-wielding princess. Dr. Ridley and her husband, a pediatric anesthetist, completed the image with matching fairy-tale costumes and plastered-on cheesy grins. I brightened at the sight—she was living a dream that seemed nearly at my fingertips.

"I also shared a love for internal medicine and physiology, which is what drew me toward obstetrics," Dr. Ridley explained, as she told me how her clinical focus in cancer and inflammatory bowel disease in high-risk pregnancies afforded her the ability to navigate the worlds of medicine, surgery and obstetrics. I confided in her that, other than OB/GYN, I was seriously considering internal medicine as well, drawn to the pathophysiologic (disturbances in normal physiology associated with disease) complexities that defined the specialty. "The beautiful part about medicine is that you can tailor your career to blend different areas of interest into your practice," she advised.

Two weeks prior, when I had joined Dr. Ridley in her Brampton-based outpatient obstetrics clinic, I had seen exactly how this blend materialized. We were counselling a woman in her late forties who had recently found out that she was expecting a baby—which should have been a joyous surprise after dealing with over a decade of infertility.

Heartbreakingly, this joy was blunted by her pre-existing diagnosis of terminal cancer. I sat in silence as Dr. Ridley counselled her through the logistics of an impossible dilemma: the pregnancy itself would not advance or worsen the state of her malignancies, but the length of time without treatment could allow the metastases to grow and threaten her long-term prognosis. On the other hand, they could plan to deliver the baby shortly after the cusp of viability (twenty-four weeks) to allow her to resume her chemotherapy, extending her own life, while potentially increasing the risk of morbidity and mortality for her precious child. Dr. Ridley shape-shifted from obstetrician, to internist, to psychiatrist as the patient's needs and queries morphed in the span of the thirty-minute appointment. I watched as the patient's emotions evolved through the excitement of impending motherhood, fear, helplessness, confusion, and ultimately hope tethered to unshakable bravery. I hardly uttered a word throughout that appointment, but I left the room knowing—beyond the shadow of a doubt—that medicine was exactly where I belonged. There was no greater privilege in life, for me, than holding the hands of patients through their darkest hours, through the stories of humanity that previously had seemed to exist only within pages of fiction and reels of cinema.

When I reunited with Dr. Ridley weeks later, on the maternity wards, as we ate our late dinner from the hospital cafeteria, I longed to be immersed in the stories of her training. I craved to know the moments that came to define her career, how she knew obstetrics was her calling above all the other specialties that piqued her interest. I wondered how she dealt with the emotional devastation of counselling patients on the precipice of life and death, whether these moments clung to her skin well after her scrubs were thrown into a pile of laundry, ready to be cleansed of the evidence of a traumatic day. I wanted to know the tales of triumph that kept her pushing through the gruelling hours on call as an obstetrician and the nights that she spent away from her kids. As a child whose mother spent more time at work than at home, and still managed to make the force of her love the guiding light in our lives, I wondered if my mother was the anomaly, or if this magic could be struck by other women—including Dr. Ridley and me.

"Boundaries are important," she imparted to me, as I fished the last piece of baked sweet potato out from the bottom of my container with a fork. I wished for another bite to eat, already feeling depleted from the fast-paced rounds on the OB floor. I resolved to treat myself to something devilishly caloric and yummy after the shift, a habit I had started to form as I was still learning how to heal the relationship between me, stress regulation, and food.

"I make sure that I can always drop my girls off at daycare and school before the start of the day—that is non-negotiable for me, especially as I'm not always home when they are done school." Her eyes softened at the thought of her daughters. I knew that doctor-moms carried the unspoken burden of negotiating their roles as mothers and doctors, often feeling as though the balance was impossible to strike.

Maybe it wasn't magic after all, but the ferocity and devotion of a mother's love that enabled us to do the impossible when presented with the infinite challenges of womanhood.

Dr. Ridley's gaze swung from me to the patient-monitoring screen at the nurses' station, close to where we were seated, which intermittently beeped with alerts of fetal heart rate accelerations and decelerations.

As I readied another question for her from my arsenal of queries, an urgent page echoed overhead as Dr. Ridley was beckoned by the charge nurse. "Let's go, now!" she said. Any curiosities I had I needed to save for later.

Before I could even register what was transpiring, Dr. Ridley sprinted from her seat toward the obstetrical emergency room. When we arrived, specialized nurses were already rushing to the patient's side.

"The bleeding started this evening," said Yvette, a third-year obstetrical resident tasked with briefing Dr. Ridley on the urgent details of the case.

"At first, she described it as a bit of spotting that got progressively heavier throughout the last hour, with painful abdominal cramps radiating toward her lower back," Yvette continued. "The pregnancy has been uncomplicated, and both babies were growing well at the last obstetrical ultrasound earlier this week."

My focus shifted from Yvette to our patient, a heartbroken woman in her early forties who lay gripping the underside of her swollen belly. Her husband stood at the bedside, in a state of shock, evidently struggling to grasp what was unfolding before him.

I learned that our patient was an expectant mother of identical twin girls, currently at thirty-three-weeks' gestation. It was her first pregnancy to make it past the critical twelve-week mark. Yvette reported that she had struggled with infertility for fifteen years, and after several miscarriages and rounds of in vitro fertilization, she had finally carried this pregnancy into the third trimester. These were her miracle babies, after years of disappointment and grief; each life inside her was an extension of her soul.

"*Why, God?!*" our patient cried out, in a shriek that tore through the wards.

Shortly after her arrival at the labour and delivery emergency department, a bedside obstetrical ultrasound confirmed the unimaginable: a partial detachment of the placenta from the uterine wall, known clinically as a placental abruption, and undetectable fetal cardiac activity in Baby Girl A. In obstetrics, this is one of the most critical cases, as the lives of both the mother and the remaining twin hang in the balance.

The sudden loss of one of their long-coveted children was inconceivable. Our sentiments of consolation fell woefully short on what was presumably the worst day of their lives. I searched my mind for words that could serve as a salve for their despair, but there was no time to waste.

"We have to get to the operating room, immediately," said Dr. Ridley calmly, yet with a commanding seriousness that let me, and everyone present, know this was as urgent as it could get. The plan was to bring our patient into the operating theatre for an emergency Caesarean section. If she continued to bleed, she could go into hypovolemic shock (a condition in which severe blood loss makes the heart unable to function appropriately) and succumb to the blood loss—ending not only her life but the life of Baby Girl B. What had started as the devastating loss of one twin could quickly end as the life-shattering loss of an expectant father's whole world.

Under the glare of operating room lights, Dr. Ridley pulled her surgical gloves over her hands and assessed the sterile field. I, too, had scrubbed in to the surgery, but due to the sensitive and urgent nature of the operation, I was asked to simply observe from the sidelines. I stood with my arms hanging rigidly by my side, careful to not disturb the sterility of my preparation in case I was summoned to join in at Dr. Ridley's side.

The sweet, crooning serenade of acoustic music filled the brightly lit corridors of the operating theatre, requested by the patient's husband. He sang along loudly, his voice overpowering the speakers, as if he was calling out to the spirit of their departed baby girl, or pleading with their remaining daughter to stay. A tear swam at the corner of our patient's eye, then flowed in a direct line down her face, onto the surgical bed. It cleared a path for other tears to follow. She sang along in a familiar cadence often reserved for funerals and home-goings. Her eyelids squeezed tightly in a pain that clearly extended beyond the physical realm.

After creating a clean incision across our patient's lower abdomen, Dr. Ridley and her assisting surgeons began a coordinated sequence of manoeuvres to quickly—but masterfully—deliver Baby Girl A and save the lives of Baby Girl B and her mother. The process went on for several minutes, a push and pull between the womb and outside world. The immense pressure elicited a painful whimper from the patient until, finally, her children were presented earthside. Baby Girl B was whisked away by the neonatology team to the resuscitation field for stabilization, as Baby Girl A was taken by the nurse to be wrapped in a blanket and given to the parents to say their goodbyes.

The room stood still for a moment. This wasn't the pregnancy ending glorified on social media timelines or celebrated on WhatsApp chain messages; it was a bittersweet and crushing ending to a saga of infertility that had spanned decades. There would be no immediate announcement card mailed to loved ones and doctors' offices. What lay before the new parents was a road paved with uncertainty, as Baby Girl B—whom they named Grace—went off to the NICU to fight for her life.

Dr. Ridley and the surgical team began the intricate art of closing the patient's incision, working their way from her uterus, through the layers of muscle and flesh, and ultimately suturing together the top layer of epidermis.

In that moment, my mind conjured a string of intense philosophical and existential questions. At what point did an unborn child develop a soul? Was it at the instant of conception, the moment when the first neural connection was sparked, or when the baby was earthside? Did this child have any concept of how much she was loved, how badly she was desired, or the intense pain of her loss? Was there a meaning behind the soul-testing misery of what this patient had endured, or was it simply just a terrible stroke of misfortune? How would this couple balance the pain of loss and the joy of a new life, knowing that every time they looked into their daughter's eyes, they would also be staring into the face of their lost child?

I shook the questions from my mind, tasking myself only with the burden of doing exactly what was asked of me as a junior medical student: assist with writing the operating note, refrain from contaminating the sterile field, and stand by for further instruction.

I was reminded that evening that frequently, despite the advancements and innovations in medicine, tragedy is a component of our work. Although doctors are trained in the school of science and evidence-based practice, we are humbled by the reminders that there are no guarantees in medicine. We do our best—our very best—and the rest is a combination of fate, luck and maybe some kind of cosmic intervention. What is asked of us thereafter is to try to make sense of the unthinkable, and usher our patients on the path forward.

▼

We were warned by upper-year students that the second year of medical school would be the hardest year of pre-clerkship, academically. Our first few blocks of the year were neuroanatomy, neurology, neuro-ophthalmology and psychiatry—a deep dive into the complicated world of the brain and mind. The mastery exams would remain as frequent, every two to three weeks, and would now be accompanied by anatomy bell-ringers.

Any medical student can resonate with the distinct, gut-wrenching fear that bell-ringers provoke. These are high-pressure tests of knowledge and composure, where pins are placed onto a cadaver, with adjoining anatomical questions, and medical students have two minutes at each station to correctly identify the anatomy and answer the questions before the bell rings and they must move on. As one can imagine, should you not be able to identify the anatomical feature (whether muscle, nerve or tissue), you would struggle greatly to answer the adjoining questions correctly. A frantic mind, silly mistakes and intense perspiration could ensue. The ring of the bell could startle you into cardiac arrest.

Failure lurked in the corners.

Unless you were prepared.

Having been an anatomy TA in Health Sci as a fourth-year student at McMaster—my second part-time job alongside being a barista—I adored anatomy and was particularly fascinated by neuroanatomy.

Now, at U of T, I would spend hours at my desk in the living room, often rising before dawn, to sketch the beautiful contours of white and grey matter: the corpus callosum, the thalamus, the hippocampi, caudate nucleus, and several other structures that come together to create the most intricate organ in the body. I was mesmerized by the understanding that our identities, our memories and our behaviours are all housed within this stunning organ, which is paradoxically both fragile to different forms of trauma (physical and emotional) and incredibly resilient and able to heal through neuroplasticity.

After class and during mornings on the weekend before exams, I would head to the anatomy labs in the basement of MSB, where I would study the cadavers alongside my classmates, grateful to the donors who had lent their bodies for the advancement of science. My printout questions would be secured on a clipboard, with red ink circling the concepts that still eluded me. By mid-afternoon, my white coat and papers would be stained with formaldehyde, and I would rise from the basement assured in my knowledge.

By late September, well into the thick of the neurology block focusing on localization and movement disorders, I had developed a routine that was tightly scheduled and militantly followed. When not preoccupied with studying, I dedicated my evenings to weekly classes and assignments for my master's degree, EISC meetings, co-chairing BMSA alongside one of the first-year Black medical students (of which there were six, prior to the implementation of BSAP), attending BSAP advisory meetings, calls where I provided mentorship, presenting at conferences as a guest speaker, and writing the Faculty of Medicine *Daffydil: A Matter of Time* musical script with my co-writer, Adam Katz.

My agenda, a grey Leuchtturm notebook, was full of bullet-journal-style annotations, hand-drawn daily, monthly and weekly calendars, itineraries down to the half-hour, and quotes by Maya Angelou written in cursive across the bottom.

"Nothing will work unless you do," I whispered to myself habitually when my morale needed lifting and my arms were weary from long days and even longer nights. I realized quickly that I needed more ways to shore up my morale when I met emotional, psychological or mental roadblocks on my path to becoming a physician.

"I think I want to write a new poem," I told Vic one afternoon in early October, while she stared quizzically at a jigsaw puzzle of famous feminists throughout history, which sat in the living room of our shared condo. The face of Frida Kahlo was partially constructed, a circuitous line cutting through her features, severing her signature eyebrow, as Vic searched for the piece with Kahlo's frayed hairs feathered in the middle.

"Ooh! So fun! Do you think you'll perform it?" she replied, while I searched the kitchen for a snack and started a coffee for her.

"Mm, I'm thinking about it," I said, spreading some hummus over a toasted slice of rye.

I had recently been invited to give a poetry set at a moody café in downtown Toronto, and my performance of "SKIN," among some other favourite poems, had me turning over an experience with a preceptor in class. The words of the doctor continued to dance in my mind, and I couldn't keep quiet about it.

I had asked the staff physician when we were going to learn how to deal with racism and sexism as medical students. We had spent the majority of first year learning about how to be culturally sensitive physicians, identifying our subconscious biases and meeting the unique needs of marginalized populations, but we had not yet touched on how racialized physicians confronted and processed instances of discrimination. Simply, what do we do when we are *also* part of the marginalized?

"Medical school," the preceptor replied, "is about teaching you how to develop as a doctor and take care of patients." I could sense the disappointment swelling within me.

"We don't really teach you how to deal with racism and sexism during medical school. When you're a resident, then you can take on that responsibility individually—it's a time for independent development. Or maybe you can connect with another Black faculty who can help you with that," the physician concluded, as, no doubt, an unmistakable look of defeat rested on my face.

I rebutted, knowing that not only had I already been dealing with racism and discrimination since the start of medical school, but I would undoubtedly face it from patients when I started clerkship. How, I thought, could I be expected to perform at a high level without the tools needed to unpack that kind of trauma? It was clear to me, from the preceptors, lecturers, tutors and lecture material, that the medical school curriculum had not evolved to create an inclusive space for racialized learners or to prepare them adequately for working in the outside world.

When the story broke of Dr. Tamika Cross, an OB/GYN who was barred from helping a passenger having a medical emergency on a Delta flight because the flight attendants didn't believe she was a doctor without formal proof of her credentials, I felt more immediately spirited to channel my frustration into advocacy.

"What does a doctor look like?" headlined articles about Dr. Cross, spurring a global discourse about who belongs in medicine, what the face of a physician has collectively been, historically, and how this has been starting to shift with respect to both gender and race.

If Black folks truly belonged at U of T, as I believed and echoed through the BSAP campaign, then these issues needed to be identified and corrected. I raised these same concerns during the BSAP advisory meetings, stating that it would be unethical to invite more Black students into U of T Med while racism and other discriminatory experiences were roaming the institution, unchecked. The faculty members on the board agreed.

It needed to be safe.

I wanted to *feel* safe. As a Black woman, navigating what was historically a white man's domain.

"I want to write about what it's like being a Black girl in medicine," I said to Vic, as the Keurig machine chugged behind me. When it churned out a stream of black coffee that splashed at the bottom of her "Reading is Sexy" mug, she rose to swirl cream into the deep brown centre, and I scurried away to my room to mull over my percolating thoughts.

I woke up the next morning at around 5:00, with the words "Black, woman, doctor" running laps through my mind. I pulled out my laptop, sitting with one knee nestled under my chin and the other leg tucked atop the chair, and I let the stanzas pour out of me. A few hours later, my poem "Woman, Black" was born.

"Wanna listen to this new piece?" I asked Vic, as she rubbed the sleep from her eyes. I was still in my pyjamas and engrossed in a world of words, new lines and rhymes popping into my brain each minute like crackles from a bonfire.

"Totally!" she replied.

I slid the cursor to the top stanza, excited to breathe life into my newest creation.

Woman, and Black
Doctor and woman, doctor and Black,
Doctor, Black woman,
Doctor! Doctor! We need a doctor!
Is there anyone on this plane that can help?

My desk transformed into a miniature stage in front of me, my cold teacup into a microphone, and Vic into my audience. The poem continued for several more stanzas, and though it was far from finished and this was my first pass through the verses aloud, I spontaneously generated the rhythm, cadence and intonation for the lines that I would use for a potential performance. My hand gestured through the air like a maestro conducting a symphony while I spontaneously edited the lines with words that felt more organic and fitting to the stanza, pausing for moments to write my edits down before continuing. Vic observed me in awe from the kitchen, a mad scientist spinning magic from metaphors and similes who would stop abruptly mid-sentence, stare blankly into the air, type furiously, then keep performing.

As I reached the final stanza I had written, still unsure how to conclude the poem, I told Vic I would catch up with her in class. As she left, the final line germinated in my mind.

I am woman. I am Black. I am doctor.
And I am here.

▼

"I think being so vocal like this is a bit risky," one of my mentors shared with me, after receiving a copy of my newly finished poem, "Woman, Black." I was planning to record and release a spoken word video performance of this new piece on a popular site for physicians and the public to engage in debates concerning health care.

"You are quite vulnerable as a medical student, Chika. You don't have the protection that is afforded with seniority. I support you, I truly do, but I want you to understand the risk that you're taking," they warned me. "Why don't you wait until you're a staff, or resident even, to do this kind of work?"

But I couldn't, I told them.

Institutional changes often take years, and art was the purest form of advocacy for me; poetry was my voice when I felt voiceless. I needed a way to process the pain I was feeling.

Before staffhood.

Before residency.

I hadn't been supported often enough through the curriculum in the way that I felt was necessary. My concerns were being either erased, minimized or pushed to the fringes. My art felt critical. I was compelled to speak up for every Black medical student who had ever felt silenced or was made to feel that their plight was irrelevant. For every Black physician who didn't fit into the mould of what a doctor looked like.

Like the *Toronto Star* article and the BSAP advocacy, I knew that the move was risky. But as I had noted in my keynote speech at a youth leadership awards night a month before, the question is not whether to do the right thing but *how* to do the right thing.

A week later, my spoken word video went live on the website Healthy Debate, as threads of pride and reticence wove through my spine. I had gone against the recommendation of my medical mentors, who wanted to protect me within an institution that would swiftly penalize a Black, fearless girl like me. But I did what I thought was right, in the best way I knew how. Through words.

Chapter Fourteen

Truth be told, the allure of silence in medicine was appealing, and for some Black docs who came before me, it was the only path to survival when they faced adversity in the profession. Those who dared to speak up against injustice in the decades prior were sometimes met with material consequences—being overlooked for promotions and academic appointments, losing their jobs, being rejected from residencies or fellowships. At the very least, they could experience a not-so-subtle social othering. The goal, I had been advised, was simply to get *through*, then challenge the system from a position of power. But what many had come to learn is that "power" is simply an illusion, even when you've accrued the accolades, titles and distinctions. Blackness cannot be escaped, nor can the systems of discrimination that come with it; these systems need to be destroyed.

"Woman, Black" was the next step in my effort to deconstruct the culture of silence around the Black experience in medical school, one that caught the attention of many who were accustomed to the pristine reputation of medicine—including journalist Ishani Nath.

I met with Ishani inside the Rogers Media building in early January 2018, after passing through the heavy security that guarded the entrance.

"I think the working title is perfect, straight from your poem and capturing the essence of the article," said Ishani, as she pulled open the doors to *Flare* magazine's head office and led me toward the photo shoot set. We had connected via email just a month before, when she pitched the idea to me of writing an article about my experiences at U of T for Black History Month 2018. It would be the first time that I'd be at the helm of telling my story to the world through the media, with no journalist serving as an intermediary. Although I continued to wrestle with the potential risks of being an audacious Black medical student, I embraced a quote from Black, queer, feminist revolutionary Audre Lorde—my silence would not protect me.

"In this white coat, I am more Black than ever" headlined the working drafts of my piece, which had passed through two rounds of editors on its way to being published.

I would come to explain, in keynote Q & As and panel discussions for years after, that this line was a double entendre of sorts. Wearing a physician's coat, quite literally, brings out the hues of my dark skin because of the stark contrast. More metaphorically, however, it's a direct challenge to the people who try to question the intelligence of Black students, those who try to make us feel that we don't belong in medicine. In rebuttal, when I wear a doctor's coat, I am actualizing my personal full potential as a Black woman; I am owning my brilliance and the gifts that are often hard-won for people like me. I am, as I stated, Blacker than ever in my physician's coat.

The studio was draped with backdrops that hung from the ceiling. There were large reflectors and soft lights to influence the exposure and brightness, monitors that displayed the photos as they streamed in, and cameras with lenses that were larger than I had ever seen and more expensive than I could even approximate.

The editors and photography team huddled around the monitor as they debated which shot would be the best one to go with the piece.

"Let's get one without a smile," the main photographer said. "Something more serious to match the tone of the article."

The camera whirred, and I steeled myself for the multiverse of potential public, personal and professional reception that would ensue.

It had been two months since the public release of "Woman, Black," and its positive reception, initially from the Canadian medical community, had left me windswept. Hundreds, then thousands of views started to accrue across the internet within days of its publication in mid-November. People began widely sharing the video, which spread across social media and circulated through email and other international platforms.

Instead of vitriol staining the comment section, there was a flood of effusive approval.

"Very powerful! Thank you, can I be your patient when you graduate?"

"Powerful, Dr. Chika. Bless you, keep going."

"Brilliant poem! Powerful. Beautiful. Important."

Poetry is transcendent. That's something I have always known, but my understanding was reinforced by this experience. There is something profound and unparalleled in being able to communicate soul to soul, reaching out and bringing someone into the light of your lived experience. Poetry does that, and that's why I needed to use my poetic prowess to let the world know what it was like to have my dream of being a doctor repeatedly questioned, dismissed and stolen.

Would the medical and general community respond to my vulnerability in this article as they had to "Woman, Black"?

In the interval between the *Flare* shoot and the article's launch for Black History Month 2018, I busied myself with studying the newest medical lecture material on pediatrics and finalizing the script for the Faculty of Medicine *Daffydil* musical—which we titled *A Matter of Time*—that was set to take the stage in mid-February. I attended a couple of the rehearsals with my co-writer, Katz, who would become an incredible friend, playwright and family physician. Watching our characters come to life off the page was a breathtaking experience, and this quickly became one of my most cherished artistic accomplishments.

BSAP had also officially launched the August before, and the interview season for the first candidates for medical school admission through the stream was taking place in late January. As the co-president of BMSA and a vocal advocate of the BSAP initiative, I led interview prep sessions, had several mentorship calls and coffee dates, and organized lunches to welcome BSAP candidates on the day of the interviews. I encouraged them to join U of T Med, attempting to persuade candidates who were being offered admission to other renowned medical schools in Canada and abroad (including Harvard and Yale). I understood what I was asking of them—to enter a space that had caused me grievance and hardship, with the blind faith that things *really would* be different in the years to come. They needed to be, for all of us—enriching the medical experience for every learner and the overall health care system as a byproduct.

When several asked me, "How bad is it?" it was clear that they were referring not only to the academics but also to the experience of going through the medical world as a Black student. Cognizant that the goal was to recruit them, not scare them off, I told them that, should they choose U of T, I would be there for support. And, unlike me, they would also have a family in the other BMSA students in their year.

The entire goal of my advocacy, which served to help them but also heal my wounds, was to ensure that no other Black student faced what I had within the walls of U of T medical school. No one, I promised myself, would do this alone. That narrative needed to stop with me.

A few of the interview candidates mentioned that they had seen my article in the *Toronto Star* and had written about my advocacy in their "Why the BSAP stream?" essay for the application. My heart swelled with pride and purpose, and I grew more nervous for my *Flare* article to be released. I needed the world to understand just how crucial it was to have this initiative, not only at U of T but at other medical and professional schools across the country.

When it was published a few weeks later on *Flare*'s major social media platforms to launch Black History Month, the cover shot the magazine chose was one that stopped me in my tracks. It displayed me with my hands cradling the stethoscope draped around my neck, my eyes earnest and forward-looking, my expression austere and commanding. It was a striking depiction of the kind of strength I had always wished to possess; when I looked at this photo, I saw my mother and grandmother looking back at me. I looked like the kind of doctor I wished four-year-old Chika could have seen in her sleepy suburban community.

I then remembered the classmate who had told me that I "just look intimidating," for no reason. Intimidation was not what I wanted to communicate with this picture, but maybe it would evoke discomfort in the reader, which is the only position where real change can occur.

"*In my white coat, I'm more Black than ever*, by @chikastacypoet" filled the limited character count in *Flare*'s tweet, with my article linked and picture attached to the post. The magazine's platform, which across all social accounts reached over one million readers, catapulted me to a level of visibility and virality that I had not yet encountered. I was beginning to receive so many notifications that the Twitter app prompted me to collate them or turn them off unless I wanted my phone to be rendered non-functional.

The article began spreading like wildfire. It did not take me long to become engulfed in the flames of public opinion.

"@Flarefashion and @chikastacypoet The average IQ of a black American is 15-20% lower than a white American . . . If she wants more blacks in her class she can go back to Africa."

My head spun from the blatant ignorance and inaccuracy of this person's claims. Racist scientific research conducted within the past century to try to prove that Black people and Africans were less intelligent, as a justification to uphold systems of slavery and discrimination, was inherently flawed and proven later to be flat out wrong. Moreover, I was advocating for more Black people to earn their MDs, but having more Black PhDs would be a great thing for *everyone*, too. Lastly, I was born in Ottawa, Ontario, Canada. I am a proud daughter of Nigerian immigrants and would love to see where my parents were born and raised. But I am Canadian-born and will only "go back to Africa" to meet my extended family, travel, assist in medical missions, gorge myself on jollof rice, egusi soup, pounded yam and pies before returning home and continuing my work as a Canadian-rooted doctor.

Trolls love to create stories that fit their outrageous narrative, I learned. But my intellectual dismantling of this person's claims would be futile. I knew better than to "feed the trolls," and clearly this person was not the kind of thoughtful debater who would engage in reasonable discourse. My palms grew damp as I watched, powerless, as the hateful responses mounted.

"@chikastacypoet Why's this a thing? She's black, so? Maybe black people don't want to pursue medicine? . . . WHY IS THIS NEWS?"

To which another person replied:

"@chikastacypoet cuz there's a monkey on campus"

This one pierced through my gut like an archer's arrow. Comparing Black people to monkeys is neither creative nor novel; it is a long-standing trope that dehumanizes our race and justifies our mistreatment. But it remains highly effective in provoking anguish.

That's the wild thing about racism. Within an instant, it can strip the recipient of power, irrespective of the initial power imbalance. It is the kryptonite of our society.

My eyes stung with fresh, hot tears that rolled down my cheeks and gathered onto the slate-grey surface of my laptop.

"@chikastacypoet Maybe not many colored people are able to present the necessary requirements . . . maybe because when competing to whites you are just a fraction!! Perhaps we should do the same Hollywood did . . . to make you feel better, bitch!!"

I broke down, logging out of the Twitter app, and shook with a palpable ire. I wanted to yell so loudly that the screams would reach the faceless trolls and drown out their hurtful, hideous words. Despite the waves of support that tried to wash the trash off the shores of my advocacy, remnants of their comments remained in my mind, rotting and festering like rancid refuse.

One half of my spirit yearned to delete all my social media accounts, retreat into the shadows of anonymity and wait for the spotlight to fade. Parts of me questioned myself, whether this effort to shed light on an experience that was commonly shared among many Black physicians was a futile endeavour that threatened my medical ambitions and made me a martyr.

The other half of me, however, realized that this was exactly the goal of the trolls. They wanted to berate me into silence, to make me question my own intelligence, my own personhood. They wanted to resolve the cognitive dissonance between what they believed and what they were viewing: Black women and men weren't smart enough to become physicians, yet here was this outspoken Black girl boasting otherwise.

I understood that a Black woman who realizes her own power is one of the most threatening forces in the world, and those who attacked me online likely recognized this as well.

I put my phone away and turned back to my laptop screen. A lecture on the five most common infections in infancy and how to perform a clinical exam waited for me, ready to be transcribed and dedicated to memory.

They could not, and would not, stop me.

An audience member snuck through the backdoor entrance of the auditorium, past a bright pink and white "Women's College Hospital (WCH) International Women's Day (IWD) 2018" sign, and searched for an empty seat in the packed crowd. As there were no available seats left, they joined the growing group of researchers, physicians, medical students, clinicians and community members who either stood in the back or sat on the steps in the aisle. The CEO of WCH remarked that the hospital had never drawn an audience this big for any other speaker it had hosted.

"This is something special," she stated, welcoming the crowd to the event before introducing me. The lights in the auditorium were dimmed, with just a few spotlights centred on the stage; beyond the front row, where reserved seats were waiting to be filled by my parents, I could hardly make out the faces of other audience members. I knew that my entire clinical skills group, including my preceptor, would be in attendance. As would Vic, Adam, Katz and even other classmates who had told me they "wouldn't miss it," asking to be released from small-group learning early to attend my IWD keynote address.

I asked one of the event organizers to keep an eye out for my mom and dad, requesting that they be ushered to the front as soon as they arrived. I didn't want them to miss a moment.

I wanted to give my mom the gift of witnessing her baby shine.

But the show must go on, and not on African time. So, even though they hadn't arrived yet, I drew a slow, steady breath as I was called up to stage. I walked over to where a sole mic stand stood, already adjusted to my height. I bent my head forward, letting my mid-back-length twists fall in front, interwove my fingers, and thrust my head up toward the audience. I was now calibrated to performance mode.

> You've waited one week,
> No words were heard when the doctor begins to speak.
> Your fingers tightly interwoven on your lap,
> Head slightly tilted back when he says, "your scans are
>   clear"
> Eyes begin to well with tears,
> Because at thirty-six years you could not have imagined
>   that you would find yourself here.

My arms ascended and fell in a theatrical accompaniment to each line;

the words rolled off the tip of each finger and floated into the crowd for careful digestion.

When my parents arrived, late, in between my second and third stanzas, I tried to not let their scuffling to their seats distract me. Over the years, I had performed through every conceivable disruption; I needed to call upon that professionalism now to get me through the piece.

It was the first time that I had ever performed the poem in front of a crowd. I was terrified of forgetting a stanza, or blanking on the poem entirely, which wouldn't have been surprising given its novelty, intricate wordplay, length and the intimidation I felt from the crowd.

When I arrived at the last stanza, near-perfect execution of my poem in sight, I slowed the tempo to match the message I was trying to deliver.

> But she finds hope in the four walls of that room
> Where faith lingers in the air like perfume
> Within a hospital that conquers the impossible
> For everyday women with concerns
> Ranging from abdominal to oncological
> Gynecological to optical
> With doctors, nurses, and health care workers
> That bravely face every obstacle
> Spinning miracles out of the improbable
> At Women's College Hospital
> Health care for women is revolutionized
> Where the gaps that once seemed so wide are being drawn
>   to a close
> Leading women through the ebbs and flows of their
>   darkest hour
> Reminding them of their power
> Pressing for progress in every direction
> Professionals of the finest collection

Are gathered here
For women,
For us,
And so we thank you.

I took a deep breath and stood back from the microphone as the audience broke into a roar of claps and approbation. I bowed in gratitude. My mom's smile shone from the front row as she cheered so vigorously that I thought she might fall out of her chair. I giggled internally, my frustration at their tardiness immediately melting away.

This day was as much hers as it was mine. I've only ever wanted to make her proud.

I walked to the podium with conviction, carrying the energy from a flawless performance to commence the formal part of my address.

I spoke of my childhood, what it was like growing up as a little Black girl who struggled to fit in, wishing away her Blackness, changing the way I spoke, only to still be othered, despite my earnest attempts at acceptance. I regaled them with tales of confronting sexism within my community— being asked what specialty of medicine I wanted to pursue, only to be warned that I would never keep a husband unless I learned how to cook.

"I am proud to a be a young woman of colour in medicine," I closed. "Hopefully, I will be the last person to say that I am the only Black student in my medical school year." They hummed and clapped in agreement.

"To my sisters, from all walks of life.

"Remember that though there are hurdles to clear, you are not alone, and success is all the more rewarding because of it. Be fearless, for there is so much you have to offer. Be loud, proud, intelligent and beautiful.

"Be your own woman, without reservation, without apology.

"Be you.

"Thank you."

Chapter Fifteen

I cried and kept crying.

Deep, heavy, unyielding sobs that emerged from the core of my body, taking me, and everyone else present on the BSAP advisory committee, by surprise. The kind of weeping that demands a bit of space instead of consolation; no soft-handed back rub, no emotional support check-ins. Just me sitting at the boardroom table, head curled toward my chest, trying to stifle the growing shivers that reverberated through my body.

It was a river of tears that burst through the dam of repose that I had built over the past two years; a chink in my armour of strength cracking straight through on that late April 2018 afternoon.

Mere moments before, the chair of the admissions committee, and one of the members of the advisory committee, a cardiac surgeon named Dr. David Latter, had announced that there would be fourteen Black medical students matriculating through the BSAP program that fall.

Fourteen.

Black, brilliant, deserving medical students.

Fourteen Black medical students who would never have to know the pain of walking across the stethoscope ceremony stage wondering if they would need to brave the next four years alone. Fourteen Black medical students who, even if they didn't become the best of friends, could lean on one another in moments when their humanity, ability and merit were challenged. Fourteen Black medical students who could find a space of solidarity, who could unburden themselves of code-switching and relax into their Blackness without reservation. Fourteen Black medical students who would shift the discourse among their classmates, bringing forth issues as they related to Black health, and creating safer spaces for Black patients to receive medical care. Fourteen Black medical students who would improve the learning environment for every other student in the MSB auditorium and foster a richer, more diverse dialogue.

Fourteen.

The number struck me like a meteorite; a blazing projection of hope whose impact was unprecedented. I had spent the past several years absorbing racial aggression in the face of my aspirations to become a physician, the past two years devastated that I was the only Black medical student in my class—absorbing further macro- and micro-aggressions— and the past year and a half advocating tirelessly for change, lending my voice and narrative to a cause that threatened professional and at times personal extinction. I had stepped into the public spotlight, against the warnings and omens of being blacklisted within the medical community, and got harassed mercilessly and violently online. I had unapologetically occupied space when my dissenters dared earnestly to push me out.

At times, the war was within myself, as I wrestled with disordered eating and anxiety in the throes of my isolation, in front of the world.

But in that moment, when I learned that fourteen outstanding Black medical students would be admitted that fall, I nearly collapsed from the gratitude, shock, relief and sheer anguish.

I relished knowing that no other Black medical student would walk through U of T alone, ever again, so long as BSAP remained in place— and we were certain that it would. That was my primary and initial goal in my advocacy, and it was achieved.

Amazement filled my mind considering the stark difference achieved in only two years, from one Black medical student to fourteen, in part due to a wildly successful campaign that gained national headlines and drew in dozens of worthy candidates. Every single media interview and anonymous racist comment, every midday mentorship meeting before an exam, every interview prep session or essay edit, and every blatant plea to the Black candidates on interview day to choose U of T was worth it.

We were changing the face of what a doctor looked like.

But within the tears of unbridled happiness were also those of pain.

I immediately wondered how different my journey would have been if I'd had thirteen other Black medical students in my class. How I could have avoided, from day one, facing certain moments of racism alone. How I could have brought my Blackness more comfortably into the space from the beginning, instead of hiding it for fear of being ostracized.

I felt robbed. I felt deceived for choosing U of T based in part on the school having a BMSA, only to arrive and find no one else in my year would be a member. I felt the anger of being disillusioned, the ripe, raw disbelief that had struck me during orientation week.

I cried knowing that, although there would be a seismic change in the years after me, my position remained fixed. I would need to weather the next two years of clerkship even more alone, and face more instances of discrimination from patients and staff, as I was told was often the experience of Black learners.

They would have each other, and I would still be the lone soldier.

As I wept in a room full of senior faculty physicians and administrators, I could hear more sobs slowly emerging from across the table.

It was Lisa, wiping away her tears. I'm sure she felt what I did in that moment: relief and pain, gratitude and grief. We were connected in our journeys and our laments.

"We should give Chika a moment, as we can imagine that this is a particularly special but difficult thing for her to process," said Onye. The sleeves of my grey sweater turned charcoal from the dampness of my eyes, and my sobs made my breaths short and sharp. Onye, too, was overcome with emotion at the gravity of this announcement.

There was not a dry eye in the room.

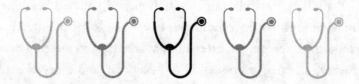

By the third week of my pediatric neurology elective in my second year of residency, I was well into the thirty-first week of my second pregnancy and already regretting my tendency to constantly hustle. It was a month before I discovered the wonders of a pregnancy support belt, so I walked through the lively halls of the pediatrics unit with the characteristic waddle of a woman braving her third trimester. Mothers with their little ones could empathize with the heavily pregnant resident doctor who passed them by, recognizing the things we quickly forget when we see the tiny toes and smell the intoxicating newborn aroma: a pause every few minutes to clutch the underside of our bellies and wince from pelvic pain, a laboured breath through the Braxton Hicks, and finding the nearest seat to rest our swollen feet.

The forward weight of my belly pulled taut the muscles of my lower back as I walked, reminding me with every step of the ways in which my second pregnancy differed vastly from my first. This time, I was blessed with a daughter, a gift that my mother reasoned was the explanation behind some of my pregnancy woes: girls (she said) make their mothers sicker (in my case, *very* sick for most of the pregnancy). Maybe it was the hormones, or maybe it was a slight taste of the headache my sisters and I gave my mother during our adolescent and teenage years, she joked. But by the seventh month of gestation, nothing seemed funny when each moment was coloured with nausea, searing sciatica pain or the fog that clung to my brain from the moment I woke. The closest thing to relief I felt was in the tiny moments when my sweet, but wildly energetic toddler, Eze, would pause amid his tornado of activity and snuggle up to me for a hug. He would quickly follow with raspberry kisses on my tummy before unexpectedly smacking it and running off to topple his fortress of Lego.

"Nkiru is just letting her presence be known," my husband, Dale, would say while rubbing my gravid belly in support. "She's strong-willed like her mama."

I knew that, like my unborn daughter, I had inherited this will from my mother, and she from hers, and so forth. It was woven into the blueprint of our DNA, a connection spanning generations and geographic locations. So, when my mother asked me why I hadn't lightened my packed key-noting schedule, or why I'd decided to go back to residency in the short time frame between my two maternity leaves, I chuckled, knowing that she would have done the exact same to provide for those she loved most. And I had witnessed her do so time and time again over the past twenty-nine years.

"I'm my mother's daughter" was my only response.

But there was one singular moment in my pregnancy with Nkiru that I knew would be etched into my mind forever, long after the pains had faded away.

Louis, a premature baby boy born at just thirty weeks gestation, lay in an incubator within the neonatal intensive care unit. His delicate yet swollen frame was wound in a tangle of tubes emerging from his nose, mouth and navel, with tape and monitoring electrodes spun around him like a spider's web. A sprawl of purple veins was easily visible through his thin, underdeveloped skin. The most petite blood pressure cuff I had ever seen was wrapped around his arm, connected to a monitor that dinged, beeped and flashed wildly behind the incubator.

When a group of us arrived at his bedside, his parents were taking their short respite at home, entrusting their only child's life to the dutiful hands of NICU nurses, doctors and other specialists on the ward. Our pediatric neurology team was consulted to assess Louis due to radiologic findings on an initial cerebral ultrasound.

"Infants born before thirty-two weeks in the womb are prone to spontaneous brain bleeds because the epithelial lining of the ventricles is fragile, which is what we are monitoring for in Louis and a few of the other neonates on the ward," said Cameron, the neonatal neurology fellow. He carried an ever-present confidence and composure despite the calamitous cases that he handled daily. I strove to mirror his equanimity, even though my heart ached at the sight of baby Louis.

"Chika, why don't you don some gloves and a gown to assist me in the neurological exam?"

I obliged, mentally rehearsing the sequence of exam steps as I waddled past the line of incubators to reach the donning and doffing vestibule.

After pulling a set of powder blue latex gloves over my fingers and tying the gown above my protruding belly, I stood on the opposite side of Louis's incubator awaiting further directives from my senior. Abruptly, I felt one of Nkiru's swift but powerful kicks pummelling me from the inside, ensuring that her presence was still not forgotten. I gripped my abdomen in response, holding it as my gaze fixed on the tiny, fragile life in the incubator before me.

In that fleeting moment, I realized that Nkiru was nearly the gestational age at which baby Louis was born. The trajectory of their lives had split in an instant—one thriving and growing at thirty-one weeks in the womb, the other inexplicably delivered prematurely and fighting for his life from the very moment that he took his first breath.

I imagined Louis's mother, whom I'd never met but felt connected to, rubbing her belly and singing sweet lullabies to her unborn son, daydreaming of the milestones to come: the first ultrasound when she could see and hear the heartbeat, intricately connected to her own, changing her purpose in life forever; the hours spent agonizing over the right stroller, nursery decor and furniture; the feeling of the first flutter within her womb, when the ability to create life feels puzzlingly real and magical all at once; the prenatal classes and plans for skin-to-skin bonding post-delivery, where the baby is soothed by the simplicity of her touch. These were the same moments that deepened my understanding of life, beyond medicine, beyond public speaking and writing. I was soon becoming someone's mother, once more, and the composite of my existence would be born anew.

But what if things didn't go as planned?

I wondered how the devastation of Louis's preterm labour, birth and hospitalization had shattered his mother's hopes for a healthy pregnancy, delivery and baby. I wondered how she found the strength to survive it, whether it was innate to her character or mustered when facing the unthinkable. My mind struggled to reconcile how the cards of fate were dealt, as fear began to wrestle its way through my gut and into my thoughts.

Please, Lord, keep my baby safe, I thought to myself, imagining what it would be like to fill the shoes of a mother in that room. Would I be able to show up brave-faced for Eze, moments after breaking down outside the NICU, praying for a miracle? Would I be strong enough to move forward in the face of peril, or succumb to it?

Medicine, especially this rotation on pediatric neurology, taught me that there are no guarantees in life or in motherhood. The line between tragedy and joy can be frighteningly thin.

"The baby is too medically unstable to be examined right now," said the NICU nurse, who hurried from her station to Louis's bedside as the monitor started blaring. A swarm of respiratory therapists, the general neonatal medicine team and other NICU nurses gathered around the incubator and began a coordinated dance of repositioning tubes and adjusting ventilation to attempt stabilization. Our neurology team took our cue to exit, stepping back from the incubator and watching Louis's laboured, sporadic breathing continue.

Nkiru had settled within me, lulled by the commotion and gentle rocking while I manoeuvred through the NICU on my way toward the back of the room.

"We'll write our recommendations into the chart," said Cameron, as I doffed my gown and gloves, exposing the silhouette of my tummy in front of another set of battle-worn parents who stood heartbroken in the hallway. I caught the mother with tear-stained cheeks peering at my belly, then making eye contact. A smile broke through the grief that cocooned her. I didn't know whether to smile back, cry or apologize.

I smiled, as her husband placed a comforting hand on her shoulder.

"Congratulations," said the mom, pressing a wet tissue to her cheek. I had heard this several times throughout both pregnancies, but this time it landed with an understanding to hold dear the life within me, for it could be gone in an instant.

"Thank you," I replied, crossing my hands in gratitude over my chest. I paused for another beat, our gazes briefly lingering in silent commiseration. No more words needed to be said. She softly grinned once more, before heading toward her baby in the incubator opposite Louis's.

We were connected in that moment, not as doctor and patient, or strangers intersecting coincidentally in time, but as mothers. I was reminded that tapping into what binds us together as humans is a force that, at times, is more healing than any medication or remedy. To be truly seen in life's daunting moments is a powerful thing.

I further understood that in the pursuit of being known as a percipient resident physician, which often calls on us to give all of ourselves to medicine, I needed to slow down, step back—otherwise, I'd miss out on what truly matters in life.

I thought of Eze and Nkiru, how quickly they would grow, and how important it was for me to never take for granted the beautiful subtleties of their childhood: the first time they babble "mama," the adorable mispronunciation of "truck" as "tuck" or "purple" as "pupple," the newborn snuggles and toddler cuddles, the wonder that sparkles in their eyes at butterflies, the last time they'll grab our fingers for help down a step. I thought of the mothers who would never get to share these moments with their children, and vowed to hold my babies a little tighter, hug a little longer, and kiss their supple cheeks for every mama who couldn't. I vowed also to set an example for my children that strength is found not only through hustling to provide and accomplish but also in seeking out moments of rest, softness and connection.

From that day on, I was reminded to look for opportunities in my day in the hospital that truly grounded me in my humanity: complimenting a stranger in the elevator, asking the security guard how their day was at the end of a long shift, pausing to pick up a toy that fell from a stroller, or simply sharing a smile with a parent who just wanted to take their baby home.

Chapter Sixteen

At the start of my first shift with an attending in the emergency department, I introduced myself as "Chika, the third-year clerk who is working with you tonight."

The doctor let out a high-pitched snicker.

"*Chika?* That can't actually be your real name?" he said, his face contorted into an expression that read as *Don't bullshit me.*

"No, I'm being serious," I replied, completely taken aback by the exchange. I had introduced myself dozens of times to different preceptors within the first four months of clerkship, and the response was usually "Ooh, *Chika*, is that Spanish?" or "I LOVE that name. It's so fun, I could say it all day long. Chika, Chika, Chika!"

But never this.

"Why would your parents name you that?" He chuckled, as humiliation enveloped me. I searched for an explanation worthy of his acceptance.

"It's Nigerian. It's my real name," I replied, before scanning his badge to see what his idea of an acceptable name was. He had a standard English name, reminding me of my parents, who go by Steve and Kate. Although they have beautiful Igbo names that they use with family, using English names professionally was one of the ways they survived as newly landed Nigerian immigrants in the 1980s.

I was confused by my attending's remarks. Had he never come across anyone who had an English name, like his own, but also a middle name that reflects an aspect of their background—or simply no English name at all? I knew I had the option to use my middle name, Stacy, at any time during my schooling, but I had so far staunchly refused. In any case, the encounter stood as a clear reminder that assimilation was the goal in Canadian culture.

I was encouraged, during lectures transitioning us to clerkship, to report situations of harassment or inappropriate behaviour through the anonymous reporting system at the faculty. These kinds of interactions are not tolerated, whether from attendings or otherwise. The learning environment should be a secure space, I was reminded by mentors often. But I doubt this particular attending had questioned other clerks about the validity of their names. I'm sure he would have remembered the only Black third-year clerk who had worked with him that year.

I instead filed that experience away, along with the egregious encounter with another male attending just two weeks prior on a different rotation. We were working in a busy clinic when a male patient entered and saw me and the staff waiting in the office.

The gentleman sat in his chair and looked over at me with a flirtatious grin.

"What do we have here today? Do I get to take her home with me as a present?"

The physician laughed heartily before calling the patient a "jokester."

My stomach twisted.

I could hardly look either of them in the eye for the remainder of the appointment, during which the patient continued to share inappropriate jokes with the doctor. I didn't laugh once, while my attending didn't stop laughing. He didn't put an end to the nauseating banter. He didn't take issue.

"You got some real serious students here, Doc," said the patient, toward the end of the appointment. I spoke only to ask pertinent medical questions or answer them. My lips were hot with anger. I kept them pressed tight; I was afraid of what might slip out if I didn't.

"These new medical students have to learn how to take a joke, or you'll never survive in medicine," said the attending, to the patient and to me. "You can't be so sensitive."

I forced a smile onto my face, like a crack breaking through hardened cement.

I returned to the hospital that afternoon still trembling with indignation. The resident on the team listened patiently as I recounted the events of that morning. He sat there, mortified. After witnessing my performance that week, he had been trying earnestly to recruit me to the specialty. "We need more residents like you," he had stated at the end of one of our workdays.

I flirted with the idea, but that morning had soured my experience.

"Report him, you need to report him," he begged me.

I badly wanted to, but the lack of anonymity afforded to me, and the heightened visibility of my advocacy, made me terrified of further rocking the academic boat.

"I just appreciate you listening," I told the resident, who swore to keep a close eye and ear out for any other missteps from that staff and report him promptly.

"It's the least I can do," he said, with a sombre look on his face.

Over time, I had grown accustomed to the ways in which issues of race and gender rear their heads within medical encounters. Many people of colour can appreciate "that feeling" that you get, without a single word being spoken, when someone, subconsciously or not, carries racial bias— if not outright ideals. Sometimes, it's the woman clutching her purse when you walk by. Sometimes, it's being followed down the aisles in a store—which has happened to me on occasion. Sometimes, it's the energy the patient emits when you walk into the room—cold and curt— but then they light up when a non-Black person enters. Sometimes, it's a remark dressed up as a "joke."

Often, it's much less threatening, like racism *lite*. The patients who ask, "Where are you from? No, no, where are you *really* from?" The questions that constitute gatekeeping of the true Canadian identity.

"Brampton," I say, followed by "I was born in Ottawa. My parents are from Nigeria" because the initial answer isn't usually sufficient.

During my clerkship, I wondered if the nationality of my other classmates was incorporated into the opening pleasantries in patient encounters. I also thought of my parents and peers who did immigrate to this country, or maybe trained outside this country. Did they have the same frustration when interrogated on their origins time and time again? Were the questions a byproduct of well-intentioned curiosity or driven by a subconscious bias? I often found myself calibrating my sensitivity and questioning my own interpretations of exchanges in a way that was self-protective while still preserving the reality of what had transpired.

"Are you used to the winters yet?" I was asked frequently during the colder months. I hate the winters, not because I had to acclimate to the weather after immigrating here from Nigeria, but because my body has yet to master thermoregulation. I joke with my family that the African blood is just too strong, and I can never really get used to the bone-chilling temperatures in Toronto.

"I was born here," I would reply politely. Then I'd pivot the conversation toward their medical and personal history.

"So, what brings you in to see us today?"

The rest of the conversation would remain lighthearted, and they would most often thank me for my care. Most of my patients were kind and appreciative of my detail-oriented, comprehensive and compassionate work as a clinical clerk. My attendings would often remark on this during feedback sessions, which made the cuts of racial slights sting a little less. I was capable and deserving of being in medicine. I needed to tell this to myself repeatedly.

Unpacking the micro-traumas of these clinical experiences was a necessary skill for survival. I continued to see my therapist and lean on my mentors, including Pier, Onye and Lisa. They would often take me out for coffee or lunch, listen to my grievances about the discriminatory experiences I faced as a clerk, and impart some wisdom to usher me forward.

I thought I was doing everything right, having an upbeat disposition, showing interest in the specifics of each specialty, reading around the cases, and presenting new information at rounds the next morning. I even applied the recommendations from a dearly trusted mentor, who had given me a heartbreaking but necessary lesson in respectability politics on the wards.

"I wouldn't wear my afro out," he told me. "You don't want to garner unwanted attention or make your patients feel uncomfortable."

This bothered me deeply. I rejected the implication that what grew naturally out of my head was an imposition. It was reinforced to me that I should navigate the world of medicine almost colour-blind, even to my own identity, and shouldn't try to bring racial politics onto the wards, or I'd risk leaving a poor impression with patients and staff.

We need to work harder, I thought to myself, reminded that I didn't have the privilege of simply existing in my natural state. I needed to conform, I needed to alter the part of myself and my Blackness that could be seen as untoward. I put away the colourful headscarves that I would use to tie my hair on days when I felt too drained to style it, and instead alternated between braids kept in a tidy ponytail or my natural hair slicked into a bun. I was careful not only with my words but also with the tone of my voice. Even in moments when I felt accosted, and my anger was justified, I dared not convey my frustrations openly and risk being labelled "aggressive" and thereby really endanger my chances of getting a recommendation letter. The margins of error that I and other Black medical students were afforded were too thin, and I was always acutely aware of this. When a Black charge nurse on my general surgery rotation told me I needed to look more "put together" in the twenty-fifth hour of my call shift, because I didn't have the luxury of appearing exhausted as a Black female doc, I knew that I was operating within a system that governed every facet of my humanity.

I wondered how much easier learning medicine would be without the added pressures to adhere to undue respectability politics, while also spending every spare minute studying for exams or advocating for equity within the medical institution.

I learned to instantly calculate whether it would be helpful or futile to correct a patient or staff in the moment. I kept quick phrases in my back pocket and pulled them out if the situation seemed fitting:

"I am actually the medical student, not the [insert: nurse / ward clerk / custodial staff]."

"Yes, Chika *is* my real name. No, I don't go by my English name."

"I was born here, but my parents are from Nigeria, so I am second-generation."

Never let them see you cry, I would tell myself in the midst of each encounter.

I saved my tears for when I got home and felt comfortable enough to let them fall. I leaned heavily into the "strong Black woman" schema, one where we are expected to course through a life acquiring strength by silently and complicitly subjecting ourselves to trauma and suffering. Scholars define this archetype by three central themes in Black womanhood: emotional restraint, caretaking and independence. It is the same narrative that kept many of the African aunties in my community shackled to loveless or abusive marriages with a smile, their plight preordained. It afflicts the single mothers left with children whose fathers were torn from them. I had seen this archetype play out in so many contexts: from civil rights history, where Black women did the bulk of physical and mental labour in community organizing, to the Black faculty across academic institutions doing the same, to my own reflection in the mirror.

This path proved to be a self-protective mechanism in the short term, allowing me to absorb the impacts of my precarious position, but a maladaptive strategy in the long term.

Often, in quiet moments on the wards, or during days spent pulsing through clinics and keynote presentations at major conferences, I craved softness. I craved the weight of the endless responsibility to right society's wrongs to be lifted from my shoulders. I yearned for a moment to cry on stage, to be held, to be vulnerable. I wanted, and eventually came to demand, that others in leadership positions take up the burden of change. Or, at the very least, value the work that often lands on our desks—or kitchen tables.

I would soon learn that despite wearing a heavy, invisible superhero cape, there would come a day when the algorithm would fail, and my professional and calm demeanour would be shattered.

I would be reminded that I am simply human, and people could say things that would sometimes make me break.

Chapter Seventeen

The elevator doors slid open to the green-blue walls on the highest hospital floor, releasing a herd of medical students, patients, physicians and nurses onto the internal medicine ward. Toronto's skyline broke through the blend of orange and champagne that painted the clouds before melting away, offering the perfect restful view to still my racing mind.

As a clinical clerk on internal medicine, I was responsible for arriving to the wards early, before 8:00 a.m. rounds, and briefing myself on the newest labs and test results for my patients. The presenting pathologies were varied: those dealing with infections secondary to intravenous drug use, those with end-stage complications from years of alcohol misuse, and a few who had terminal cancers that were not detected early enough to save their lives. Each day underscored the fragility of our existence, reminding me of the immense privilege it was to provide care to some of the city's sickest patients.

In the tiniest font I could write that was still somewhat legible, I noted the new blood work results in the margins of the printed patient lists. Any new radiographic findings would also be checked, as I prepared to brief my staff on the pertinent clinical news, as well as how my new knowledge would inform the ongoing clinical care.

I strove to be a diligent, independent and driven clerk who would leave a lasting impression on our preceptor. At this point in my medical school journey, my third year of medical school, in 2019, I had determined that I wanted to pursue either obstetrics and gynecology or internal medicine; as such, it was imperative that I perform to a high standard of excellence.

The core internal medicine rotation was and still is regarded as the most difficult, mentally rigorous and brutal phase of clerkship, partly due to the one-in-four call schedule. This translated to an in-house twenty-six-hour shift (which sometimes stretched even longer) every four days, with tedious consults throughout. Clerks would be paged in the dead of night, jolted from sleep and asked to see a patient. We would then, groggily, document our encounter in a cleanly formulated note to be presented to the team during handover the next morning. Our presentations were usually done in a semi-delirious state where basic words would escape us and we would beg our bodies not to collapse mid-questioning. The post-call days, where we would go home and rest before we returned to the hospital the following morning, would be littered with hours of studying as there was an impossibly dense amount of physiology and pathophysiology to master for the internal medicine exam.

More than during any other specialty in medicine that I rotated through as a clerk, I was the most acutely aware of my race in the halls of the internal medicine unit. This was in part due to the highly conservative and prestigious reputation that internists had; they were lauded as the wisest of the wise, possessing wide-ranging medical knowledge that was drawn upon to solve the most complex and elusive medical mysteries in the hospital. The quizzing of medical knowledge was ever-present, and clerks needed to interpret a radiograph or ECG at a moment's notice, or be asked to determine a differential diagnosis for a confusing and challenging case presentation in front of the entire group. There was also a palpable energy of competitiveness to prove yourself as the most knowledgeable and intelligent medical trainee. As a Black, female medical clerk, I felt that it was the ultimate arena to prove my merit as a budding physician, and I was reminded often that the stakes were all too high.

"Good morning, *Doctor*," said Cheryl, a Black senior nurse who had been with the hospital for decades. "I got you a snack," she said, pulling out a warm croissant from the bakery in the cafeteria downstairs. They were my favourite, and Cheryl knew this.

A few weeks before, she and another, younger Black nurse at the station had spotted me coming down the hall at the tail end of my call shift, dishevelled and spent. My once slick bun was just a messy cornrow with hair fraying in every direction. I had barely slept that night, given the time spent doing consults and editing my documentation for the presentation at rounds. When I had finally made it to my call room at 4:00 a.m., there was a code blue, and as a clerk I had to attend it to provide life-saving resuscitation for an elderly patient. I learned within a few minutes of providing chest compressions in CPR that it is one of the most taxing physical exercises to do, yet I was carried by the adrenaline rush and desire to save the patient's life. They survived, and shortly after the adrenaline drained from my body, I dragged my feet back to our team room for rounds.

As I walked dizzily through the hall, Cheryl and Bernice, the younger Black nurse, waved me over to them.

"Are you one of the medical students?" they whispered to me, as I shuffled the weariness from my muscles and searched for the simple response in my scrambled mind.

"Hi! Yes, I'm Chika. I'm one of the third-year clerks from U of T on internal this rotation," I said, reading the faded "RN" on their badges.

"We are *all* so proud of you, girl!" she replied, placing a loving hand on my shoulder and giving it a tight squeeze. "We have been working here for a long time and rarely see Black doctors or medical students around here."

"Yes, it's definitely an issue . . . not having enough of us as medical students and doctors. I'm the only one in my class, so probably the only one you'll see on the wards in my year."

"Oh my goodness!" said Bernice, in shock. "*You're* the one in the news? The one Black student in her class who is helping more students in our community become doctors?"

I smiled. "Yes, that's me," I replied. The heft of exhaustion lifted.

"Thank you for what you're doing, Doctor. I know you're not a doctor quite yet, but we are so proud of you and what you've done that we are going to give you that title now," said Cheryl, and Bernice nodded in agreement.

"We've got your back. You're one of the few to walk these halls, and we know that you must work harder to be seen as equal. We're going to protect you."

From that moment forward, every morning they would greet me with a jubilant "Good morning, Doc!" accompanied by a full-face smile, wave, and "You got this, girl!" and "We're so proud of you, keep it up!" If they ever caught me waiting in line at the cafeteria, they would tell the cashier to combine our orders and offer to pay for my morning snacks or midnight call shift pick-me-up. "We must," they insisted, and gave me the loving but stern look of *Don't try to turn this down, you will pay it forward in time*.

This was my goal.

The Black nurses on the wards ensured that I never felt alone, especially when the pressure felt all-consuming. Their daily check-ins, cheers of support and assurance of my wellness was a protective force that shepherded me through the hardest rotation of medical school. I cherished the maternal protection that was gifted to me by them, and I always stopped to chat with them whenever there was a lull in my busy day.

I thanked Cheryl now for the warm croissant, and for her endless generosity, and headed back to the rounds room with a stack of freshly printed and stapled lists. As the long arm of the clock struck 8:00 a.m., the residents, clerks and elective medical students trickled into the windowless room, illuminated by dim overhead lights and a large screen affixed to the wall. The senior medical resident toggled through the electronic medical record system on the computer and projected the labs for the first patient onto the screen.

Dr. Griffins, our attending on service for two weeks, had been an internist and palliative care physician for the past three decades. He was a commanding presence in the room. I was warned by other clerks who had rotated through internal medicine that he was a tough nut to crack, asked difficult and unpredictable medical questions and might be hard to elicit a letter of recommendation from. I wasn't terrified of him, per se, but when he entered, I definitely adjusted my posture, put my phone away and rehearsed my patient updates in my head so as not to fumble over the complicated medical jargon.

We paced through our list over the ensuing hour, listening to the overnight residents hand over the consults. Before they were relieved of their duties, they and the rest of the team were required to join the attending to see the newest consult and patient on the list. I gathered my phone, list, pens and notebook, and arranged the items within my fanny pack, before swinging my stethoscope onto my neck and rising to exit the room.

Through the consult, we had learned that the patient was an elderly gentleman with complex medical morbidities and cognitive decline that might be signalling dementia. He was refusing medical treatment for a bowel obstruction, despite being in great discomfort, which had prompted his admission. In the emergency department, the resident turned to find his chart while the rest of the group filed into the patient's room.

"Hi there, I'm Dr. Griffins," said our staff, shaking the patient's hand. "I'm the staff physician overseeing your care here with my team of residents and medical students." He informed the patient that everyone in the room was either a doctor or doctor in training, and since this was a teaching hospital we would be there to observe and participate in his care for our medical education. There were fewer than ten of us in the group, including Dr. Griffins.

The patient grew visibly upset almost immediately, stating that there were people in the room who should not be there.

"Everyone here is a medical learner," said Dr. Griffins, calmly but sternly, "and either a physician or about to become one."

The patient grew more irate.

"No," he replied. "There are people in this room who don't deserve to be here." His agitation was steadily ballooning. He began to pull at the tethered IV lines and attempted to lift his frail body from the bed in protest. "Anyone who is not a part of the medical team should leave," he declared.

"Everyone deserves to be here and wants to take care of you," said Dr. Griffins, more sternly.

I scanned the room as if it were full of new faces, as if I hadn't just spent the past three weeks working with these same residents and clerks. I was trying to guess who the patient was talking about. Our group was approximately half women and half men, partly white, but there were other ethnicities as well. I started to shift uncomfortably and dart my eyes from the patient back to Dr. Griffins, who was struggling to contain the elderly man's growing frustration.

"Not her," the patient said now, with his wilted arm half extended and a slender finger pointed straight at me. The only Black learner in the room.

"She is not a part of the medical team," he said, his agitation peaking, "and if they're not part of the medical team, they should leave."

"Yes, she is. She is a medical learner," said Dr. Griffins. "And we do not tolerate these kinds of actions toward our learners," he concluded, while the patient continued to protest.

My head spun as my vision instantly blurred with hot tears that dragged the mascara off my eyelashes and down my cheeks. It felt like I was outside my own body, watching the interaction unfold, watching my spirit crumble. It was clear that my presence in the room was making the patient more upset and hindering his ability to receive proper medical care. There was no algorithm to apply in this moment, nothing I had learned in pre-clerkship to guide me through this heated clinical encounter.

I thought of the preceptor who had told me that my "independent development" would occur in residency, and that I could wait until then.

But I couldn't wait.

I only knew that I had promised myself never to let a patient make me cry, yet I had already broken that promise before I could leave the room. I tore my body from the frozen mould that had settled over me when the patient singled me out from the group, and I pivoted quickly toward the curtain, pulling it back and exiting in haste.

My tears broke into heavy sobs that drew attention from the RNs and ward staff in the emergency department. Lenny, a first-year psychiatry resident doing his mandatory internal medicine rotation with the team, joined me in the hallway, extending an arm in consolation. Soon, other members of the team emerged. The other third-year clerk on my team hugged me and whispered, "That was horrific, I'm so sorry."

Lenny encouraged me to return to our team room and offered to join me. I thanked him and asked for a moment alone to gather myself and process what was happening.

Another team member joined us as I wiped the tears from my eyes and tried to steady the shaking.

"Are you okay?" she asked, with a tone that didn't immediately offer comfort. I sensed by the look on her face that my exit was unanticipated. I nodded and asked to excuse myself.

"You really needn't be so sensitive," she stated boldly.

Searing shame washed over me as she continued.

"Patients never believe that I'm a part of the medical team either because I am a woman. That doesn't mean that I leave the room crying. You have to be stronger than that," she urged me. "You need to stay in the room and prove to them that their words have no power over you."

But they did, and I had never been trained on what to do when I was being openly discriminated against in a medical encounter. I thought that, as a woman, she would commiserate with what I was facing. But we are not a monolith, and she stood as a painful reminder that solidarity isn't always found in the places I would expect it.

I apologized, before turning toward the elevator to return to the rounds room.

I could barely make it through the door before the heavy sobs broke through once again. The totality of the situation was too much to process, and there was only one person I felt I could call within an instant to soothe me.

"Hey, babe, what's going on?" said Dale, my boyfriend of seven months at the time. He was just settling into his workday as a senior policy analyst with the Ontario government at the Ministry of Health and wasn't expecting me to call during my busy shift at the hospital. He picked up his phone after the second ring, taking the call in the privacy of his boss's vacant office.

Through sniffles, I explained to him what had just transpired with the male patient, and the further invalidation I felt from the team member who took the opportunity to chastise me instead of lending comfort. I could hardly let the words escape between the sobs, and he tried in earnest to get me to take deep breaths. "That is truly horrible. I am so sorry. It makes me sick that someone could say something like that to you," he kept repeating, unsure what words he could offer to remedy the situation. Dale had never encountered racism before in his life, because he is white.

Dale was the only white person I had ever dated, and initially I battled with the extreme uncertainty of venturing into an interracial relationship when not only was my advocacy staunchly pro-Black, but I was terrified of facing more racial insensitivities in my personal life through him, his family or his network of friends. There were many mornings when I would confide in him that I had barely slept the night before, because I feared being in an interracial relationship, I didn't want to be hurt any further, and I didn't want the Black community to think that my advocacy was disingenuous. I spent many hours over the phone with my mom, sisters, friends and family debating whether I should leave him, though Dale was a loving, nurturing, attentive boyfriend and incredible ally. He took deep interest in my work, attended my keynotes at every opportunity, read several books on anti-racism, and was deeply committed to sitting with me in the raw discomfort of the adversity I faced. When we walked hand in hand in public, prompting turned heads and protracted stares, or entered gatherings to thinly veiled looks of disgust, Dale encountered racism-by-proxy for the first time in his life, and it changed his understanding of the world instantly. He admitted that he lived a privileged, sheltered life as a white man, and wanted to learn as much as he could to be the best boyfriend I could have.

And he did.

So I fell in love with him, though the fear of the implications of our love haunted me daily.

"Take a deep breath," he instructed me, and he asked me if I wanted him to leave work to come and see me.

"No, it's okay, I'm feeling better," I replied, salty streaks of tears drying on my cheeks. He promised to check on me throughout the day and bring some dinner after work. "We can watch that movie you like— *Bridesmaids* or something?" He chuckled, softly, as I sniffled through a laugh and took him up on the offer. Comfort food, humour and reassuring arms were the elixir for a tough day on the wards.

"You're so strong, even though you shouldn't have to be," he said, before saying, "I love you" and ending the call to return to his office.

Though I had stopped crying, my body continued to feel numb. I ran through the scenario in my head dozens of times, wondering if I should have stayed and challenged the patient's demand for me to leave. I wondered if I had shot my chances at getting a good recommendation letter from Dr. Griffins. I wondered if my peers would ever respect me again, and questioned if being incensed was even justified. I thought through each situation until my head throbbed.

I crossed the hallway into the nearby bathroom and cleaned up my face, knowing there was little I could do about the puffy, red eyes.

Rebecca, my classmate and fellow clerk, returned to the team room first.

"That was the most blatant and disgusting display of racism that I have ever seen in the hospital," she said, consoling me. "I am here for you, and I'm so sorry. I don't think you needed to stay there and tolerate that." Her words soothed me.

I thanked her for her support, and we continued chatting while the rest of the team trickled in, Dr. Griffins in tow.

I was terrified at how he would interpret my behaviour. Would he tell me that I did the wrong thing? That I should have stayed in the room and toughened up, like my team member told me? Would he view me as weak, unfit for medicine?

He sat down at the head of the table and looked at me directly with his crystal blue eyes behind thinly framed glasses. He cleared his throat as the room fell silent.

"I'm sorry, Chika," he said, with a tone of sincerity that provoked a well of tears back to the corners of my eyes. I told myself that I wouldn't cry anymore, but I couldn't help it.

"I want us to take this time to debrief what just happened," he said, "and if you feel comfortable, Chika, I want to give you the floor to steer the conversation."

I was in shock, not only because we had a busy day ahead and a long patient list to tackle, but because he wasn't angry with me. Instead, he was committed to tackling the discrimination head on together, instead of leaving me to unpack the trauma alone.

"As an old white guy, I gotta say that I didn't know what to do back there. I haven't faced racism before, and I'm not sure if there is a better way that I could have supported you. I'm open to learning, if you feel comfortable enough to tell us how we could have handled it better."

Dr. Griffins created an emotionally safe space in the cramped team room, where we spent the next hour talking about discrimination that faces medical learners and physicians. I felt secure enough to be vulnerable about my experiences in medical school thus far, recounting the times during clerkship and throughout my first two years when I had felt othered because of my race. I told them about the trolls online who, over the past two years, had been trying their hardest to push me away from medicine and stop my advocacy. I spent nearly the entire hour in tears, which gave way to calm and gratitude as Dr. Griffins and the team listened attentively, carefully and committedly.

When the hour had elapsed, he thanked me for my bravery in that moment but also in front of the patient. This changed not only the trajectory of my day but my entire experience throughout my internal medicine rotation.

"This is a teachable moment for us all, especially me," Dr. Griffins finished.

We picked up our stethoscopes, notebooks and folded patient lists, and continued with our duties for the day.

Chapter Eighteen

Spencer followed closely behind me as I led him and his five-year-old daughter, Thea, down the hallways of the clinic.

"Hi, Thea! I'm Chika, the senior medical student working with Dr. Ali in the family medicine clinic today," I said, turning back to ensure they were still in step. Thea held tightly to her father's hand, periodically looking toward him for reassurance. With her free arm she cradled a taupe-coloured stuffed bunny, clearly well loved over the years, with a scruff of loose threads where a beaded eye had once been and the fuzz of its tail matted.

As we passed a stretch of office doors, she squeezed her father's fingers a little tighter and let out a tiny whimper.

"No pokes today, sweetie," he promised her, sharing with me that she wasn't the biggest fan of needles or doctors' offices.

Thea started to cry, pulling her father in the opposite direction. "No, Daddy," she pleaded.

Spencer paused and knelt to Thea's height, levelling their gazes. "You're a brave girl, sweetheart—and I can see that you're scared. But we're just here to take a peek in your ears and make sure they're all better."

Thea looked toward me, unconvinced.

"No pokes, sweetheart," I said, also bending to Thea's height. "I'm just going to take a super quick look at your ears to make sure they are healthy! Like this," I continued, pretending to use my stethoscope to peer into her stuffed bunny's ears.

She giggled and took a turn looking into the floppy ears as well.

"Daddy will hold your hand the entire way through," Spencer reassured her.

We continued along the hallway. "Just a bit further down," I said, as we rounded the corner.

The corridors in the newly built family health centre were long and winding, with doctors' offices lining the passageway and towering windows ushering in the eastern sun. The waiting room was filled with patients from the local community waiting to have their chronic and acute ailments assessed: follow-ups for diabetes care, refills on their prescriptions for anti-hypertensives and anxiolytics, well-baby developmental visits, and run-of-the-mill coughs and colds. I had ranked this clinic as my top placement choice to do my family medicine rotation because it was situated in a historic neighbourhood in Toronto that was predominantly Black and racialized—like Spencer and Thea—housing many immigrant and refugee families.

Dr. Ali, one of the preceptors for my six-week rotation in family medicine, was seeing another patient on our roster just a few doors down from me. By the third week of my rotation, we had settled into a beautifully synergistic routine on the shifts that we worked together. We would start our day with an overview of the schedule, dividing the list of patients to be seen between us. She would endeavour to give me cases that would pique my clinical interests, anything along the lines of women's health, Black health, mental health and pediatrics. After assessing each patient, I would tap lightly on her door and request to review the case, summarizing the encounter in a concise, linear presentation that outlined my history taking, physical examination, clinical impression and management.

"I wish we could hire you in the clinic right now," she would sometimes share after debriefing a patient case. I dreamed of nothing more than working alongside her.

I grew to cherish and eagerly await the days I would work with Dr. Ali, with whom I had grown to share a special bond. As a half-Indigenous, half–East African clinician, she was the first Black female preceptor that I had worked with in my clinical clerkship year, and one of the most engaging and compassionate doctors I had ever met.

Dr. Ali's primary office was decorated with emblems of her core values and identity; her walls were adorned with vibrant Indigenous and East African prints, drawings of Black mothers cuddling their babies, thank-you cards from past medical students and residents, and culturally sensitive guidelines for pre- and postnatal care in Indigenous and racialized communities. She possessed the uncanny ability to make each patient feel at home in her presence, and I would often dawdle after the clinic had wrapped, melting into one of the chairs in her office as though it were the couch in my living room. We would swap stories about our experiences as Black women in medicine, and she uplifted and protected my deep dedication to offering service to the community.

When Thea's name appeared that morning on our schedule for the day, Dr. Ali tapped on the monitor's screen and said, "She will be perfect for you to meet, you'll love her." She tossed me a smile as she adjusted her long, curly, dark brown hair. Her beaded, Indigenous-crafted earrings sparkled under the clinic's light.

"Here we are," I said to Thea and Spencer, pushing open the doors of my temporary clinical office and welcoming them inside. Spencer helped Thea onto the examination bed, as she placed her stuffed bunny, named Daisy, close to her side.

I punched my password and identification into the desktop computer and brought Thea's records onto the screen. Her growth and pediatric development charts, which monitored her weight, height and developmental milestones since birth, revealed a healthy girl who was always exceptionally tall for her age. She had met or exceeded all motor and language milestones and was up to date on her vaccination schedule, despite the needle-phobia that plagued many children her age. Luckily, I had learned, she always had Daisy nearby for any scary moments—from pokes to thunderstorms to monsters that reared their heads at bedtime.

Thea had no significant past medical history other than a few recurrent ear infections, successfully treated with a course of antibiotics, in the past few years. Upon probing for more information around their last visit to the clinic, I learned that Thea had recovered from a viral upper respiratory tract infection a couple of weeks ago, which was accompanied by a bilateral ear infection requiring a further course of amoxicillin. Spencer wanted to ensure that her infection had cleared, citing concern that Thea would intermittently complain about an earache or tilt her head to the side in discomfort.

"How is your ear feeling today, Thea?" I asked her, as she brought Daisy closer to her chest and scanned the tiny office. She reported that her ears felt "okay, sometimes they hurt, but okay for now" and asked if she could get a sticker and lollipop after I checked her ears. This was a common practice reserved for kids after braving a vaccine poke, not typically given for a regular checkup—but I happily agreed.

"Of course!" I replied, lifting the otoscope from the clinic wall.

"May I take a peek in Daisy's ear first?" I asked Thea, who lifted Daisy's floppy ear to expose an imaginary eardrum. "Ah! I think I see a carrot!" I joked, letting Thea take a look as well. She squinted through the lens and giggled, stating boldly that it was a pink carrot with purple polka dots.

"Can I check to see if your ears have any carrots in them?" I asked comically, while Spencer placed Thea on his lap.

I carefully scanned her eardrums for any inflammation, bulging or fluid—signs of a new or inadequately treated ear infection. Minimal fluid remained. It appeared that the infection was responding to the treatment course, and I reassured her father that the residual fluid should clear over time but can sometimes cause irritation to the eardrums, leading to the symptoms Thea had demonstrated. Still, it wasn't a major cause for concern, and if her symptoms persisted, he could always come back in for another checkup. Spencer sighed in relief and kissed his daughter's forehead as Thea tried to harvest the purple-spotted carrots from Daisy's ears.

As I typed my assessment into her electronic chart and started scouring the cabinets for the cartoon-themed stickers and lollipops, Spencer thanked me for my patience with Thea.

"Of course, my pleasure," I replied, sharing that I loved seeing children in the clinic, especially ones as sweet and charming as his little girl.

"You and Daisy can come by any time." I winked at Thea, who handed me an imaginary carrot and giggled. "Why, thank you! I'll bring this to Dr. Ali while I review what we discussed," I said. "Then I'll be back shortly with the box of stickers!"

Thea's face lit up with glee.

"Sorry, Chika, before you go, can I ask you something?" Spencer whispered, still holding Thea and Daisy on his lap.

"Certainly." I could sense from the outset that there was something else that pressed heavily on his mind, beyond the gripes of repeated courses of antibiotics and the fatigue that comes with tending to a sick child.

He placed his hand over Thea's coily, shoulder-length hair, which was bound together with a satin scrunchie that matched her polka-dot dress.

"I don't know if Dr. Ali mentioned anything," Spencer continued, his gaze briefly breaking connection with mine. He stared out the window toward the greying sky. "But my wife, Jacklyn, passed away last year from ovarian cancer." His voice faltered over the last few words, while he looked toward his only child and choked back tears.

"My goodness, Spencer, I am so sorry," I replied. "My sincerest condolences. I can only imagine how devastating that must have been for you both."

"Thank you." He sniffled. "It has been hard. Jackie was our guiding light, and ever since I lost her, I feel like I've lost myself. But I stay strong for Thea, and we've been in therapy, even before Jackie passed. She wanted to make sure we were prepared for the transition—just like Jackie, always the planner." He smiled, chuckled softly and wiped away a tear.

"You're so strong," I responded, as Thea continued fiddling with Daisy.

I learned that in the days following Jackie's diagnosis, when the grim prognosis was delivered, Jackie told Thea that whenever she felt scared, or alone, or missed her mama, she could hold Daisy close to her heart and know that her mommy was there in spirit. I marvelled at the resilience housed within this small child, who had already weathered one of the worst storms life can throw our way.

As we continued chatting, Spencer pulled out a snack and a colouring book from Thea's backpack, finding ways to keep her occupied.

"I try my best to fill the shoes of two parents for Tee, but there are things that Jackie did that I struggle to do now that she's gone. Like baking Tee's favourite banana pancakes or painting her nails without making a mess," he said.

"I'm trying to master these things," he went on, "and I've gotten close. But more than anything, I wish I knew how to do Tee's hair. Her mother had her wash days down to a science—it was their thing, you know? Mother-daughter bonding. Jackie always knew how to detangle Thea's hair gently and could do a million different styles that made Thea feel like a princess. Now, after long days as a mechanic, I pretty much throw her hair into a bun. I can't comb her hair without her crying, and I've noticed it's not as healthy or long as it used to be.

"I know this may sound strange, but as you were taking notes, I realized that I've never met a Black doctor whose hair is like Thea's and Jackie's—and I've never felt comfortable enough telling a physician how much I've struggled with this, especially since it could be a nutritional thing, or maybe the stress of losing her mother?" he continued. "I wasn't sure if they would know how to help us, and I did not want to be judged."

He shared with me that he, like many Black women and girls, had never learned how to take care of natural, afro-textured hair. As Thea's curls were 4c in pattern, and even tighter and coilier than mine, her hair was incredibly delicate and sensitive to how it was handled. Spencer shared that he'd watched his mother and aunties chemically relax their hair over the years, but he wanted to keep his daughter's natural, as it was important to Jackie before she passed. He had taken Thea to the salon on a couple of occasions, where they experimented with getting her hair pressed and braided with extensions, but he realized quickly that her hair was sustaining damage. It was also quite costly, and he couldn't afford regular salon visits on his wages.

I immediately noticed some traction alopecia, a common concern among Black women and girls who wear their hair in tight braids and weaves, resulting in a receding hairline. Her hair was also different lengths around the crown and nape and looked as though it had not been detangled in weeks.

"Can you tell me how you keep your hair healthy?" he asked, with a pleading look in his eyes that made my heart ache.

"Of course," I said to him immediately, studying Thea's hair and making a determination of which products might be beneficial for her unique afro-textured hair needs.

We spent the next hour diving into my secrets of natural hair care. My hair that day was worn in chunky twists, which was one of my go-to protective styles during the winter. "I've tried protective styling before, but I haven't been able to master it," he admitted, admiring the twists fashioned into a half-up, half-down ponytail. Realizing that I needed to impart wisdom on the foundations of hair care before we got to protective styling, I pulled out a piece of paper and wrote down my tips and tricks for how to wash, deep condition and treat her coily hair.

"You don't have the standard doctor scribbles," he joked, as I ran the blue pen across a sheet torn from a yellow notepad and chuckled. I took extra care to make the instructions as legible as possible, numbering each step and underlining the key features.

"Always try to finger detangle her curls. I use a good amount of deep conditioner during my wash days, and either use my hands or a wide-toothed comb to gently tease apart the locks, reduce breakage, and make it easier to style afterwards."

Spencer nodded diligently, studying my tips like a keen student on the first day of school.

I gave Spencer a list of low-cost household items that could be used in place of the brand-name deep conditioners, a page straight from the Black girl hair codebook. I drew upon the years I had spent curating my own hair care routine, from hundreds of hours spent watching natural hair gurus online, and gave him a recipe for a homemade deep conditioner: half a cup of olive oil, a quarter cup of honey and one or two eggs.

"Blend it on high speed, or bring it together in a bowl if that's easier," I said, scrawling each instruction onto the piece of paper. I was running out of room, so I tore another sheet from the notepad and continued, excitedly.

As a natural-born teacher, I was in my element, and I savoured each magical moment spent in this rare opportunity where my professional and personal worlds collided.

By the end of our appointment, nearly an hour later, Thea and Spencer were equipped with a refreshed hair care routine, different strategies for how to care for her natural hair, and a follow-up appointment within a few weeks to see if they had made any progress. Ensuring that I was doing my due diligence as a medical student, I educated him on the medical reasons that might be predisposing her to thinning hair and hair loss, including anemia and autoimmune disorders—even underlying stress. Spencer agreed to have Thea complete some preliminary blood work to rule out any medical causes of her hair concerns. I printed out a lab requisition and took it to Dr. Ali for revision.

"Thank you so much," said Spencer, as he pulled a wool cap over Thea's hair and zipped up her sweater. "We're so lucky to have met you," he continued, "and I hope you'll come back to work here full-time."

We shared a silent moment of understanding how special and rare our encounter was. A feeling of purpose rose within me, as I was reaffirmed in my ability to create safe spaces for Black patients to explore the wholeness of their human experience.

"You are spectacular!" said Dr. Ali, as she read through my notes in the electronic medical record, signed off on the lab requisition, and gave approval on my assessment and plan.

"Thank you," I said, blushing, further informing her that I was going to bring the patient back within a few weeks for a follow-up on how her hair care journey was coming along. "It was so dope being able to chat about Black hair for an hour," I said, elated from the encounter with the patient. I felt teleported back to a time before medical school, when I would take every opportunity to informally teach little Black girls how to take care of their natural hair, revealing to them the limitless options of what our curls could do. How they could defy gravity and unlock their beauty, if they knew how to handle it with the proper care.

My cousin Ijeoma had done this for my sisters and me when we were less than ten years old and still grappling with the aspects of ourselves that didn't feel beautiful.

I never wanted another little girl, or woman, to feel that way.

"I think I want to create a printable handout for patients with afro-textured hair that can be given to them if they have concerns similar to Thea's," I said, the idea blooming on the spot in my mind. "Maybe I'll do it as my longitudinal family medicine project."

Dr. Ali agreed cheerfully, coaxing my brainstorming, saying she would champion any initiative I brought into the clinic. As there were many Black patients who came through the doors of the centre daily, it would be an advancement of the equitable health care they were striving to achieve.

I stayed up that evening creating a printable handout and poster version of my natural hair care manual, with detailed steps on how to maintain growth and retention of coarser, kinkier curls. I rewatched my favourite natural hair gurus' tutorials on YouTube, infusing myself with the most up-to-date knowledge from NaturalMe4c, TheChicNatural and Naptural85.

"Always wear a bonnet to bed to reduce breakage. Use the LOC method (leave-in conditioner followed by oil, then a cream) to enhance growth. Tuck your ends in with protective styles, and reduce manipulation through frequent styling as much as possible," I typed into the manual, adjusting the font and size for a clean look.

Within a week, I had a stack of posters that I had printed out on the kind of glossy, high-quality paper for which Staples charges customers top dollar. I paid the extra price happily, thrilled to have the final product put up throughout the clinic.

Dr. Ali pushed metallic tacks into the corners of the poster, affixing it to the wall of her clinic above the digital scale and directly across from the entrance. It hung beside a long, pink cloth that had drawings of Black children with picks, hair lotion and wide-tooth combs dappled throughout. It was one of the first things I'd noticed in her office, on the first days of my rotation, and I'd known instantly that she would be someone special on my medical journey.

I stood back proudly as we admired the eye-catching image of a Black woman with bouncy, healthy curls at the margin of the poster, mirroring the Black women who would frequent Dr. Ali's office, and the very woman providing their care.

By that afternoon, the other physicians and clerical staff had caught wind of my natural hair care guide and came knocking on my office door for copies for their offices and the front desk. I made my rounds through the rest of the staff, offering copies of my posters to put up in their rooms or take home to their children. That afternoon, a doctor from another clinic across town was visiting our site and requested a copy of the poster for her office. It was situated within a community that wasn't like ours and didn't serve a large population of Black patients. Still, the message that we deserve to be acknowledged in all spaces and places was being disseminated.

My joy grew at the positive reception, as I pictured a little Black girl staring up at the welcome desk in the clinic and elsewhere and seeing someone like herself represented within the medical community.

The Black patients, against the odds, would be seen.

Chapter Nineteen

I gasped in the mirror as the first flexi-rod curler I unfurled from my still-damp lock of hair spiralled precariously on the edge of the bathroom sink before toppling to the ground. The sectioned, wet lock recoiled toward my nape, returning to the natural, tight, 4b/4c hair pattern that I had wrestled with throughout my life. The same pattern I'd been trying frantically to tame the night before. Where were the looser, spiralled curls I had envisioned?

My mind marched through the steps that I had followed on You-Tube from TheChicNatural for using the perfect flexi-rod curling set: wash hair; finger or wide-comb detangle; part into thin sections for more volume; apply leave-in-conditioner and oil in light quantities; squirt mousse into your palm and saturate each strand of hair; install the turquoise and violet flexi-rods onto each section, rolling them toward your scalp and securing the ends firmly with a bit of extra mousse; sit under a domed dryer, or let air-dry overnight. The instructions didn't include but should have: try to sleep through the discomfort of having dozens of flexi-rods protruding from your head, without disturbing their position (most Black girls can identify with this profound struggle, like the challenge of sleeping with fresh single braids). By the next morning, *voilà!*, the perfect set of curls for your 4c hair, without any risk of heat damage.

In the video, TheChicNatural's hair was transformed from mois-ture-shrunk 4c hair to stretched, luscious and healthy beach-wave curls that bounced as she tousled her hair within the frame. The video ended with her signature grin and kiss blown toward the camera.

I studied this video like a hawk after searching the internet for the perfect hairstyle to wear for my photo shoot in the morning. The pic-ture would be one of the most important I would take in my life, as it would be submitted with my residency applications during the fourth-year Canadian Residency Matching System (CaRMS) process. It would be a key feature of my file, and undoubtedly impart a first impression that could colour how the rest of my file was interpreted, graded and ranked.

I wanted to not only look but feel beautiful, confident, intelligent and worthy.

As I had been taught, there was "no room for an afro on the wards," although throughout my clerkship years, I gradually started to wear my natural hair out anyway, daring to step into my authenticity despite the looks that it could draw. I would remark, during my keynotes and presentations, that stepping boldly into my identity was a form of heal-ing for me and allowed me to show up more confident in my skills as a doctor-to-be.

Yet I knew that the CaRMS photo was a historic rite of passage for fourth-year medical students and necessitated judiciousness down to a granular level, much like my initial medical school interview at U of T. Hair, makeup, lighting, choice of jewellery and blazer/blouse, back-ground, intensity of smile (teeth? no teeth?), placement of hands, angling of head and neck—every detail was magnified when we were choosing which photo would go along with the most important application of our medical careers.

The process of residency applications, known colloquially among medical students as "matching," was further marred by uncertainty and strife for me as I had been warned throughout my entire medical school journey that I had blown my chances at matching the day I started my advocacy in first year. Everything, including my photo, needed to be as perfect as possible, the last Hail Mary to persuade any closeted dissenters.

By this point in my advocacy, I'd had mentors, friends and family plead with me to shelve my vocal concerns regarding the institution and the medical system until I was several years into my practice, beyond the checkpoints that were heavily guarded by more conservative-leaning physicians (residency match, fellowship, staff appointments). But I had persisted, doing what I believed was the right thing to do. I maintained my speaking engagements, travelling across the country and internationally to deliver keynotes on the importance of diversity in medicine, while maintaining my high standard of performance and grades during each clerkship rotation. Despite the slander online that claimed I was engaging in advocacy to leverage my "failing grades," I received glowing letters of recommendation from preceptors, within specialties I coveted and even those I was keeping in my back pocket, just in case. Throughout my advocacy work, I performed my poems "Woman, Black" and "Press for Progress" to open and close different conferences. I manoeuvred comfortably within my element—from wards, to stages, to clinic offices—steeled by my conviction to create an enduring change in the world.

At Mac's Health Forum in 2018, when a group of young male undergrad students heckled me during my talk and said, "Don't you think if [Black students] were smart enough they would just get in?" I held the stage confidently, despite their barely stifled laughs and jeers, and dismantled their asinine remark, point for point, leaving them silent.

But I wasn't naive when it came to the very real professional risk that could play out in the matching process. During one of my keynote presentations at a Global Health forum for medical trainees, a resident remarked that I was courageous for doing this work, because she had always wanted to speak up and advocate as a medical student yet felt that she couldn't. When I asked her why, she informed me that she had observed the way that medical students were blacklisted from other programs when they were deemed "too outspoken" and "unbecoming" of a surgical intern, for advocacy similar to mine. Her suspicions were confirmed when she became a resident and spoke with residents in other programs who had access to the inner workings of the matching process.

"I didn't want to risk throwing away my career," she stated, with the same solemn eyes that I saw in my concerned mentors, family and friends.

Neither did I. But I couldn't rest under the crushing weight of inaction. I tried to remain poised in the belief that the right program would value my work and want me to show up unapologetically as a Black female advocate in their specialty.

When a classmate approached me during one of our mandatory third-year lectures and told me, without prompting, that "there are people in our class who don't agree with what you're doing—I can't say who, but you should know that it's going around," I felt a wad of unease settle into the pit of my stomach. I knew that it was impossible for everyone in my class to agree with me, though no one had openly dissented against my work to my face. It was just painful to have my suspicions confirmed, and to play the cruel guessing game of who it was that really felt that way. I would never find out.

Though I had been able to dismiss their words through therapy and self-affirmations, their remarks rushed back to me the moment my drenched curl sprang through my fingertips, still dripping with the residue of SheaMoisture leave-in conditioner and drugstore mousse, mere hours before my photo shoot was scheduled.

As I unfurled the rest of the rods from my curls, fooling myself into believing that maybe it was just one failed installation, the full reality of my hair situation hit me like a freight truck.

My hair was still soaking wet, retaining its tight, coily state from crown to nape, forming into an afro that fell just below the swoop of my ears. Though I loved my hair in its natural state, I understood that CaRMS was no battleground for racial politics, and Black hair is inherently politicized. When Angela Davis, an outspoken civil rights activist and professor, walked boldly into the courtroom in 1972 to challenge her federal charges of conspiracy, she intentionally wore a full, booming afro as a symbol of Black resistance and liberation. It was a direct challenge to the Eurocentric ideals of professionalism, intellect and beauty. I deeply admired Davis and channelled her energy when I dared to wear my afro on the wards and in the clinic, but I felt that I couldn't risk triggering any reflexive subconscious biases that an application reviewer might have when they saw a Black girl in an afro. I had already created an undetermined amount of jeopardy for my application, and I didn't want to draw any untoward attention.

My natural hair, in loose flexi-rod curls, would have allowed me to retain my authenticity as a Black woman while playing into the presentability politics that seemed inescapable. Or so I thought.

I immediately broke into a panic and attempted to FaceTime my sisters to pull from their well of expertise and crisis management. Because they are night owls and rarely answer the phone before 10:00 a.m., my efforts to reach them were met with voicemail tones and prompts to leave a message.

A stream of tears started to steadily flow as Dale appeared behind me in the bathroom mirror and asked what was wrong.

"My hair, the curlers didn't hold," I said through feeble sniffles. He studied my curls from behind as I caught his reassuring smile in the mirror.

"I love your hair in an afro, babe. Just rock it."

I didn't have the energy to explain to him the nuances of Black hair, professionalism and respectability politics when I had to meet the photographer within a few hours and needed to find a swift resolution. I thought about rescheduling to a new time when I could be squeezed into my stylist's schedule instead of risking another failed attempt. As I scrolled through my calendar, I realized this wasn't an option as I was on the cusp of starting a busy and intense three-month stint of back-to-back electives throughout the country in internal medicine, family medicine, shelter-based medicine and consult-liaison psychiatry.

I even flirted with the idea of running out to the drugstore and purchasing a flat iron but didn't want to attempt a silk press. While I took immense pride in my natural texture, I equally embraced experimenting with versatility; I celebrated the ways in which our hair can be worn in a multitude of styles, day to day, completely transforming our look—therein lies the essence of Black girl magic. But as a realist, I knew that my inexperience with straightening my own hair could easily leave me with limp, heat-damaged strands that would lose their ability to revert to their original pattern.

I needed to decide, and act quickly.

But an unanticipated tranquility washed over me as I looked at myself in the mirror—eyes stained pink from panicked tears, bathroom littered with flexi-rods, combs and half-empty bottles of conditioner—and stood in front of my reflection in silence.

This is me, I thought to myself, my eyes catching the brown tint in my curls illuminated under the bathroom lights. I took in the features that I had spent my earliest years wishing away—my full lips, broad nose, dark skin with imperfections, melanated gums that crowned my teeth, and my dare-not-be-tamed, enough-is-enough, kinky, tight coils.

I had spent my entire medical school career challenging what a doctor looked like. *Why not now?* I thought to myself. Yes, just a few years prior, U of T had seen an unprecedented number of medical students go unmatched (nearly 10 percent), and there was a fright that gripped each fourth-year student as the CaRMS November deadline drew closer, but I didn't come this far not to live within my truth.

Black hair is beautiful.

To deny its suitability within the world of medicine is to imply that I don't belong.

As my hair slowly dried, the afro continued to shrink and the definition in my curls was lost. Just an hour earlier, it had felt as though I was struggling to contain a full-blown crisis. But, standing before the mirror, I felt ready to redefine the face of professionalism in medicine.

When my photos came back from the photographer a week later, I stared at the shot that I had selected to be submitted with my residency application. I was wearing a pink, three-quarter-sleeve blazer, a crisp white camisole and the diamond necklace that Dale had given me on our one-year anniversary.

My curls at the front were parted to the side, framing the contours of my face and underscoring my reclaimed afro-centric beauty.

I looked just like my grandmother and every woman in my lineage before our beauty was robbed and distorted by colonial forces.

I thought of the final lines of my poem and felt that I was *truly* embracing the words: "I am woman, I am Black, I am doctor. And I am here."

The cursor blinked at the end of the final line of my statement letter for U of T Psychiatry, the residency program that was among my top choices. I had read through the essay maybe a hundred times since its inception two months earlier, grooming the grammar and syntax, pruning the sentences like a flowerbed within a manicured garden.

Psychiatry had become more competitive in the last few years, with almost all spots at U of T being filled in the first round of residency applications. Having recently discovered my passion for clinical psychiatry, I knew I needed to formulate a compelling statement that would compete against ardent psychiatry gunners.

Throughout medical school, I had been certain that I would follow either obstetrics and gynecology or internal medicine with a focus in obstetrical medicine. I was drawn toward the complex pathophysiology, had a dedication to women's health and felt destined to carve out a niche for myself that blended both worlds.

But by the end of my third year of clerkship, heading into the elective period (where medical students get to select clinical rotations within the specialties of their choice, at different schools across the country), I had finished my last clerkship rotation, in psychiatry, and become instantly infatuated.

Psychiatry is often regarded as the underdog of medicine, tainted with a checkered history of brutality toward marginalized groups (not unlike some other specialties) and questionable medical practices, despite the incredible scientific advancements and groundbreaking discoveries that the field continues to make. Medical students have mythologized the specialty, claiming that it is grossly underpaid, overworked and—no pun intended—a depressing environment in which to work. A mentor of mine during one of our coffee dates, when I first disclosed my interest in and also reservations about pursuing psychiatry, told me that psychiatrists are sometimes viewed as auxiliaries to medicine instead of real doctors, despite the lengthy medical training and daily application of scientific knowledge to the care of our patients.

The stigmatization of mental health within society is often extended to the practitioners, and there are those who question whether psychiatry is even "real medicine."

Yet anyone who has spent even a day on the psychiatry ward or in an emergency room, or shadowed a psychiatrist, can understand just how imperative psychiatrists are to the functioning of our society and our medical system.

Despite the stigma, I was drawn to psychiatry not only due to the rapidly evolving brain science that I had loved since my second year of medical school but also because of the wealth of psychopharmacology that was embedded in the core knowledge of the specialty. Even though we were not required to memorize the neuro-receptors targeted in different psychopharmacological agents for our exam, I thoroughly enjoyed mapping out how the various drugs worked on different neurons in the brain, and how their "sloppy targeting" led to the frustrating side effects of anti-depressants and anti-psychotics. Understanding this complicated interplay within the neuro-network allowed me to conceptualize how other medications are used to treat undesirable side effects and helped me to consolidate the knowledge before the exam. Even after my rotation had concluded, I would listen to psychiatry and psychopharmacology podcasts in my spare time, vying to absorb as much knowledge about the field as I could.

Like in a whirlwind romance, I fell hard and fast.

The medicine of psychiatry fascinated me, in part because it lies at the intersection of art and science, as it necessitates an understanding of psychological and societal nuance, incorporating how different factors affect mental health—including race. The connection to my advocacy seemed clear, and the practice of psychiatry on the ward spoke more intimately to my core values than any other rotation. Having the privilege of being deeply immersed in a patient's story or inner world, and then having the responsibility to package and retell that narrative through detailed documentation and case review, also brought me a joy that I had not yet felt in my clerkship year.

The intellectual challenge of psychiatry is matched by the immediacy and the challenge of working directly with patients. It's not an exaggeration when I say there is a never a dull day in the in-patient psychiatry ward or emergency psychiatry department. I woke up each morning of that rotation eager to get to the hospital, happily stayed late chatting with patients or their families and finishing the notes, and even went in on the days that I wasn't scheduled to work.

There were stories that stuck with me long after I left the wards.

During my rotation, while leading a family meeting, I consoled a grieving wife whose husband had not died but had suffered a stroke that left him with a protracted course of vascular dementia and stuporous catatonia (a complex neuropsychiatric processing disorder in which the person can appear sedated, but is actually withdrawn, immobile, mute, and has abnormal posturing). In essence, the husband appeared deceased in his bed, despite the unremarkable vital signs and blood work, a kind of death that occurs long before the body actually dies. The person she had known and loved dearly for ten years no longer existed, and all efforts at remedying his catatonia were futile. She grappled with the guilt of confronting his impending institutionalization, especially in the face of mounting pressure from his adult children to return him to his seniors' residence. We not only managed his medical care but also helped them navigate this new, unexpected and terrifying frontier in their lives. There wasn't a day she didn't stay by his bedside, inconsolable, wishing to bring him home.

Psychiatry, like poetry, required an unflinching examination of some of the most devastating narratives of patients' lives; being a clerk on that rotation made me feel most like an artist, the part of myself that was drawn toward the often unexplored reality of our existence.

What further compelled me was the understanding that psychiatry, like most other specialties in medicine, had very few Black physicians trained in the field, and there was an overwhelming need for mental health resources within the Black community. Given the history of psychiatry, which has been weaponized against Black people historically (as, for example, with drapetomania, the fake psychotic label given to enslaved Black people who tried to earn their freedom), Black community members didn't always feel safe seeking mental health help from predominantly white clinicians. This—coupled with the understanding that Black Canadians experiencing first episode psychosis are at greater risk of involuntary psychiatric admissions, Black children are more likely to be labelled as having behavioural/psychiatric issues compared to non-Black children during their educational course, and Black youth are far less likely to have access to adequate mental health care—impressed upon me the critical need for more Black psychiatrists.

However, having just discovered my interest in psychiatry so close to the CaRMS deadline, I knew that I was at a disadvantage. My only psychiatry research was from my undergrad thesis, I had just one elective in psychiatry at U of T, and I had to compete against people who had strongly demonstrated their psychiatric interests over the last four years.

I continued to type, delete and rewrite the closing sentence of my U of T statement, praying that it would be strong enough to earn me an interview, against the odds I knew were stacked against me and those that were beyond my foresight.

I spent the rest of the evening toggling through my other statements for different specialties and schools, spreading my chances across internal medicine, family medicine and psychiatry. Although I knew psychiatry would be most well-suited to my future career, I struggled to let go of my dreams of being an obstetrical internist, or a family medicine physician who delivered babies and focused on maternal health as well. And as much as I loved obstetrics, I knew that since I hadn't removed my psych electives in order to stack my electives with surgical rotations, I wouldn't stand a chance, so I pulled that application from the list.

Over my fourth year, I had grown increasingly upset with myself. I was frustrated at my lack of certainty in specialty choice, especially since my character is one of strong convictions and I'd always had a clearly envisioned career plan. Ever since I was a child, I had always known that I wanted to be a doctor. During my first CTV interview, with Lisa, I had told the world that I wanted to be an obstetrician. Now, I was convinced it was psychiatry. I began to second-guess myself, floundering about in my indecision, certain only of my dedication to be a leader and way-maker, and unsure what kind of doctor I was meant to be.

I read the final lines of my statement once more before retiring for the night.

Nikki Goldberg was the chief medical resident on internal medicine during my clerkship rotation in the chilly winter of 2019. She was a passionate ally for racialized communities and would often make herself available during a busy day on the wards to check in on how I was faring. One thing about Nikki that holds true to this day is that she doesn't shy away from uncomfortable conversations about how medical learners experience racism and sexism. Her superpower is her dedication to learning, and her willingness to vulnerably admit that she is on a lifelong path to truly understanding what it means to be anti-racist. Like Dale, she would read books on anti-racism, buy resources for her small children to foster an environment of anti-racism at home, and challenge her biases as a white, Jewish woman. She acknowledged that for Black learners the discrepancies in privilege and social capital exist, as there are networks within medicine that are kept within social circles, and those who are well-positioned to enter medicine years before admission also benefit from these same connections through medical school and residency.

Nikki was one of the allies who sought to level the playing field for me and members of other historically marginalized groups, and she lent her support in every way possible. When an unwell patient told me, "If I brought a friend home that looked like you, my dad would shoot her off the doorstep," I texted Nikki immediately and sought her consolation. "That is absolutely horrible, and I am at a loss for words," she replied, as three little dots appeared while she continued to type. "I wish I knew what to say to make it better other than I am sorry, and it must be hard for you to continue the day." Nikki had mastered the simplest and most effective form of allyship that a colleague, friend, preceptor or ally can lend to someone who has experienced discrimination: validation. Even though Nikki was not Black and couldn't truly understand exactly what it felt like to be a visible minority targeted in their place of work, she ensured that my trauma was seen, acknowledged and validated. This made it easier for me to process, heal and move forward from racially aggressive encounters. I thanked her for simply being there in support, as too often I have had peers, tutors and people online strive to invalidate the trauma I experience as a Black woman in medicine.

During one of my panel engagements at a women's leadership conference for Western University in mid-2019, another white, female panellist told the group of undergrad students that sexism didn't exist because she simply wouldn't allow it to: "I didn't see gender growing up, and neither should you." While this advice was about gender, not race, it made me and other attendees shift in discomfort. I took the mic and cautioned the crowd as to the hazards of ignoring discrimination, especially when you are the recipient and are subject to its effects, whether you are cognizant or not. I further stressed the idea of intersecting privilege, such as having wealth or being non-racialized, as this may buffer one's experience of hardship.

Unfortunately, I have even had people within my community try to derail my advocacy, as they adhered to the tenets of meritocracy—if you work hard, your race shouldn't matter—and didn't believe that they were affected by systemic racism. I came to understand, and stress in my public speaking engagements, that I do not strive to speak on behalf of every Black individual, as we are not a monolith and should be respected for our individuality and differing perspectives. I seek only to share my story and traumas, the evidence base as it pertains to anti-Black racism that permeates the judicial, political, educational, medical and social fabric of society, and the hundreds of anecdotes told to me by other Black professionals in health care and beyond whose stories are similar to mine. What further complicates this situation is the understanding of internalized racism and survival; though almost every Black person is affected by systemic racism in some form (whether subconscious or explicit), they may repress these effects in order to assimilate, remain focused on their work and reach their goal. I understand the protective mechanism underpinning this narrative and appreciate that some Black people may have had more positive experiences in their place of work and study, even if they were alone.

But that is not my truth, and not the truth for many others like me.

"I hope you find a way to take care of yourself tonight," said Nikki, forever a vocal proponent of self-care. I planned to watch reruns of *Say Yes to The Dress* and prepare for my upcoming keynote address for the African Students' Association at Western University.

Navigating my advocacy proved to be challenging at times, yet it remained an important facet of my self-preservation throughout my fourth year of medical school. Though my keynoting had slowed during the months when I was travelling for electives, when I arrived back in Toronto in November to focus on my CaRMS submission and local electives, I also swiftly re-engaged with public speaking. I had gigs lined up at McGill medical school, Queen's, Western and U of T before the Christmas break.

There is nothing more potent and healing than empowering others to not only deal with discrimination but also become an effective ally. As my public speaking platform grew, I moved toward speaking passionately about authentic leadership, organizational wellness, the power of curiosity in leadership and—of course—mental wellness.

As a voracious reader and lover of all things art, I encouraged my audiences to diversify the stories they read. "Take stock of the things that you consume—books, food and film—ensuring that you are learning from a diversity of voices, as this will inform the lens through which you view the world." I would share a list of my favourite reads from authors of Indigenous, Southeast Asian and African descent at the end of the presentation, and a list of podcast suggestions for the non-readers in the crowd. Further, I encouraged them to differentiate anti-racist from non-racist from racist, making the point that non-racist is another form of indifference that upholds racism through inaction.

"Only through action, and navigating uncomfortable conversations, can real change be done," I would close.

My advocacy work almost always met with an overwhelmingly positive reception, and this carried me through the daunting last leg of my medical journey as I inched closer to match day, convocation and residency.

The first-year class of medical students at U of T was now more reflective of the population that we were serving, through the efforts of BSAP, but I knew that my work was far from over.

And as the final chapters of my medical school journey drew to a close, unbeknownst to us, the world was edging toward an unprecedented global pandemic set to challenge all we'd ever known.

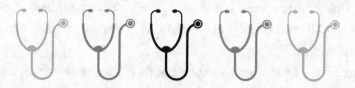

"Our children will either come to you a thousand times," I said to Dale, with our infant daughter on my hip and concern in my eyes, "or they will come to you once."

"The path they take will depend on how you respond the first time," I continued, fighting my urge to cry and storm off. Marriage is hard, and it can be even harder when the partners come from separate worlds, like Dale and me. He grew up as a white male with relative affluence and I as the Black daughter of African immigrants who did all they could to make ends meet. Over time, I had learned that leaning into vulnerability in the face of conflict, instead of turning away, could mean the difference between a marriage that persists and one that is in peril.

We stood in the corridor outside our bathroom, just a few steps from our son's bedroom, moments after he had settled into slumber. It was not the ideal location or timing for a heavy conversation around race and parenting, but the matter at hand couldn't wait.

We'd had iterations of this discussion before, at length, before our children were born and increasingly in the days, weeks, months and years after. It usually started with exploring the kinds of parents we wanted to be, the values we wanted to instill in our children, and how to ensure we provided them with the most enriched and loving home possible. The discourse would then wade into what it meant for us to raise biracial-Black children in our society, and how our vastly different lived experiences impacted the lens through which we parented and loved.

"I need you to know how to show up for them," I would often tell Dale, and he would sincerely agree. Protecting our family, in every way a father and husband is called to, is of paramount importance to him.

But that evening in the corridor, I felt as though Dale had fallen short.

"When I came to you to unpack the racist comments left under photos of our child, I could sense that you were clearly angry, but it seemed like you chose to mentally check out instead of sitting with me in the pain," I went on, referring to a photo that I had posted on Instagram. Dale inched closer to console me. I took a step back, wanting him to truly appreciate the gravity of disappointment and hurt in my eyes.

"I felt completely alone . . . and I never want our children to feel that way if they ever come to you to talk about race," I ended, leaving us in a moment of silence.

Admittedly, Dale had tried, as he always did, to validate my pain in the wake of experiencing anti-Black racism or sexism. When we first discovered the slew of racially violent remarks left under my posted maternity photos, some of which showed the hands and feet of our son, Dale's initial response was "This person is clearly sick, and I'm so sorry." His indignation was obvious, as was his desire to protect me and our children from the online harassment that I had faced for years while doing my advocacy work.

"Babe, I hear you, and I'm sorry," Dale responded now, respecting the distance I wished to keep between us until I felt seen and heard. "But I thought I validated you, so I don't understand where I went wrong."

He was right—he did start with validation, a tool that I frequently speak about during my keynotes on how to be a better ally. When I provide audiences with my "Prescription for Allyship and Advocacy," I explain that validation is the easiest and fastest thing you can do to display allyship and create an arena of emotional safety, whereas invalidation is the quickest way to other someone experiencing discrimination.

The difference was, however, that I expected Dale, as my life partner and strongest ally, to not only validate but *really* stay with me in the mire of the experience, so that I didn't have to face it alone. No, he would never have the experience of being Black or understand how racism feels on a visceral level, but I needed him to grapple with the discomfort we, as Black people, face instead of turning away from it.

"Babe, you jumped straight from validation to problem-solving by contacting our lawyers and sending another cease and desist," I explained. "Then it was like your brain just turned it off. You were done with it, and when I kept going with how dehumanized and hurt I felt, you reiterated that we will speak to the lawyers and offered no further emotional support."

After five and a half years together, I understood Dale in a way that no one else did, and vice versa. I knew that when he was confronted with tough emotions, he had a propensity to shift his mental gears immediately into a solutions-oriented mode, and then let his emotional well run dry. I knew that dealing with racism, proximally through me and our children, threw Dale into a rage—but he had the privilege of emotionally opting out, whereas my children and I did not. This is where I needed him to really show up for us as an ally, husband and father, or risk alienating us within our own home.

"I hear you, sweetheart. I really do," Dale went on. "I'm sorry I wasn't there for you like I wanted to be. I suppose I was so focused on how to protect our family through legal support that I neglected to meet you where you were emotionally."

I accepted his apology, as he swept away the tears brimming on my lashes and pulled me into his embrace.

At the start of our relationship, a conversation such as this one would have been challenging; Dale was, at first, uncomfortable with deconstructing the nuances of white privilege, fragility, white saviourism, subconscious bias and the real magnitude of racial dynamics at play in structures of power. After raising these topics on our second date, I realized that, like some Canadians, he had a superficial understanding of racism that was more or less limited to distancing himself from those who used racial slurs or consciously discriminated against a racial group. Initially, I bore the responsibility for educating him more deeply, prompting many impassioned conversations about race, implicit bias and intersectionality. I realized fairly quickly, though, that I could not move forward in a serious relationship with someone who didn't understand the core of my humanity—especially when it was integral to my advocacy. Most importantly, I wouldn't dare raise children with someone who wasn't wholly dedicated to understanding the toll of anti-Blackness. Quickly thereafter, Dale recognized that to truly operate within an anti-racist frame of mind and become the partner I would need in an interracial relationship, he needed to take the onus of education upon himself and spur knowledge into action. So he sought to immerse himself in anti-racist literature, podcasts and documentaries, often pushing me to further expand my own knowledge of anti-racism and the impacts it has. He took a genuine interest in Nigerian and Igbo culture and history and even endeavoured to learn bits of the language (yes, his accent is terrible, but the effort is appreciated).

When we found out years later that we were pregnant with our son, and then our daughter, we mutually agreed on the importance of giving them Igbo first and middle names to precede their English surname. We understood that names carry power and hold strong the connections to our heritage—one that I didn't want to be lost as my children grew up in Canada. We further promised to bring them to the village where my parents were raised and deepen our collective appreciation for the rich beauty of my motherland.

Still, like all of us, Dale and I are fallible. There would be many moments when I would feel exhausted by needing to explain things about my lived experience, wishing that he would just *get it*. There would be times when I would feel lonely even when he was right there beside me. Yet we knew that the journey of growth and learning was not linear, and there were moments, such as this, where we would stumble. What mattered most was that we continued to move forward toward understanding and healing.

Our two-month-old daughter, Nkiru (affectionately dubbed Nki), cooed happily in my arms as Dale kissed her cheeks and retreated to the living room.

That evening, I cradled Nki in my embrace while we swayed in our rocking chair and read the board book *I Love My Beautiful Hair* by Elissa Wentt, pulled from her nursery library. The cover displayed a little Black girl with afro-puff pigtails rejoicing against a backdrop of bows, butterfly hair clips and pink afro picks. Nki's nursery was thoughtfully curated with several

books like Wentt's that celebrate Black beauty and the boundless potential of women. The rest of her room was adorned with paintings of Black
ballerinas leaping through the air and reaching for the stars, a personal-
ized affirmations sign, and a wooden name carving displaying "Nkiruka
Nmeka," her first and middle names.

As we turned the final page of the board book, Nki's eyes becoming
heavy with slumber, I paused to study the little human who captivated my
heart. I drank in her features—the almond eyes that she got from me, the
button nose from my mother, her father's eyebrows—falling more deeply
in love with the daughter for whom I had always prayed. I knew that my
greatest job, above all other purposes in life, was to love, protect and nurture my children. Still, as a mother, I was constantly analyzing whether my
performance in this job was adequate, or whether I was falling short. I intimately understood the risk of the latter, having met many children who had
slipped through the cracks.

Peering down at Nki drew me back to my four-month residency rotation
in child and adolescent in-patient psychiatry, during which I was heavily
pregnant with Ezenna. In Nki's face I saw the high volume of biracial-Black
children under my care who were experiencing mental health difficulties
as a direct consequence of racism experienced at home and school. The
recurrent narratives of anti-Blackness from non-Black family members or
peers in the form of microaggressions, invalidation, use of racial epithets
and differential treatment scarred and traumatized my patients; they did
not feel safe at home, a place where they should have felt safest. Con-
sequently, many experienced mood and anxiety disorders, increased
thoughts of suicide, and self-harm. The urgency to fortify the wellness of all
children, especially racialized children, was underscored on this rotation
as I challenged how we clinically formulate our patients (integrating racial
trauma as a core component) and volunteered to counsel parents as to
how to meet the unique needs of their Black children. These conversations
were often uncomfortable but desperately critical, as their child's life hung
in the balance.

Dale and I understood that were we not careful and intentional in how we handled matters of race in our home, our children could face similar trauma. These pressures have even led us to have hard conversations with others around race, nuance and bias, and to make the painful—but necessary—decision to distance ourselves when these conversations soured. The health of our children, and sanctity of our home, depended on it.

I laid Nki down in her bassinet, turned on the white-noise machine and watched her doze into a deep sleep. Dale slipped in through the door and grabbed a hug as we soaked in a rare moment of stillness in our bustling lives with two children under two years old.

Parenthood is messy and difficult, even on the best days, but we are dedicated to making sure our children feel safe enough to come to us whenever they need to—not just about race, but about anything else that weighs heavily on their hearts.

Our journey won't be easy, but it will be worth it.

Chapter Twenty

Dale had promised that he would follow me anywhere.

"Wouldn't it be cool if you did a fellowship in neuropsychiatry out west, and we relocated to Vancouver? We could go hiking every weekend!" he exclaimed, while his mind ran wild with adventure. "I could find another government job easily out there, and in the winters, we could go skiing in the mountains."

He wrapped his arms around me from behind as we lay atop the freshly laundered hotel linens.

I chuckled, knowing that the closest I would come to the ski slopes would be the nearby chalet, sipping on a cup of hot cocoa made with oat milk—extra hot, no foam. I would probably have my journal and blue pen in tow, as there is no better milieu for introspection than the quiet hum of the wilderness and a view of dusted mountaintops.

"I'll leave the skiing to you, babe," I replied, tilting my head toward the floor-to-ceiling windows that overlooked the Caribbean Sea. A grand cruise ship was pulling ashore. Tourists and locals were dotting the sidewalks along the streets of Port of Spain. I imagined the uneven asphalt would be scalding to the touch, and the air would smell of freshly baked rotis and sweet iced tea.

The beaming equatorial sun shone through the window and brought out the stark difference in our hues, bathed and darkened in the Trinidadian heat.

Dale and I were dissimilar in many ways beyond our racial differences. He found peace in the outdoors, craved the salty ocean on his skin, devoured fantasy novels and opted for punk rock playlists on Spotify. I yearned for the comfort of a cozy night in, under a quilted blanket, tucking into a psychological thriller, autobiography or other non-fiction work, playing Solange's album *A Seat at the Table* on repeat, and falling asleep on the sandy beach under the fenestrated shade of a coconut tree.

But we slipped into each other's lives seamlessly, and the love we shared washed away any uncertainty and reticence I'd had about entering an interracial relationship. Dale started to explore the musical world of Afrobeats and would discover new songs from Wizkid and Davido before I had even heard them. He would even do a little bop to the rhythm, which improved over time with a bit of finesse. Though I wasn't a sports nut, I was pulled into the masochism of being a Toronto Maple Leafs fan, and endured nail-biting playoff games while we cheered, groaned and fell in disappointment onto our couches. We had hard, uncomfortable, raw conversations about race, privilege, sexism, activism and intersectionality. We ran through scenarios: How would he react if someone made a racist comment while we were together? Could he identify a microaggression when it occurred? What would we do if we had children and they faced discrimination within his family? No stone was left unturned in our discussions, and the end result was always the same: *I will learn from you while taking responsibility to teach myself, protect you and love you.*

Dale made me feel secure, even in the spaces and places I felt most scared. Over time, his ability to discern racial aggressions grew more sensitive, as did his desire to vocalize the concern, leverage his privileges and safeguard our relationship.

He was my home, and there was no one else I would have wanted by my side on the fateful morning of match day—Tuesday, March 6, 2020.

Any physician can relate to the heart-stopping, breathtaking moment in fourth-year medical school when they find out what program they are matched to. It's a fear that grows subtly throughout medical school, rising exponentially throughout the final year of our clerkship training. As medical students, we had to rank the residency programs from which we'd earned an interview from most to least desirable, with the understanding that whatever program we matched to, we had to attend. This meant that we had to ready ourselves to uproot our lives, if need be, potentially living in a city or starting a specialty that wasn't necessarily our top choice. Training in this new field and location could last anywhere from two to five years.

Dale tried to steady my nerves as I grabbed one of the hotel pillows and cradled it close to my chest. His smell was familiar and comforting; I nestled closer to him, having been terribly homesick for the past several weeks. I was grateful that he had travelled to join me.

Dale had flown from Toronto to Port of Spain, Trinidad and Tobago, where I was completing my final master's practicum from February to March 2020. Immediately after wrapping a busy CaRMS interview season that January, during which I had travelled through blizzards in my cramped sedan and caught red-eye flights between interviews, I'd boarded a flight to embark on a six-week international elective in pediatric oncology. My practicum (which earned me credit for both my MD and MSc) was split between clinical work and research, in which I bore the responsibility of being a health care consultant focused on quality improvement on the pediatric oncology ward. Though I was homesick, the experience was engrossing. I had the privilege of working with a medical team composed almost entirely of Black physicians, and for the first time in my medical career, I didn't carry the weight of always being acutely aware of my race.

The residents and staff doctors were brilliant and worked skilfully with the limited resources available to them in an underdeveloped island nation, caring for children and their parents caught in the most unimaginable challenge a family could face—childhood cancer. I acquired an incredible amount of knowledge about global health and was fascinated by the opportunity to spur innovation within the space through leadership; I delivered ideas that could minimize administrative burden, optimize mental health resources for the patients and improve sanitary practices on the wards.

The physical and mental distance from CaRMS was protective in the days leading up to the match, though flares of anxiety would peek through. Although I felt confident in my CaRMS essays, my performance during interviews and the strength of my recommendation letters, I knew of many strong candidates who had not matched to their top choices in years prior.

I also wondered what, if any, impact there would be from my highly visible and vocal advocacy. Did I really stake it all, and at what cost?

As the minutes ticked closer to 11:00 that Tuesday morning, my hands broke out in a rhythmic tremble. I tapped the bedframe mindlessly with my jittery feet and swung my gaze from the clock, to the laptop screen, to the unfazed tourists by the crystalline ocean, back to the screen.

Dale and I sat hand in hand in silence, the takeout containers holding our half-eaten breakfast teetering on the edge of the king-sized bed. My mom was waiting back home, ready to pick up my FaceTime call and share the result; she had always wanted me to be an obstetrician and deliver babies, but she'd grown to realize, respect and eventually embrace my choice to pursue mental health and neuroscience instead. When I told her that psychiatry had a sub-area of reproductive psychiatry, where I could still work with pregnant women, she was sold.

We waited. Each minute passed more painfully slowly than the last.

The throbber swirled in the middle of the page as the portal to our results became available, congested by the traffic of hundreds of anxious medical students trying to get onto the site at once. My body was wired with the rush of adrenaline and sleeplessness from the night before, my crossed legs growing numb beneath me, as my eyes locked on to the screen and Dale recorded the life-changing moment on his phone.

I drew long, deep, intentional breaths as my heart thumped so fiercely I thought I would faint. I kept my gaze fixed forward as the world seemed to hold still on its axis.

When the webpage finally loaded, revealing my results, I held my breath as my eyes widened in anticipation.

"Congratulations! You have been matched to U of T Psychiatry."

I read the message in a matter of milliseconds and cupped my face with an audible gasp, followed by sobs of happiness.

I had matched to my top-choice residency program.

Despite the sleepless nights, rife with uncertainty and overwhelmed by the fear that my dreams would slip through my fingertips, I had beaten the odds.

I called my mom immediately, sharing the news, and she broke out in cheers and started giving praise to God.

"My baby is a doctor! You're going to help those most in need and do the work that few are called to do," she cried as she passed the phone around to my father, brother and sisters, waiting to share their congratulations.

She was right, I would be committing to a career that was subject to both scrutiny and fear; psychiatrists grapple with the checkered past of the specialty (for instance, homosexuality and epilepsy were once characterized as psychiatric illnesses), constant questioning of our place in medicine, and decisions that often strip patients of their agency and autonomy in order to safeguard them and others.

But I was ready, and more excited to embark on the next leg of my training than ever before.

Dale and I celebrated with a four-course seaside dinner, the Caribbean sky dancing with deep oranges, reds and yellows that spanned the horizon where ocean met atmosphere.

I blew out candles on a tiered tiramisu cake, with *Congratulations* written in cursive around the golden rim with chocolate sauce, and watched the sun fall behind the sea.

▼

"I hear there's a case on the island, a girl who travelled from the UK and brought it back home to her family," said the taxi driver, as I sat in the backseat, praying to get to the airport faster. From the teal backpack, I took out an old, blue surgical face mask that I used on the wards and pulled the elastic loops over my ears, securing it snugly to the bridge of my nose.

"She real sick, yuh know," he said in a singsong way that seemed ill-fitted to the subject matter. He whistled cheerfully as the green landscape and multicoloured homes whirled past us.

His dust-tinted sedan bumped over the uneven roads, as the salty Trini winds blew in through the window. I craved the taste of one more street-side double Bake and Shark on the beachfront, salted plantains from the local restaurant, and one more hug goodbye from my friend Shari. She was off sick from work when I got the email.

I had to leave the island, urgently, as instructed by administrators at U of T medical school. Though I had a few weeks left in Trinidad, I rushed to book a last-minute flight back to Toronto as global concerns rose over the rapidly spreading COVID-19 virus. Every U of T medical student doing an international elective had to return home, as there were concerns that international flights would be cancelled and airports shut down to limit the spread of COVID.

When we first heard about cases of the novel coronavirus spreading overseas in China in late 2019, most everyone naively assumed that it would be another epidemic swiftly contained and extinguished before it spread to international shores. When I was leaving for Trinidad in February, and the global panic was steadily rising, my master's professor assured me that Trinidad had no cases and I would be safe. By early March, when I arrived back in Toronto and the world quickly went into an unprecedented lockdown, I knew that we were facing a health care crisis that would shift the course of history forever.

The nightly news told horrific stories of illness and death sweeping across nations around the world. U of T, like other institutions, had transitioned to virtual learning, and my master's practicum presentation, final exams and last lectures for medical school were all online. We, like the rest of the world, were assuming that a couple of months of sheltering in place, social distancing and contact tracing would flatten the curve and bring a rapid end to the frightening pandemic.

As the weeks paced by, and the cases and death rate continued to climb, the full gravity of the situation fell upon us, leaving a collective anxiety that upended our sense of reality.

The days, then weeks, then months spent inside seemed to mesh into an indistinguishable blur.

Dale and I tried to retain some normalcy. We strove to get outside once a day for a socially distanced walk, still fearful of being near others as we didn't quite understand how the virus spread: one minute, they said masks were unnecessary and pushed hand hygiene above all; the next minute, there were alarm bells rung that the virus might be airborne, and N-95 masks became scarce. Local grocery store shelves were empty, while mothers made public pleas online to source formula and diapers for their newborn babies. There was a palpable and ever-present fear within society as we looked for answers to questions science and medicine had only just encountered.

All we knew for sure was that COVID was extremely contagious and potentially fatal for the most vulnerable in our society, especially those with pre-existing illness, and those within long-term care homes or precariously housed in shelters. Headlines were grave and left many, including me, feeling hopeless and afraid.

My friends who were already in residency shared stories of the tsunami of cases that filled the hospital emergency departments and intensive care units, while they watched their colleagues fall ill to the virus. They tweeted in earnest about the extraordinary suffering, observing hospitalized patients in isolation saying their final goodbyes over video calls while holding the gloved, unfamiliar hand of a nurse or doctor. The layers of death and grief, they shared, were leaving them burned out, numbed and traumatized.

As members of the next graduating medical class, on the cusp of our residency and joining the ranks of those regarded as "frontline health care heroes," we waited in the metaphorical wings, eager to lend our services as newly minted physicians but terrified of the unknown landscape before us.

Like others, I quickly took stock of the mundane things in life that I took for granted. I missed getting dressed up just to sit in a café and study or write—how I achieved my best creativity and focus—while sipping on a freshly made latte and nibbling on a pastry. I missed the background chatter of café regulars, and the birds that always flew too close to our drinks, scavenging for crumbs of food. I missed catching up with my friends over a candlelit dinner, before a time when seeing someone outside your social bubble was one step short of sin.

More than anything, I missed the comfort of my mother's warmth. Throughout the first few months of the pandemic, I was unable to see her or anyone else in my family, even though Dale had proposed to me just days after my return from Trinidad. When I showed her my engagement ring over FaceTime, she gasped for joy and promised me that we would celebrate someday soon, "when this is all over."

All she had ever hoped for me was that I would marry a good man who would "treat me like a queen" and avoid the mistreatment that many African women faced within her generation. I wanted the same for myself and was thankful to have found that in Dale.

My anxiety was quieted by her reassurances, as it always was, while I begged her to delay her return to her job as a PSW until the pandemic receded. In December 2019 she had undergone knee replacement surgery and was on disability leave while she was rehabilitated, but she was eager to get back.

Stories were circulating on the news, and through the African auntie network, of racialized PSWs dying on the frontlines of the pandemic after contracting COVID. Cognizant that my mother's health was already in a precarious state, I was terrified of her returning to work, despite her explanation that the bills were mounting and she couldn't afford to stay home. My father, who also served on the front lines as a part-time registered practical nurse in a nursing home, was barely earning enough to make ends meet, and the household required my mom's financial contributions to stay afloat.

After a short, emotional conversation with Dale, we decided to gift my mother with enough money to cover three months of work pay and resolve some of her outstanding debt. The potential catastrophic consequences of her joining the front lines haunted me, stole my breath, and reminded me that saving, extending and enriching her life was one of my ultimate priorities. She wept in gratitude and informed her work immediately that she would be extending her leave.

Thankfully, though my semi-retired father was still working, my mother stayed safely at home as the pandemic continued to intensify and the world struggled to adjust plans made for the future. As graduation was being planned, with nominations for the valedictorian opening in April, U of T announced that all convocations would be cancelled in-person and shifted online.

Our collective dream of crossing the stage within the historic Convocation Hall on U of T's central campus, getting our medical degrees in front of proud family and friends, vanished within an instant. Cancellation and postponement of weddings and graduation parties swiftly followed, as the threat of grave illness, long COVID and death loomed over us like a dark, ominous cloud.

It had been fourteen years since U of T's Faculty of Medicine last had a female valedictorian, the students in my class learned, through murmurs and by digging into the medical school archives. This fact, especially given the nearly equal numbers of men and women that had been in the class over the past two decades, came as a shock to us all.

The list of ten nominees for our year was mostly made up of men, but it also included a few women who had the honour of being nominated by the class, including me and the president of the medical society. I had learned that Vic and a couple of my close friends from the *Daffydil* musical had nominated me, stating that I perfectly fulfilled the criteria of what a valedictorian should be: someone who embodies the ideals of a diligent and compassionate physician, a leader, an advocate and an excellent student. But for a name to make the short list, multiple people needed to nominate you. So, when I saw that I was short-listed, I was overwhelmed with gratitude and astonishment. I was elated by the idea of being honoured in this way in medical school, as I had been in high school, but I knew that my advocacy and work beyond our studies weren't accepted by everyone in my class. I remained disquieted by the statement from a classmate who warned me that there was a growing distaste for my equity efforts among a small group of my peers, hinting that there might be some faculty who felt the same.

I was also acutely aware that, on a factual level, I, as a Black woman, did not represent the average student in my class.

However, I was reminded by Dale, Vic, Adam and other friends in my class that my endeavours transcended the bounds of race or gender and bound our class together through an inspirational narrative; I was a dedicated medical trainee who catalyzed a seismic shift in the future of medicine at U of T, an ally and advocate and a seasoned public speaker who could rise to the occasion of delivering a virtual address to a graduating class about to be lauded as health care superheroes.

As the election polls opened, I rested assured knowing that, irrespective of the outcome, I had garnered the respect of those within my class who had nominated me. They believed that my work was of value and understood that, though I was unique in certain ways, I could still be the perfect representation of the future of medicine.

The following afternoon, as I sat on the couch and distracted my mind from the scary headlines and looming election results, an email from our class co-president Justin appeared.

"Valedictorian Results" filled the subject line. I opened the message with trembling fingers, steadying myself to accept whatever result lay before me.

"Chika Stacy Oriuwa has been elected as the valedictorian for the 2T0 graduating medical class of 2020. Congratulations!"

I dropped to my knees in surprise, and I picked up my phone and shared with my mom the news that would change the course of my life forever.

Chapter Twenty-One

The relentless vibration of social media notifications caused my phone to creep toward the edge of my nightstand, threatening to throw itself overboard; maybe it, too, was growing weary. I grabbed it quickly, saving it from peril, and disabled the push notifications from Twitter, Facebook, Instagram and LinkedIn. I turned on "Do Not Disturb" and activated my self-protective strategy for navigating the media spotlight: check tags and mentions periodically, stay away from Reddit, and try to focus on the positive, uplifting messages of support from friends, family and strangers.

My inboxes across all social media accounts were filled with dozens of messages from people all over the world, as my notifications neared the hundreds.

The communications team within the faculty cautioned me to stay offline, as the messages on Twitter and Reddit were becoming especially vile.

Just forty-eight hours prior, the *Toronto Star* had released its article titled "The only Black medical student in a U of T class of 259, Chika Oriuwa graduates as valedictorian," written by renowned journalist Royson James.

James, a Black male writer who had worked for the *Star* for decades, had interviewed me the week before the article's release and openly shared his pride in my accomplishments. "We need to celebrate you," he said over the phone, during our interview in late May 2020, only days after the headlines swarmed with news of George Floyd's death. The world was in the midst of a racial reckoning, in the aftermath of the brutal and inexcusable murder of Floyd, a Black man who was killed by excessive and undue police brutality in Minneapolis by a white cop named Derek Chauvin. Videos of his murder filled social media timelines, as Chauvin's knee was captured crushing Floyd's neck for eight minutes and fourteen seconds, leaving him begging for mercy before the last molecules of oxygen were starved from his lungs. I, like many Black people on social media, had grown traumatized by the passive consumption of Black suffering. For the first time, however, the incubator-like scenario created by a worldwide lockdown forced every gaze, Black or not, to become fixed on the horrors of the Black experience. The racism was not new, nor were the cameras, but the pandemic-driven attention to social media caused an acceleration of a civil rights movement that has been coaxed forward since the days of Dr. King and Rodney King.

As news of my selection as valedictorian broke beyond U of T circles, picking up interest within the media circuit, massive protests against anti-Black racism were happening worldwide, urging systemic changes and policies safeguarding Black people on the streets and across institutions. Black Canadians like Desmond Cole were centre stage in the media, drawing attention to policing practices prejudiced against Black Torontonians. In the latter half of 2020, the Ontario Human Rights Commission published its findings revealing that Black people are more likely to be arrested, charged and killed by police in Toronto than non-Black citizens. These revelations, in tandem with the horrific history of colonialism and anti-Indigeneity, as well as mistreatment of other racialized groups, shattered the pristine image that Canada had as the "Friendly Neighbour of the North."

The confluence of this reckoning and news of my valedictorian achievement led to a media kindling that had explosive results, garnering national attention for my speech and further cementing the balance between my career as a physician and my dedication as an activist.

The *Toronto Star* article hit the internet on a late-May afternoon, just three days before I was scheduled to graduate, share my virtual valedictory address and earn my medical and master's degrees. It detailed the trials that I had faced as a Black medical student championing advocacy throughout medical school while confronting the adversities of racism. James further explored how, through the efforts of BSAP, U of T had recently admitted the largest class of Black, talented medical students in Canadian history—twenty-five outstanding students. I had learned that many of the applications that were submitted that year had referenced me as inspiration in their essays, drawing them toward U of T to pursue their dreams of medicine as future Black docs. This, I shared, was one of my greatest achievements in life and a legacy I felt honoured to leave behind.

The article, though boasting an eye-grabbing title, was meant ultimately to be one of inspiration. I was lauded as the first Black woman to be named sole valedictorian (there was a Black female co-valedictorian in 1992, Dr. Kristine Whitehead), and first female valedictorian in fourteen years within the faculty. I often feel uncomfortable leaning into my accolades publicly, but I came to learn that there are moments to celebrate yourself and bask in the light of your shine. There are moments where we must take up space, without apology or reservation.

The face of medicine was changing, for the better, and the story was meant to unite a society that was rife with racial division, especially under the influence of political leaders like Donald Trump, who perfected demagoguery and coaxed derision along racial lines.

Within hours of the *Toronto Star* article being posted online, hundreds of comments began to accrue on social media posts. Like my *Flare* magazine article, it drew attention from online commenters.

"@chikastacypoet, @TorontoStar I would never let her treat me or give me medicine."

"@TorontoStar She only won this because she is a Black immigrant."

"@TorontoStar, this is a clear political move by U of T, if she wasn't Black, she wouldn't have been named valedictorian."

"She was literally barely passing medical school, I'm in her class and can confirm."

"I go to U of T medical school as well and try to avoid her at all costs in the hallways or whenever she has a talk on campus. Her energy is off-putting."

"I fear Blacks in positions of power, so less is more."

Of course, the accounts were anonymous. Faceless, spineless trolls who tried to rob me of my merit, accolades and joy in my achievements. They tried to push me to the fringes and string caution tape across the doors of the hospital.

I fluctuated between quivering in indignation, breaking down in defeat, being fortified by the overwhelming avalanche of support and encouragement from people of all ages, races and genders across the world, and feeling completely numb.

I put my phone away and tried to breathe and reiterate positive self-affirmations.

I was less than two days away from my pre-recorded valedictorian address going live during convocation, a speech I had crafted over three weeks, pausing my studying for my licensing exam to meet the deadline. It would be one of my best speeches ever delivered, and I was honoured to have the privilege of representing my graduating class. I stood on the precipice of becoming a newly minted physician, a goal I had kept for a lifetime and worked passionately toward over the past four years. I was just weeks from starting residency at my top-choice program and bravely stepping onto the front lines of a deadly pandemic.

I am enough. I belong. I deserve this.

As I had always done throughout my advocacy journey, I turned to the power of words to grapple with processing the pain of prejudice and othering. When an editor at the *Toronto Star* asked me to write an op-ed about my experiences of dealing with racism as a Black Canadian, I took them up on the offer, just twenty-four hours before I earned my medical degree.

"The [hateful tweets] reminded me," I wrote, typing my thoughts out hastily, "poignantly within a day of becoming a physician, that there is no escaping the vise-like grip of anti-Blackness. It exists in the fabric of our society, throughout all systems, and strikes with impunity."

I further detailed the disillusionment that struck me in the wake of the racial violence I was confronting online; I had waded through medical school with an unspoken, misguided belief that earning my medical degree would confer upon me immunity from racism. Surely, I thought, once they saw that I had graduated from one of the most prestigious medical schools in the country, while also earning my Master of Science in health systems leadership and innovation, as valedictorian who advocated for a paradigm shift not only at U of T but at other medical schools across the country, I would no longer face the pain of racism. *They* would see that I had proven my merit, I had gone above and beyond, I had worked twice as hard to earn my spot—I should be allowed to feel welcome in a career I adored, taking care of the sick and the vulnerable.

But I wasn't.

Instead, I was met with further racist invalidation of my own worth and of the credentials that were freshly applied to my name. I was told that I wasn't worthy of practising medicine, touching patients or being near children. I was reminded that, despite everything I did, I still wasn't enough and never would be. This kind of hatred would later escalate when a single, persistent harasser so terrified me and Dale that I sought police protection and retained legal counsel. I would be forced to change the settings on all my social media accounts, remove myself from the hospital rosters at work, and even have security guards chaperone me to and from my car in the parking lot.

It's a kind of targeting that leaves you incredulous and gasping.

Fortunately, allies and colleagues from near and far, as well as complete strangers from different cities and continents, battled with the trolls online.

Past clinical preceptors came rushing to my defence when trolls claimed that I was a "lazy, failing medical student who didn't deserve to be named valedictorian," and let them know I was the antithesis of what they claimed.

The Nigerian community came out in droves, calling me their "collective daughter who has put Igboland on the global stage, making them proud."

Dale, though not much of a Twitter user, tried his best to refute the comments that aimed to discredit me; he was the only person who had an in-depth view of my pain, and he knew that despite the "strong Black woman" cape I wore, I was still human. And I was still hurting.

We placed our phones down in silence, knowing that at the end of the day, it was us against the world.

What was it like to watch George Floyd have a knee pressed against his neck for eight minutes and fourteen seconds?" asked the television reporter, abruptly, as the red recording light of the camera flickered behind him, capturing a wide-angle shot of my reaction. The videographer held the camera steady, while the reporter focused his gaze on me, eyes narrowing. As my face distorted in shock, I wondered if this was more about the ratings than it was about me.

I tried to quickly remould my expression, knowing it would be broadcast that evening to the entire country.

That morning, the day before my graduation, I had agreed to do an interview for a national news network. There would be millions of Canadians watching the segment, which had a prime-time spot on the network. The reporter and his videographer had agreed to conduct a socially distanced interview in the park, with the gorgeous June day acting as the perfect atmosphere for a light, positive discussion about me as valedictorian. Or so I thought.

The red recording light continued to flicker, the reporter waiting for my response.

It was reinforced to me that morning, and throughout the following day of my convocation, that while most media outlets strive to uphold integrity, there is a danger that Black pain can be exploited. In that moment, rather than the subject of a story about my achievement, I felt used as a caricature of Black suffering.

Unfortunately, this feeling was only amplified for me by other journalists who prodded and dissected my experiences with racism, like biologists over a Petri dish. "My editor wants more details," said one of the journalists, who was writing an article about my experiences at U of T for a popular magazine. I had already given her an hour of my time during my convocation week, as I was attempting to salvage every spare moment to prepare for my licensing exam scheduled just two weeks later.

"We want to bring the reader into your shoes with more stories of racism from patients. What's the worst experience that you've had? Tell me more about how you felt, in that moment."

I spoke with this journalist for another hour, laying bare my soul until I was an emotional wreck. While journalists are under pressure to get the story and move on, they can leave behind those they interview—like me—to lick their opened wounds alone.

The social media frenzy continued to beat along in the background, a stir of positive, negative and neutral reactions. I would sometimes cave to the seductive allure of tapping into public opinion, before quickly realizing that it was a pitfall for my mental well-being. Whether the comments were good or bad, I learned that I needed to strengthen my self-worth, not only internally but also with the sentiments of those who truly loved and cared about me.

The night before my convocation, I pranced around the living room in my velvet graduation gown and cap, snapping pictures to send to my mom and sisters, pretending that we were in Convocation Hall. Dale had decorated the walls with blue and white balloons (U of T's colours) and hung a string sign that read "CONGRATULATIONS" across the mantel.

As the pandemic was still raging on, I was unable to spend the following day with my family, despite my graduation being a monumental feat for us all. This was heartbreaking for me, as I wanted to share it most with my mother, the first person who believed in me above all else.

The most important person in my world.

"I am proud of you, Nnem, so proud."

I was choked with gratitude. Her opinion was the only one that mattered.

It was already sweltering hot on that June morning, and thanks to my velvet gown (which I wore purely for the fun of my own private celebration) and the nervousness of my address going live, I broke out in a sweat. Dale interwove his fingers with mine for comfort.

As my face appeared on the screen, I drew an inaudible breath and squeezed his hand. I appeared wearing a simple white blouse and my anniversary necklace, with my hair in a booming, unapologetic afro.

"Good morning.

"Dean Young, Vice Dean Houston, esteemed professors, physicians and faculty members, mentors, family, friends and especially my fellow graduating class of physicians at the University of Toronto, Faculty of Medicine, Class of 2020.

"I am Chika Stacy Oriuwa, and I have the absolute honour of being the valedictorian of our graduating class here at U of T. I'd like to start by thanking you, my fellow graduates, for the opportunity to share my address, during what will be the final time that we convene before our respective journeys take flight."

I could feel Dale tightening his squeeze as he sniffled and held back tears.

I continued my address, referencing my belief that physicians are often called to make sense of patients' complex medical narratives, synthesizing them into a coherent story that leads to our differential diagnosis and treatment. I reframed our profession as "sense-makers" who help patients navigate through some of the most difficult parts of their lives.

"But what do we do when it stops making sense?" I inquired, following up with the idea that, in these moments, we should remember that the most important skill we possess is not our ability to make sense of things, but our ability to connect, remain human and bring comfort.

"Or, as Hippocrates is thought to have said, 'Cure sometimes, treat often, comfort always.'"

Over the next fourteen minutes, I drew wisdom from Michelle Obama, reminding my class to "get out there and define yourself, or you'll be quickly and inaccurately defined by others," while also exploring the journey of the last four years that we embarked on together. I remarked on the earliest days of medical school, the countless hours spent committing a mountain of medical knowledge to memory, honing our clinical skills within the hospital, laughing as much as we learned, and leaning on one another when the tears couldn't be held back.

I stated that during clerkship we had learned about the fragility of life, as we ushered it into this world and held its hand on the way out. I thanked the patients who patiently let us learn, through trial and error, as we upheld our promise to first do no harm.

I vulnerably shared my story of advocacy, and what it was like to venture through the halls of U of T Med, and the hospital wards, as the only Black medical student in our year. I shared the moments of being othered, asked to leave the room by patients who didn't believe I was a part of the medical team, being mocked and ridiculed online and left hopeless. But I also thanked my classmates, for their unrelenting allyship and protection, showing up for me at my keynotes as comforting faces in the crowd, and defending me online when I felt voiceless and afraid.

In true Chika Stacy fashion, I closed my address with a poem dedicated to my class, as poetry has always been the purest way for me to express my gratitude and encompass the gravity of any moment.

To my fellow graduates
To this cohort of brilliant physicians with boundless potential
To the people who are quickest at thinking of a differential
Who have finally earned the credential of MD
We had a vision of 2020,
though the picture didn't quite come out as clear as we thought
   it would be
we remained a class of visionaries

Those with the foresight to define themselves in the world
Who raised their arms with fists curled in the face of injustice
As our patients entrust us with their lives
The time has officially arrived for us to rise to the occasion

So here is to the stem cells
The first generation to graduate from the curriculum of
   Foundations
We waded through uncertain waters
The sons and daughters of hope
Equipped with knowledge, compassion and our stethoscopes

We now find ourselves, four years later
Starting residency in the face of an uncertainty that is much
   greater
Once again, wading into uncharted territory

Maybe, it's a defining part of our story
To be the class who is familiar with moving forward despite
   the unknown
We have shown that we are capable of doing what has not
   been done before
We are the class who will explore the stones yet unturned

Here is to the innovators, waymakers and healers
Who have been mentored by some of the greatest leaders in
  medicine
At an institution that continues to redefine excellence
We are ready to take the leap into the next chapter of our lives
And on the other side awaits personal and professional
  celebration
Anniversaries, weddings,
Rare diagnoses and successful resuscitations
And though we will encounter a difficult road ahead
We are united by the threads of endurance and tenacity
Within us lies the capacity to change the world

To my fellow graduates of the University of Toronto, Faculty
  of Medicine,
Class of 2020, Congratulations!

We did it.

Chapter Twenty-Two

Holding the newly printed security badge in my palm, it all suddenly felt real.

"Dr. Chika Oriuwa, Resident Physician," I whispered to myself, as I waited in line to grab a tea from the hospital cafeteria before my evening shift. I ran my hand over the bold lettering, feeling the cool touch of plastic beneath my fingertips. I had thought the surreal feeling of achieving my life's greatest goal would lift when I passed my medical licensing exam or held the physical "Doctor of Medicine" degree in my hands—but no. It was in the moment when my hospital badge reflected my newly minted credentials, and when my first patient called me "Dr. Oriuwa."

I was no longer a clinical clerk in med school protected by the seemingly infinite layers of medical seniority. I was a real physician, with real responsibilities and real lives under my care. The five-year stretch of psychiatry training would require me to make countless clinical decisions that could shift the course of my patients' lives forever. I strove to integrate best medical practices with patient preferences in every choice, whether relatively innocuous or consequential, as I endeavoured to safeguard my patients' medical autonomy and decision making.

When I encountered Adetola, and his son Demi, on my first shift in the psychiatric emergency department, my stance on patient-centred care was no different.

Adetola begged us to help him contact his wife, Tolu. He wanted to tell her himself. Initially, I obliged and sought to attain Tolu's contact information.

Demi, freshly out of university, pleaded with his father to "calm down and let the doctor help you." When I learned from Demi that his mother, Tolu, had been deceased for nearly three years, I quickly appreciated the extent of Adetola's fractured mind and broken heart.

It was his second presentation to the psychiatric emergency department within two weeks, the earlier visit prompted by his concerned son and extended family back in Nigeria; Adetola hadn't stayed long enough to be assessed at the prior visit. Demi reported that since the anniversary of his mother's passing three weeks ago, his father's behaviour had become increasingly unusual and worrisome.

I learned that when Adetola had refused to leave Tolu's gravesite over several hours that morning and had come to believe that he could contact her through the radio, Demi decided to bring his father into the emergency department himself.

"Back home, in Nigeria, before my mother passed, we noticed that my father would sometimes do and say strange things. Mama told us not to worry, but we still did. He would claim to be able to communicate with spirits through the farm animals, and he even wrote long messages to God on the walls in our home. Many community members would call Papa crazy during these episodes. Mama was always able to bring him back to his normal self—but ever since she died, it's like no one can help him."

Demi looked toward his father with concern, as Adetola retrieved a weathered notebook from his coat pocket and flipped through several pages of drawings and scribbles. I thought immediately of my father's dinnertime tales of psychics, wizards and weather-shifters in his village back home, and wondered how many—if any—were actually afflicted with mental illness in a society where it was highly taboo.

"Doctor, are you going to let me go? I have serious matters to deal with," said Adetola, as he gestured toward the door dividing our interview room from the emergency department.

The atmosphere was dreary that evening in the sprawling hospital, which was full of patients with a range of psychiatric ailments, from suicidal ideation and self-harm, to psychosis, withdrawal, substance use, and mania. Many were distressed, like Adetola, and sought a soft place to land.

"Demi, I have to tell your mother that I finally found the cure. We are wasting time here," Adetola uttered, so quickly that his words were barely intelligible. His hands were trembling so violently that I was certain the notebook would slip through his fingers. Before Demi had an opportunity to respond, Adetola buried his head in his hands, slowly rocking back and forth in the chair and whispering, "No, no, no. Tolu, don't worry, I'm coming." He flipped through the notebook again, landing on a page with a complicated diagram of the kidneys and internal organs. "We just need to get the blockage out," said Adetola, as he vigorously rubbed the flank of his abdomen. Demi shared that his mother had died of kidney failure, secondary to systemic lupus erythematosus, often known simply as lupus. His parents had been married twenty-five years before her death—and for every time that Tolu had saved Adetola from himself, he sought to return the favour, even after her passing.

"Papa, Mama is gone! We cannot bring her back! Please, you are not well—let the doctor help you, Papa."

The psych nurse and I sat at the other end of the room, supporting, observing, documenting.

It was my first year as a resident doctor in psychiatry and in the bustling emergency room. After starting my residency with two blocks of clinical research on neuropsychiatry (with a focus on functional neurologic disorders), followed by emergency medicine (at the height of the third wave of the pandemic), I was ecstatic to immerse myself back into psychiatry and start treating patients who were historically marginalized within medicine and society. Notably, during the pandemic, mental health crises rose drastically within the emergency room as isolation and social distancing served as kindling for substance use disorders, worsening depression and self-harm, suicide attempts, and an increase in episodes of psychosis; patients with and without a psychiatric history presented to the emergency department in droves.

Adetola was my first patient of the night, a sturdy, six-foot-tall Nigerian man in his early fifties, with sporadic presentations to the emergency department over the past two years. He had immigrated to Canada from Nigeria with Tolu and Demi fifteen years earlier, shortly after his psychosis began. After a brief primary hospitalization in 2018, following Tolu's death, he was diagnosed with schizophrenia and started on a proposed lifelong treatment with atypical anti-psychotics. His clinical charts revealed a remote appointment with his psychiatrist and several clinic notes during periods of mental stability, which appeared to have tapered off in recent months.

"Papa doesn't like to take his meds every day," said Demi, "even though I notice that he is more stable when he does."

"Nonsense," shouted Adetola. "Those medications just made me sick! I couldn't think straight or have the energy to get out of bed," he said.

"Listen, Demi," he went on. "Your mother said she is ready to come home," Adetola begged, his eyes wide with urgency. "They weren't able to save her. But I figured it out, Demi." Adetola pointed to the arrows and numbers strewn within his leather-bound notebook, then clutched it in his hand as he rocked in the chair.

A woman's voice suddenly boomed through the overhead speaker system, from the hospital's security team, announcing a code white several floors above.

"Tolu? TOLU? IS THAT YOU?" Adetola pleaded. As the voice disappeared, he begged for her to return. When two subsequent announcements were made, he began to cry. "She has been trying to communicate with me all week, Demi, I promise," he kept reiterating, as Demi pleaded with his father to find reason.

I tried earnestly to create a space where we could de-escalate his heightened emotions and he would feel safe, while eliciting the necessary history to determine an approach to management. I elucidated a timeline of his current presentation—his delusions and bizarre behaviour had been steadily growing over the past three weeks, worsening when he drove to the gravesite that morning.

I validated his anxieties. "Adetola, I can appreciate how deeply you want to help your wife, Tolu, and I imagine that her absence has been unbearable." I asked him to describe to me what life was like when Tolu was still around, and how he had managed in the years since she passed.

"I have been driving taxis for many years, since I arrived to Canada. After Tolu left us, I started to hear her voice in the noise between radio stations. I tried to ignore it, but I can recognize her voice anywhere, and she was calling for me. So, between driving my patrons, I would drive close to the cemetery, and I realized that her voice became more clear." Tears gathered in his eyes before spilling into the palms of his hands. I learned that he would spend more time parked by the gravesite, talking with Tolu, than actually driving customers in his taxi.

When Demi started to notice that his father would disappear for periods of time without contact, and that Adetola's prescriptions were not being filled, he grew increasingly concerned.

"I found him earlier this evening by the burial site, after not being able to get a hold of him for hours," said Demi. "He was rambling about finding the cure to Mama's illness and bringing her back to life or something. There was a shovel in his passenger seat, and I know that when my father gets like this—nothing can stop him."

Adetola's fingers tapped the notebook once more, on a page filled with numbers down the margin. "These are the stations you can hear her most clearly," Adetola went on. When he flipped through the last page, a wallet-sized, creased photo of Tolu fell out.

My heart sank, while the vision of Tolu made something in Adetola break.

His eyes began to dart from me to the corners of the room, to the nurse, to the door. "I must leave," he demanded. "Please, let me get out of here, Doctor, I don't have much time!" Sweat started to bead along his hairline. He stood from the chair and began pacing the room, growing frantic. "I won't let you guys hurt me or make me sick again! You didn't help Tolu, you killed her! You killed her! Now you're going to kill me!"

Demi begged his father to sit down, attempting to pull him by the hands to no avail.

I was trained in my first month of residency, during onboarding, to always position myself closest to the door when interviewing a patient, as situations can escalate quickly and become potentially dangerous. "If a patient stands, you stand," my preceptor said to me during safety training. Her words came back to me in that moment.

I stood.

"Adetola, I can see that you're feeling very concerned right now. Can you tell me more about how you're feeling?" I said, in my calmest voice, while my heart began to race. I wasn't scared, per se. It was just one of my first times encountering a Black patient in the psychiatry ward, and I knew that his intense distrust was not undue; Black patients have historically been treated differentially in psychiatry, especially in the emergency departments. Black men, moreover, are more likely to have physical restraints used, and higher doses of tranquilizing medications administered, driven partly by a subconscious fear that they will be more aggressive and require more sedatives. I wanted to not only "do no harm" but also reinforce the most positive experience he could have in the emergency room, as this often dictates whether patients will return when in crisis or continue with follow-up.

"You are going to lock me up like an animal again, aren't you?" said Adetola, with eyes that looked more terrified than threatening.

"We are only here to help you, Adetola, and I can't be certain what that help may look like while you're here. But I promise that we will do our best to make you feel better, and less scared." I kept my eyes on him, soft and fixed, as he paced the back perimeter of the room.

"Would you be okay taking a seat?" I asked. He did.

Demi continued to reassure his father, and shared with us more details of prior hospitalizations, visits to the emergency department, prior medication trials, and stories of how his mother was able to ground Adetola in moments of distress.

Gathering collateral information is one of the most important parts of the psychiatric assessment, as patients with psychosis or altered realities may not always remember details or will have limited insight into the initial symptoms and course of their disease.

"Demi!" Adetola cried out. "Enough! Enough! Enough!" he screamed, before bursting into wails and calling out for Tolu. He stood up and threw the notebook across the room.

"Papa," said Demi, with jagged breathing and a shaky voice, "I will take you to go and see Mama soon, but remember how she would remind you to breathe? Breathe with me, Papa."

Adetola looked at his son through tears. He fell back into the chair and began to slow his breathing through deep, protracted breaths. Demi released an audible sigh, reflecting the collective relief the nurse and I hid behind a wall of professional composure.

"He's not always like this, Doctor," said Demi.

Adetola was a vibrant, intelligent man and loving father, he shared, who was kind and helpful toward his neighbours, and had great rapport in his business. He stressed, above all else, that he wouldn't hurt anyone, even when he was "like this."

"He was restrained and heavily medicated during his last hospitalization," Demi continued. This had caused him to become distrustful of the doctors here and the medical system more broadly.

"I'm so sorry that you experienced that, Adetola. I can only imagine how unsafe and terrified you must have felt," I said, knowing my words of comfort fell woefully short of imparting a sense of ease.

"Please, just don't hurt my father, Doctor. Please. I know he might look like he could hurt someone when he's like this, but he won't. He is a good person, very loving. He just hasn't been well since Mama died. Just please don't hurt him. Treat him like the other patients you're taking care of." He broke down in sobs.

I understood, through his coded language, that, as a Black man, Adetola might face differential treatment in the emergency department, like undue force from security and other excessive treatment measures. Within recent years, media headlines had surfaced about Black people experiencing mental illness within Canada and dying in the process of getting help. Demi surely also understood that racist stereotypes portray Black men as more violent and aggressive, especially when experiencing mental illness.

It was clear that he was building a case for his father that served more than to inform his treatment course—it was to protect him.

"I understand your concerns, and I want you to know that I will do everything to ensure that your father is safe here, as will the other doctors, nursing staff and support team," I responded, as Demi grew more emotional.

"I can see that it would be hard to believe me, given everything you've both been through, but as a Black physician, I can appreciate why you and your father are scared about him being in the psychiatry department with a mental health crisis and possibly being treated differently." Demi looked forlornly at his father, while I further tried to placate his concerns.

The role reversal of son protecting father struck a chord with me, as a daughter often called to protect and advocate for her mother in medical settings and beyond.

"Doctor," Demi said. "Thank you, truly. You have no idea how grateful I am to know that there is someone like you here who is helping take care of my dad," he continued, sniffling through his gratitude.

"Can you please make sure that the other ones understand, as you do, that he is just like the other patients, and should be treated the same way as everyone else? Please, Doctor, you know how they can treat us in here."

I didn't think my heart could sink any further, but it did. I discreetly turned my head toward the ceiling, averting tears. His voice, though heavily accented with a Nigerian lilt, reminded me of my own brother's: soft, but hurting. Adetola was all he had left, and he would never give up on his father. I reassured them both once more, explaining the developing assessment and plan, and promised to relay their concerns to the rest of his care team.

Adetola agreed to take a small dose of Ativan, and soon he began to doze off in the assessment room.

I returned to the workstation to review with my staff and type out the lengthy report on his assessment and plan. As was the case with many psychotic patients, the extent to which we would be able to achieve and sustain wellness would depend on the extent of the psychosis, severity of medication side effects and adherence to treatment, responsiveness to prior antipsychotic interventions, and the length of time that the patient's disease had gone untreated. Sometimes, patients respond brilliantly and remain stable for years. Other times, sadly, every treatment seems futile, and patients can remain quite sick for most of their lives. Almost every time, we cannot say definitively why. Psychiatry is a field of limited certainty, and we as physicians in the specialty need to sit comfortably in the unknown grey areas of science and help the patients who wade through their murky waters.

I finished writing Adetola's note and reviewed the charts for the next patient waiting to be seen. Several hours later, I handed my cases over and headed home for the night.

The following week, after rounds and handover from the overnight residents on call, a psych nurse called out my name.

"Dr. Oriuwa, there is a patient's son in the waiting room who wants to speak with you."

It was Demi, who appeared much more cheerful and hopeful than when we had last spoken.

"Doc, I mentioned you yesterday to my auntie back in Nigeria and she knew your name—so I googled you and read some of the articles you wrote. Wow!" he exclaimed, reaching for my hand in gratitude. "I cannot believe that my dad will be in the care of a famous Black—and fellow Nigerian—doctor. God bless you for your work and everything that you are doing in the community. You've made our people so proud."

I thanked him, heartily but humbly, realizing that our exchange was painfully rare. Black children helping their sick parents to navigate the psychiatric system will often wrestle with the unspoken risk of being a Black body in a health care institution. Though implicit-bias workshops and diversity, equity and inclusion task forces appeared in droves during the pandemic, the risk of unmitigated biases and differential treatment of Black patients remained ever-present. Black people experiencing a mental illness in the community were still more likely to have coercive and threatening force used to bring them to the ER, to be involuntarily held within hospitals, to be physically or chemically restrained in the emergency department, and to be diagnosed with serious psychotic illnesses such as schizophrenia.

More than ever, especially within psychiatry, there was a battle cry for more Black physicians, not only to increase the feeling of safety and comfort for Black patients but to advocate for real change within the system.

Speaking to Demi served as a poignant validation of my last-minute switch to psychiatry and my call to serve a community on the fringes.

His kind words, however, also made it clear that, for better or for worse, I had, to a great extent, forfeited that privacy in the earliest days of my public-facing advocacy as a medical student. The pressure to not only represent the community but also be the "perfect Black, Nigerian-Canadian female doctor" weighed heavily on me. Failure to meet this expectation would come with a risk of falling from public grace.

I remained acutely aware that, as Michelle Obama detailed in her memoir, Black women in the public eye are held to an impossibly high standard, and even the most diligent will be dismantled and denigrated, as she experienced.

All eyes, it felt, were on me. And I couldn't slip.

Chapter Twenty-Three

Every specialty has a soundtrack—a distinctive melody that a discerning ear in the hospital can tease apart from the rest. Within the walls of the operating theatre one can appreciate the buzz of electrocautery (electric current used to cut through tissue or form scarring), surgical instruments landing on metal trays, or the surgeon's sigh of relief after a successful excision. On the pediatric floor, the uproarious laughter of children echoes through the hallways, juxtaposing the pulsing of vitals monitors above in the ICU or the wails of labouring mothers on the floors below.

In the psychiatric emergency department, there is a cacophony of sounds emerging from patients shrieking in the throes of psychosis, the rapid murmurs of those experiencing mania, and the deafening silence of patients who do not feel safe when left alone. Amidst this lies the steady rhythm of doctors, nurses and auxiliary staff who flow from the nurses' station, to the documentation room, to the emergency vestibule, answering the call to protect some of the most marginalized people in our society. If one listens closely, one can hear the patter of residents' fingers blitzing across the keyboard, transcribing notes from a consult, or the discourse between physicians, puzzled by an unusually challenging case.

Whenever I stepped into the psych emerg, despite the often-chaotic environment, I felt a calming reminder that I was where I was called to be.

It was a windswept winter day on the streets of Toronto, one that demanded a turtleneck under my scrubs and thick, woolly boots, even into my shift in the psych emerg. Our city was grappling with yet another series of pandemic-driven lockdowns and a health care system on the brink of collapse. The emergency department continued to bustle with patients experiencing mental health crises, placing its trust in both the newly minted and the seasoned physicians labouring in the ER, pushed beyond exhaustion.

After assessing an older gentleman who was brought in by police for erratic public behaviour and suspected alcohol withdrawal, I heard a high-pitched yell cascade across the department.

"That's from room three," said Nicole, one of the psychiatric nurses on service with me that evening.

Patients in the EOU, or extended observation unit, are typically too unwell to be released from the hospital following an assessment, but may not require urgent admission to the ward, or may be waiting until space becomes available on the packed psychiatry unit above.

The patient, Magda, was a brilliant young woman in her mid-thirties, with a complicated history of bipolar I disorder, complex childhood trauma, and recurrent episodes of self-harm and suicidality. When I'd spoken with her two days earlier, during an initial assessment, we'd spent an hour carefully combing through her medical, psychiatric and personal history, as well as the immediate events that had precipitated her current presentation. Magda shared that, over the past year, she was finally starting to put the pieces of her life back together following an extended stay on a mental health unit recovering from a severe manic episode. Upon medical stabilization and discharge, she had been able to return to her graduate studies and finish writing and defending her doctoral dissertation in actuarial sciences, and she had started looking for research positions at a nearby post-secondary institution. Excitedly, she shared that she had picked up recreational volleyball again, which she used to play competitively for her high school and university teams, leading them to repeated championships. Things were going well, she lamented, until her boyfriend of three months abruptly ended their relationship.

"I didn't know the reason," she shared through pressured speech (speech both fast and frenetic), further elaborating her suspicions that he might have been involved with "that woman at the gym," or that he was secretly envious of her academic achievements. When asked to explore what had prompted her presentation to the unit, she said that her mother was worried, as Magda had spent the two weeks leading up to that day struggling with insomnia and increasing thoughts of self-harm. She had also started using cannabis again after swearing off it for six months. "The medications helped," Magda reported, "but I know my brain and my body, and I wanted to treat things naturally." Like many patients afflicted with psychiatric illness, Magda had stopped taking her prescribed treatment, additionally citing valid concerns such as undesirable weight gain, mental fogginess and blunted emotions. As a psychiatry resident, I understood and commiserated with my patients about the unpleasant side effects of our medications, especially anti-psychotics, yet struggled to balance this against the potentially disastrous ramifications of untreated mental illness. The consequences, for Magda, were playing out in real time.

Once I'd gathered further collateral information from Magda's mother (with her consent), I learned that Magda had been sending multiple messages to her ex-boyfriend, Johnnie, and to Kara, "the woman at the gym," whom she had tracked down on social media.

"She stopped looking for work," Magda's mother reported, "and spent all her time on her laptop or cellphone keeping tabs on Johnnie and this woman she is convinced he left her for. She even became paranoid that her neighbours knew of the affair and weren't telling her, so she shouted at them one evening—I was scared that they would hurt her, not knowing that she was just unwell." I could hear the pain in her voice, a desperate mother who felt helpless in the face of a cruel disorder. "She must have sent maybe fifty messages to Johnnie in the past week, and he said to me that he would call the police if she didn't go and get help," her mother said, "so I begged her to come in."

I learned that when Magda refused her mother's plea and ceased all communication for several hours, her mother called the police to perform a wellness check, which led to Magda being brought directly to our department.

Magda shared that she had struggled with an urge to self-harm in the hours leading up to her presentation to the hospital, and she had ever-present passive thoughts of suicide. When asked if she had thoughts of harming others, especially Johnnie and Kara, she divulged that she "would never hurt anyone, even if they deserved it." Though reluctant, she agreed to staying on our extended observation unit for ongoing assessment and initial treatment pending an admission to the ward due to an emerging manic episode.

When, two days later, I heard Magda screaming through the halls of the EOU, I knew something had gone awry with our forlorn patient. Before I was able to pull up her charted notes and review the interval history from auxiliary staff, I was quickly beckoned by Nicole to assess Magda, who was growing angrier by the minute.

"YOU!" she yelled, extending a finger in my direction. She appeared much larger than when I had seen her last, slouched over in the assessment room, mourning a lost love. Now, her voice was boisterous and her green-hazel eyes were wild with fury. I felt dwarfed and fearful facing her much taller stature.

"You are a CON ARTIST!" she screamed, as a crowd of psychiatric nurses, co-residents, curious patients and security guards gathered. I scanned the room for my staff attending, who stood on the edge of the circle, waiting to see how I would enact my training to de-escalate the patient's rapidly accelerating agitation.

"Magda, I can see you're very angry right now. Would you kindly take a seat so we can talk?" I said, feeling the muscles of my throat tighten.

"NO! I want a REAL doctor, not you. I know who you're really working for!" she yelled, slowly rotating around the circle, demanding another doctor to take over her care.

"I looked you up online, *Stacy*, you BARELY passed medical school! Someone even said you actually failed! You are NOT a real doctor—and you shouldn't be allowed near ANYONE! Yet you said you could help me. You obviously know Kara and you're doing this for her—to keep me here, so that she can get closer to Johnnie. That's right, I'm onto you. I know you both went to McMaster University around the same time, yet you denied ever meeting Kara when we first met. YOU FRAUD!"

"Magda"—my voice was shaking as the words became lodged in my throat—"I'm not sure what you read online, and I can appreciate that you are scared right now, but I am a real doctor. I am a resident doctor of psychiatry at the University of Toronto, and I went to the same medical school to get my degree. I graduated last year, and I have never met Kara." I held my badge out to her, clearly showing my face and "Dr. Chika Oriuwa, Psychiatry Resident" in bold blue lettering across the bottom.

"NO, YOU'RE HELPING KARA!" she said, fists curling as she came within a foot of my space. My body instinctively froze, like a prey animal in the wild who had just noticed a top predator flying overhead. I had never before seen eyes widen and fix with pure rage; it frightened me so fiercely that my hands and feet went numb. I looked at my preceptor for help, but they continued to observe from the sidelines.

I had been trained in what to do, algorithmically, when a patient became increasingly agitated and threatening. Most importantly, for my safety and the safety of those in the emergency department, I needed to de-escalate, first through disarming words, then with an offer of a sedative, to be taken voluntarily or delivered involuntarily by the psychiatric nurse if the situation became urgent. Security was positioned skilfully around Magda and me, ready to intervene immediately should the situation worsen.

"Magda, I am a real doctor who is responsible for your care tonight. I want to give you the option of taking some medication that will make you feel a little calmer so we can talk about what is upsetting you." The words left my mouth disjunct, as my heart raced so brutally I was sure everyone in the room could see it.

She continued to yell and draw closer, as security inched closer behind her and the nursing staff prepared the sedatives, in both the pill and syringe forms.

"I will never let YOU give me any medication!" she yelled. "You'll all be charged with conspiracy once I speak to my lawyers!"

I had always thought I knew the feeling of what it was like to be rendered speechless, whether by joy, surprise or devastation. But for the first time in my life, I genuinely felt paralyzed by fear, my throat squeezing so tightly that it wouldn't let words out or air in. I was certain, as Magda gesticulated with her fists and inched closer to me, continuing to yell, that I would get hit before the security guards could restrain her. We were trained in what to do when a patient attacks us, how to defend ourselves without inflicting harm on the patient, but that rarely works when your brain has chosen "freeze" over "fight" or "flight."

After another fifteen or so painfully long seconds, I willed my mind and body to return to a state of composure and handle this situation as the resident doctor I was, even if Magda was convinced I was not. It was clear that in her mania she had felt driven to do some further research on me, as patients are able to keep their phones during their stay, and her persecutory delusions had latched on to the hateful messages that she had read about me online. This was not uncommonly seen in psychiatry, as patients suffering from mental illness are particularly vulnerable to what may grip the cultural zeitgeist—especially the misinformation and disinformation spread through social media and fringe internet forums. I understood that her hurtful accusations were not a personal or moral failing of Magda's but the tragic outcome of a challenging, unrelenting illness.

Her statements that I was a fraud who wasn't a real doctor and shouldn't be practising medicine sounded like a rote memorization of the comment sections on Twitter and Reddit on the articles about my advocacy. Hearing the words that I had battled with for the past four years online resurface in the form of an agitated, threatening patient sent me into a transient state of detachment.

I nudged myself to remain steadfast and determined, now more than ever, for my patient who was sick and threatening, but still my patient.

"Magda, as the doctor responsible for your care, I am offering you the choice of taking these medications that will help you relax either by mouth or through a needle administered by the nurses. You have the choice—what would you prefer?"

"I will never take any pills from you, but I'll let the nurse give me the needle," she uttered, as the psychiatric nurse moved closer to her, ready to administer the sedatives. I thanked Magda for her compliance and said that someone would be in to speak with her soon.

Magda returned to her room, muttering once more that I was Kara's accomplice and she wanted someone else. I felt my heart slow in my chest as the team dispersed to attend to their other demands.

My staff shared a fleeting "Good job back there, let me know if you want to debrief" as the circulation returned to my extremities and the feeling of surreality lifted.

I placed my clipboard down on the desk in our staff room, leaving the cursor blinking on the EMR screen for Magda's documentation, and quickly strode toward the back exit.

I stood in the howling, biting winter winds and gasped frantically for air, letting the oxygen fill my lungs.

I pulled out my phone to call Dale, steadied my frenzied nerves and returned to the workstation ready to finish the rest of my shift.

When I got home that evening, I tossed my scrubs into a pile of blue fabric on the floor and stepped into a hot, steaming shower. I tried to wash the ruins of the day from my bones, from my skin, from my mind.

But I couldn't. Nor could I brush away the feeling that I had impaired my ability to navigate my medical career with the safeguards of relative anonymity.

My throat tightened as I reflected on the interaction with Magda, the details magnified in the rearview mirror of my mind. The way her nostrils flared in anger, the vein that throbbed at her temple, her bright green irises eclipsed by enlarged black pupils, the feeling of my cotton scrubs on my skin, weighted by the woollen sweater I wore overtop.

The smell of fear emanated from every pore in my body.

I scrubbed harder to wash it away.

I scrubbed and scrubbed until my deep brown skin turned raw.

Navigating the medical world, the outside world, felt as though it would never be the same.

Shortly thereafter, I would grow panicked in patient interactions in the emergency department, feeling my chest tighten when a patient inched uncomfortably closer during an examination or spent too long peering at my badge, studying my name. Could they have seen a headline about me or watched one of my keynotes? If so, were they impressed, ambivalent or incensed? The nature of my work could be inherently polarizing, as some valued the equity-driven climate magnified during the global pandemic, and others grew to resent it.

I understood the reality of public-facing advocacy, one where my narrative online and in the media could be parsed and spun in any direction—positive or negative, salacious or accurate—to exist on the internet forever. I had seen every "version" of myself online—from heroine to villain, lazy medical student to egotistical narcissist, do-gooder to race-baiter. Although I strove to define my narrative—as Michelle Obama had advised in her book *Becoming*—I quickly learned that there will always be individuals who will work to construct a counter-narrative. Just as in the halls of the hospital wards and clinics, I was not afforded protection in the court of public opinion, and took on this great personal and professional risk in the name of doing the right thing.

Daring to trust my internal compass, the guiding light of my convictions, was the only way forward.

Chapter Twenty-Four

A gloomy, overcast mood painted the March skies across Toronto, as the frosty earth summoned spring back to centre stage. It had been almost a month since I'd concluded my rotation in the psychiatric emergency department, still intermittently quieting a heart that raced in the presence of patients and strangers who eyed me suspiciously.

I was now in the throes of the hardest stretch of my first year of residency, two months of internal medicine with one-in-four call (doing an in-house twenty-six-hour shift every four days with regular working days in between), followed by a month-long block in consult neurology and finishing the year with palliative care medicine. The COVID-19 pandemic continued to blaze through the country and world, sending an influx of sick patients into the emergency department and onto the wards. Black, Brown, elderly and marginalized communities continued to be hit the hardest, as they filled the intensive care unit and left tending staff with memories that would haunt them for a lifetime. The ever-present fear of death and illness permeated the hospital, leaving us yearning for an end to the unprecedented times, and a return to normalcy that seemed as if it could exist only in a fairy tale.

I had just finished a ruthless week on the internal medicine wards, completing three twenty-six-hour call shifts within six days, and was relishing the quiet lull of my scheduled day off. Dale was returning from a jog with his best friend, Hani, while I stared through our washroom window and debated Dale's suggestion from that morning.

"Just take a test, babe," he whispered to me, having keenly observed how I'd picked the pineapples off my pizza the day prior and slumped into bed early from exhaustion.

I tapped on the cardboard box with "Clearblue" printed on the surface, pausing before tearing the lid open and reading the instructions.

What if I really am pregnant? I thought to myself. *How would our lives change?*

Dale and I had always wanted to be parents, and when we eloped the summer prior, we knew that we were ready to start trying. Being a mother had always been one of my most important goals, driven largely by the incredible mother that I was blessed with; if I could be even a quarter of the mother and woman she was, to my children, I knew I could give them a beautiful life.

I pressed my tongue against the ridges of my teeth, waiting out the longest five minutes I had ever endured. I read the instructions over once more: "Do not interpret results before 5 minutes."

Forever possessing a rebel spirit, I flipped the testing stick over at the three-minute mark.

Two bright blue lines appeared on the clear central panel of the at-home pregnancy test, just as Dale walked up the stairs toward the bathroom.

I whipped the door open and threw myself into his arms. "You're going to be a daddy!" I said as his jaw dropped and his eyes grew wet with emotion.

They say that when someone learns they are going to become a parent for the first time, everything changes. I felt this seismic shift within my body, from a spiritual to a cellular level, as my entire life became reframed in an instant.

I was no longer just a doctor, writer, advocate or public speaker. I was someone's mother—their mama, the most important title I would ever have the honour of holding. I understood intimately—from both personal and clinical experience—the powerful force of a mother's love on a child's well-being, and the devastating effect that can be felt in its absence.

From that moment onward, as I braved my remaining weeks of internal medicine and shifted to neurology, then palliative care, the lens through which I viewed my work as a physician and advocate evolved. The sanctity of each life became heightened in a way I had never understood before, as did the pull toward ensuring this world was a safer, more welcoming and better place for me to raise my children.

My precious baby would be a person of colour and would invariably grow to encounter the disturbing reality of anti-Black racism and possibly sexism. Though I would do everything in my power to shield them from these intolerances, I knew that the insidious nature of prejudice could not be eradicated from a societal system that was built directly upon these forces of discrimination.

I could, however, inculcate within my children the famous quote from the iconic civil rights activist James Baldwin: "Our crown has already been bought and paid for. All we have to do is wear it."

Like my mother and her mother before her, I promised to teach my children that they were courageous and resilient, that they were the very embodiment of Black excellence, and I would demonstrate for them the force of resistance that was encoded in our DNA.

No matter who would try to snatch their crown—their confidence, their voice—it could never be taken from them.

It could never be taken from me.

Realizing that one is becoming a parent forces a person to reflect on their own childhood in a microscopic way, unearthing previously healed and unhealed traumas, examining their father's and mother's parenting styles in relation to their own, and urging them to confront uncomfortable truths—about the world and themselves.

One of the foremost things I understood as a child was the heartbreaking impact of not only racism but colourism and sexism. As a darkskinned Black girl, I was socialized to believe that, even within the Black community, I was at the bottom rung of attractiveness, affability and intelligence; the closer one was to being light-skinned (like my father), the more graces one was afforded within and outside the Black community. Throughout my life, I saw my beautiful, brilliant, dark-skinned mother face ridicule that she was too "dark, short and stupid" to be married to a man like my father. These comments scarred not only my mother but her children, who only ever wanted to grow up and become just like her. I also vividly recall hearing, time and time again, from Black and white boys alike, that they would never date a dark-skinned girl or bring her home to their family.

When my sister welcomed my second niece, who expanded the love within our hearts in ways that are immeasurable, the baby's lightskinned complexion was immediately contrasted with my elder niece's darker-skinned complexion by other family members. It broke my heart, and when I heard people within the community openly make insensitive, ignorant remarks toward my nieces, I would force them to apologize and rescind their words immediately. It was imperative that my nieces understand that their beauty and worth, whether light-skinned or darkskinned, could not be stripped from them.

Dark-skinned women are further mischaracterized in the media, through rap lyrics, on television shows, in movies and in politics (yes, another nod to Michelle Obama's experience within the unforgiving political spotlight).

Even before Dale and I became pregnant, people would frequently remark that we were going to make such "gorgeous children," which had never been expressed to me in my prior relationships with Black men. It was clearly implied, and sometimes explicitly stated, that having lighter-skinned, mixed-raced children, with curly, looser hair, would be one of the greatest things I could accomplish as a mother. What I would remind them is that genetics is a peculiar thing, and I have met biracial children with a darker complexion than their Black parent, and kinky, afro-textured hair, too. They were beautiful, and deserving of love and adoration, just like other children—something I wish society had reinforced for me when I was a child.

I grappled with these conceptions during the early days of my pregnancy and reflected on the times when, as a little Black girl, I had felt invisible. When I played with my dolls, they had lily-white skin, long, straight blond hair and big blue doe eyes. I would fashion them into doctors, and that play subconsciously formed my understanding of what it meant to be smart, beautiful and successful—a narrative that drifted from what I saw in the mirror.

How different would my self-perceptions have been if, as a little Black girl, I had seen someone like me doing what I didn't think was possible? What would it mean to the child growing in my womb to know from the beginning of their life that they are worthy, that they could occupy spaces in powerful places without apology?

It was while bustling through the halls of the University Health Network, eleven weeks pregnant and feeling the throes of first-trimester illness during my consult-neurology rotation, that I received an email from Mattel Canada that would answer this question in the most unimaginable way possible.

"We would like to honour Dr. Chika Stacy Oriuwa as a Barbie Role Model, as one of six women chosen around the world who have made an impact as health care heroes during the pandemic. Mattel Canada would like to provide her with her very own, one-of-a-kind Barbie Doll made in her image."

There would be no white coats fashioned out of toilet paper, no makeshift shoestring stethoscopes or imaginary curly hair and deep skin tone.

This Barbie would be real, and it would be me.

I would be doing this for the little Black girl who felt invisible on the world stage.

It was our time to step into the spotlight and be seen.

"How are you feeling? Can I get you a quick snack?" asked Lisa Perry, Barbie brand manager for Mattel Canada. She looked like the personification of the original Barbie Doll—tall, blond, beautiful, wearing bright pink lipstick. She was effusively warm and bubbly, exactly what one might imagine for someone who worked for an iconic brand like Barbie. The entire morning of the televised Barbie unveiling, and throughout the day, she kept a hawk-like watch over my needs, shuttling food and water to me on the set, remarking intermittently how vividly she remembered the discomfort of pregnancy and how it was "the least she could do."

"I'm great, thank you!" I replied, feeling the swift kicks and twirls of my baby within me. The baby had been relatively quiet all morning but had become increasingly active as the minutes ticked toward showtime. It was an unexpected comfort to know that I wouldn't be braving this moment alone, and I tapped into the superwoman strength that I felt as a mother-to-be.

The Global News anchor came out and chatted with me for a few minutes before we started. I could sense that he was trying to calm any nervous jitters so that our pre-segment repartee would ease into an effortless conversation while the cameras were rolling. I moved the pink-ribboned box containing my Barbie to the gap between us, positioning it in the ideal spot for the big reveal. A white customized mug reading "Barbie, you can be anything!" in the brand's iconic pink and italicized font was placed to my left, the logo facing toward the camera.

As the camera operator counted us into the segment, I handed my coat to Lisa and fixed my grin into a delighted smile.

The conversation started light and playful as we discussed what it meant to be a Barbie Role Model memorialized in doll form, and what implications this would have for diversity and inclusion during the time of the pandemic.

We discussed my work as a psychiatry resident, and how imaginative play intersects with mental health among children.

"Girls as young as five start to have self-limiting beliefs, and I want to change that trajectory through the importance of representation." I smiled toward the camera. It all felt surreal. My baby continued to twirl, increasing the force of their kicks and punches, unbeknownst to the rest of the world. *I can't wait to tell them about this one day*, I thought to myself, as Lisa stuck two thumbs up in approval of my performance.

"Let's unbox your Barbie, Dr. Oriuwa!" said the anchor in the perfect journalist voice, calm, cool and collected, with the ideal smattering of authentic enthusiasm.

I pulled the pink ribbon out of its bow, placed it on the anchor's desk and lifted the box's lid.

My mouth parted in an audible gasp as I pulled the Dr. Oriuwa Barbie out of the box. It almost felt like a scene out of *Toy Story*. I half expected her to come to life.

Nothing really prepares you to see yourself in doll form, let alone representing your country among other international role models.

I was genuinely elated, with a childish, rhapsodic grin that grew from ear to ear.

"Wow, this is incredible! I love it!" I exclaimed, clasping my hands in joy, almost forgetting that this was being broadcast across the country. I wished to exist in that moment forever—pure, unbridled happiness, so rare and fleeting.

The Barbie looked exactly as I had imagined her, with my exact features, the typical doctor uniform, and a big, bouncy afro that was twice the size of her head—a not-so-quiet reframing of the face of medicine. I felt like a kid again, wanting to set her down amidst the teddy bear patients and get to work.

She was perfect.

After the buoyancy of the moment settled, I shared what this meant for me, and what it would mean for little girls around the world.

"I want to redefine what a doctor looks like, and let them know that they can be and do anything."

Once the segment wrapped, the photographer took a few more shots of me with the doll as I cradled her in my hands and stared into her eyes.

This, I whispered to my younger self, *is for you.*

Chapter Twenty-Five

et's get away for a while," I said to Dale, a week after the Barbie filming wrapped. The media buzz following the reveal lingered for days,
sweeping me up in back-to-back television and radio interviews that ate
into my mornings before work and evenings after. I wished to disconnect
from the world after a particularly stressful twelve months of being in
and out of the public spotlight, especially as a twenty-six-week pregnant
psychiatry resident.

"Like a babymoon?" he asked, also feeling the lassitude of a long
summer with a heavy work schedule. He had recently started a new job
within the government and faced exhausting days at work as well.

"Exactly," I replied.

We decided to fly, three weeks later, to a gorgeous remote chalet nestled in the mountains of rural Quebec.

Our plans for the two-week trip were simple: try the best poutine,
read to our hearts' content, take a stroll through the quaint, cobble-
stoned streets of Quebec City, attend our virtual prenatal classes and
lean into our relationship.

The solitude of the picturesque escape also forced us to confront the
impending shift in our private world—we would become parents for the
first time in only a matter of months. We wondered about the common

things: What would it be like to be *truly* sleep deprived? How would it affect our marriage? Who could we turn to for support?

But we also further unpacked the unique dynamics of an interracial family: What would it be like to raise a child whose experience with race would differ from our own? What would Dale do if our child experienced racism and I wasn't there to support them? Would Dale be able to identify it? How would he handle teaching our children about how to engage with the authorities? Would he know to let them know that even their best efforts might not change the outcome?

How would Dale comfort them when they begged an answer to questions that were inexplicable?

This conversation would continue to evolve as the actuality of parenting manifested.

We had learned, just weeks before, that we were having a son. A little boy who would grow to face the pressures of the world as a biracial-Black man.

How were we going to prepare him to thrive within a social and political system that is not inherently constructed for his success?

How would we teach him that, as a man, he could still be soft, gentle and kind—circumventing the tropes of toxic masculinity?

How would we be honest about racism, colourism, sexism and all the ways in which the world can threaten the well-being of him and those he loves?

As a white father, was Dale ready to really raise a Black son?

Was I?

We had some of the hardest conversations we have ever had as a couple, strengthening the connective tissues that hold the bones of our marriage together.

In solitude, I reflected on my advocacy and the awe-inspiring journey of becoming a trailblazer throughout my medical career, despite the professional and personal risk I assumed. I thought deeply about the implications of my career for my growing family, and how it would influence my mothering; I would do everything in my power to be a devoted mom, while also showing up for my community, as a physician, writer and waymaker. The balance, I believed, would be much more challenging than juggling scriptwriting, studying and keynotes—but I understood that I carried the strength of the women who came before me, like my mother and hers.

I, like them, believed I would build a future generation of leaders who would shift the intergenerational needle farther away from trauma and the pain that held us back, as women who constructed the impossible.

In the wise words of poet Sarah Kay, we "were born to build."

"It's so important to celebrate the people who have made these accomplishments of being the first or being the only," I said, in the concluding line of my *Time* magazine feature video, shot for the "2021 Next Generation Leaders" campaign. I had been informed of my selection while away on the babymoon and was again balancing the demands of my pregnancy with the ever-present expectations to show up meaningfully in the world. "But at the same time, that should be the spark for us to realize that more work needs to be done."

The clip ended, fading into black, with "TIME NEXT GENERATION LEADERS 2021" appearing at the centre of the frame. Its release was timed for when the magazine hit the stands in early October, just a few weeks after filming had wrapped. I learned that I was in the auspicious company of other notable figures, like actor Timothée Chalamet, whose greyscale photo took the cover, framed by the iconic red borders.

I wondered how differently it would have unfolded if I had decided, that fateful day in December 2016 when I was asked to join the BSAP campaign, to follow the fear in my mind instead of the bravery in my heart. I wondered how many little Black girls would have continued to question their worth, their ability to enter medicine—or even their place in the world—had I not stood up and shown them that anything is possible. That their dreams were not only real but very much within their reach.

I wondered if I would have forged a path that led me to give international keynotes, make headlines in other countries and languages, and push for paradigm shifts in the landscape of Canadian medicine and beyond.

I wondered how different my narrative would have been had I not decided to unapologetically occupy powerful spaces, step into my authenticity as a Black woman, challenge the status quo and redefine what a doctor looks like.

My son swiftly kicked my belly, the imprint of his foot discernible through touch.

I chuckled. *Ezenna,* I thought. The name Dale and I had decided to give him.

It loosely translates to "God is supreme / King of the Father" from Igbo, which is similar to the translation of my own name.

We would call him "Eze," meaning "King," for short.

I wanted him to know that, like a "king," his crown was already bought and paid for, through the sacrifices and courage of Black waymakers and trailblazers like his mother.

All he had to do, as James Baldwin noted, was put it on.

Eze lay curled on my chest, still bound to the fetal position to which he had been accustomed in the womb. It was early December 2021, just two days after he was born and just hours after we brought him home from the hospital.

I was feeling bludgeoned by the whole experience of labour and the demands of early postpartum, still shaking off the delirium brought on by bringing forth a new life. My body remained swollen, and the anguish of recovery pulsed through me unrelentingly.

But his quick little breaths, fluttering eyes and new baby scent were intoxicating. I felt a love I didn't know was humanly possible. I was forever changed the moment I held him in my arms, as he unlocked a strength in me I didn't know I possessed.

Dale sat beside me on the couch, also in the throes of new fatherhood and sleeplessness. My mom was waltzing through my kitchen, throwing together the concoction of Igbo remedies for postpartum recovery, fixing a nutritious plate for me as she had done all my life—with love.

I looked around at my living room, letting the dizzying blend of bliss and lethargy wash over me. The details of my wall-to-wall built-in bookshelf, which over time had blurred in the chaos of my life, came into fine focus. Beside the TV was my Barbie doll, encased in glass by Dale to remain unspoiled in perpetuity. Within one of the cubbies was the poster advertising my keynote speech at International Women's Day 2018, my name superimposed on the photo from my *Flare* magazine feature, framed by my dear friend Adam. Two rows above was my natural hair care guide from third-year clerkship, perched against a row of books that held stories that informed the way we viewed the world. In the bottom right corner was a portrait of me with my stethoscope, given to me on the set of my TEDx Talk, after I dared listeners to step into the light of their truth.

I placed my hand on Eze's back, and felt it heave and fall with each breath. I felt the crushing weight of responsibility to care for something I loved so much it hurt, and to protect him in a society that would affect him while he was still young and innocent.

I gently kissed his forehead as he fell into slumber.

He would never know a world in which Black didn't equate with excellence, intelligence and tenacity, in every form, as he would be surrounded by this from the first day of his life.

As I looked at my Barbie, and all the other artifacts of my daring journey, I imagined Eze, and my other future children, knowing innately that they are worthy.

That they are seen.

And, most importantly, that they belong.

Epilogue

Dr. Chika," called a voice from the middle of the audience. It belonged to a little Black girl with chunky box braids and an effervescence that surpassed her eleven years. Her hand was the first to shoot into the air at the end of my keynote, beating the curious others in the packed room. I learned that her name was Adaline, and she was one of approximately fifty Black elementary and high school girls in attendance that late-summer morning. The conference was organized by local church leaders to inspire the young women to reach toward their dreams, and my forty-five-minute talk was in pursuit of this goal.

"When you want to give up, what makes you keep going?" she continued, as the rest of the room looked toward the podium where I stood. I immediately remembered her voice and her spunk from the start of the session, when, in response to my asking what careers they wished to pursue, she had proudly declared that she wanted to be "an architect or scientist." Speaking to her felt like stepping through a portal into the past where I could counsel my younger self, or like stepping forward into the future to share a heart-to-heart with my own daughter.

"I love this question, Adaline," I replied, sincerely. Over the course of my public speaking and my career as a thought leader, the answer to this popular question continued to mirror the evolution of my values and experiences.

"I've always anchored my determination to keep going in my 'why moments'—which are the moments that remind me *why* my voice and work have purpose," I continued, observing her eagerly scrawling notes in a blush-pink journal.

"One of my *why* moments is happening right now, speaking to young women just like yourself who represent the incredible potential right here in our community. Every time I look into the crowd and get a chance to connect with another brilliant Black girl, I am reminded of how critical it is to continue representing the importance of unapologetically occupying powerful spaces.

"I want you to remember that if I could do it, so can you, and even more boldly, bravely and powerfully," I continued.

"Another *why* moment is when I look into the eyes of my son and daughter, from whom I draw the most incredible strength. Every time I hold my babies, I am reminded that I must leave this world in a better place than when I entered it, for them and for future generations. This, in part, means continuing to address disparities in medicine, be it toward equity in medical school admissions, health care research, clinical practice, and beyond into other sectors and industries. It's part of the reason why I named my little girl Nkiruka, as it translates from Igbo into English as 'the best is yet to come.' Her middle name, which she shares with my mother, is Nmekadinma, which means 'to do good is a good thing.' At the core of all my *why* moments is the desire to do good in the world, even when it is risky, even when I feel like giving up."

Adaline smiled and thanked me from the audience, while several more hands sprang into the air with questions.

After the session wrapped, Adaline and her mother waited for me by the exit and asked to take a quick picture. I bent down to Adaline's height as we smiled brightly for the camera.

"Thank you for this, Dr. Oriuwa. I know she'll remember this moment for life," her mother said, as Adaline twirled with enjoyment. She embodied the wonder and innocence of childhood that I desperately wanted to protect from the damage of the world. She deserved this, and so much more.

"So will I."

Woman, Black

woman and black
doctor and woman
doctor and black
doctor, black woman

doctor, doctor!
we need a doctor
is there anyone on this plane that can help?
how can you be both doctor and black,
woman?
they told her step back,
they asked for credentials
what's at the top of the differential?
physician: unlikely

they did not look like me
they did not speak like me
and yet it only took me three years on this earth,
to realize that doctor is what I was destined to be
it took you 10 seconds to decimate
10 plus years of my training
I do not have my credentials,
but this man's vitals are waning

they told her step back

how can you be both doctor and black?
I ask myself the same

when they call me by name
I will say not Stacy, but Chika
Chika Stacy if you insist,
but you would be remiss if you thought I would divorce myself
from this African bloodline
when I step into this white coat
I am more black than ever

I will remember
the days when they laughed at my features
broad nose, dark skin, and kinks
caused my confidence to shrink
when they asked me
did they make it easier for you to get in here?
juxtaposed against these white walls
the message was clear.

woman, black
prestigious school of medicine
home to the discovery of insulin
my existence in this lineage felt like insolence
managing the dissonance of my identity
enigma at the epicentre of diversity
code switching with urgency
shedding the layers of culture off my tongue
carefully dissecting the vernacular
my speech becomes the disembodied phantom of my being
that I fail to resuscitate

code blue
in the deep hues of my skin remind me
that this is more like code black
meaning that there is an imminent threat
suspicious object found on hospital grounds
they asked if I felt pangs of regret
being the only black body in a sea of 259 students
they advised me, remain diligent, prudent
the margin of error is insignificant
when you dare be woman and black
when you dare be opinionated
they will misconstrue your passion for attitude
your conviction for aggression when speaking on oppression
so
be black but not radical
Shonda said we must work twice as hard to get half as much
so work four times that
think logic, think practical
think.
black, woman, physician in training

my patience is draining
when I instead deviate towards hypotheticals
what am I supposed to do when I encounter bigotry in my field,
and their condition is critical?
when do we learn how to deal with internalizing sexism and racism during
rounds
when do we learn how to heal?
is there even an option?

I was told to proceed with caution
for there was no formal training when navigating the coarse waters of
medicine
as woman and black
doctor and woman
doctor and black
doctor, black woman
doctor . . . doctor . . .
we need a doctor
is there anyone on this plane that can help?
how
can you be both doctor and black,
woman?

I quickly say back,
I know of nothing else
than to become doctor in the face of doubt
to be fearlessly melanin when the world begs otherwise
to be feminine when my narrative is challenged
and my capabilities are called into question
I will stand at the intersection of my identities and boldly proclaim
I am woman
I am black
I am doctor
and I am here.

Acknowledgements

To the incredibly gifted team at HarperCollins Canada who brought this book to life, I thank you. Special thanks go to Jim Gifford, who conceptualized this memoir, inspired me to put my life on the page, and believed in the power of my story and my ability to tell it. Thanks to my literary agent, Rick Broadhead, who was always available for a late-night call, editorial check-in or words of advice and encouragement when I needed them most.

To my superstar editor, Jennifer Lambert, I thank you for being the visionary of the architecture of my book. Thank you for pushing me to the cusp of my literary limits, only for me to discover that I had more creative and artistic potential to draw from. Thank you for believing in me, for guiding me, for being patient and flexible as my story deepened and my life expanded with two little ones. Thank you for always answering my anxious texts and bolstering me through the quagmire of writer's block. I am forever grateful.

To my fantastic legal and copy-editing teams, especially Alison Woodbury, Jeremy Rawlings, Catherine Marjoribanks and Natalie Meditsky, thank you for your patience, exceptional attention to detail, and taking great care with my story and words.

To my husband, Dale, thank you for loving me through the moments when writing this book made me a flustered, neurotic mess—and deciding to love me even more deeply. Thank you for believing in my ability to write this manuscript through my medical residency, two pregnancies and two maternity leaves in under two years. Thank you for giving me the space and grace to grow as a writer, physician, wife and mother, just trying to figure things out and juggle an impossible load. I love you, always.

To my precious babies, Ezenna (Eze) and Nkiruka (Nki), for whom I live and breathe, thank you for giving me a reason to document my life's journey so far. The love I hold for you both, and your father, is beyond any words I can string together in beautiful metaphors or poetry. Thank you, my children, for giving me the strength to keep going, and going, and going—even if it means writing and editing during nap times, in the dead of night, or at 4:00 a.m., so that I can be present when you wake up to conquer the day. To be your mother, and to tell a tiny bit of your origin story in this book, is an honour.

To my best friend and sister of my soul, Vanessa Pina, thank you for being the magical human and step-in-mother/Tia/godmother to my babies when I needed the extra support to write this book. Thank you, especially, for being by my side for the last decade and change, for helping me care for Eze in the months it took me to develop my first draft, for the constant words of support and encouragement, and for believing in me in the moments when I didn't believe in myself.

To my family and friends who checked in on my writing progress, offered to read over excerpts, and lent incredibly helpful commentary on my writing, thank you. Special thanks to my siblings and parents, who are the bedrock of my life and have gifted me with an upbringing that is worthy of narration.

Thank you to my medical mentors-turned-friends-and-family, who have guided me through my medical journey, namely Drs. Pier Bryden, Lisa Robinson, Onye Nnorom, Cindy Maxwell and Mr. Ike Okafor.

Thank you to those who have paved the way to make it possible for young, Black physicians like me to shine in medicine and beyond.

Thank you to my patients, who have taught me not only what it means to be a doctor, but also what it means to be human—and, even more so, a human in evolution.

And to the light of my life, my mommy, Nmeka, thank you for absolutely everything. This book is, quite evidently, a letter of love and gratitude to you, without whom I could not be the person I am today. Love you more.

Notes

CHAPTER 2

33 Historically, through the efforts of colonialism and slavery, afro-textured hair:

Aliya Rodriguez and Brooke Jackson, "What Every Dermatologist Must Know About the History of Black Hair," *Practical Dermatology*, November 2023, https://practicaldermatology.com/articles/2023-nov/what-every-dermatologist-must-know-about-the-history-of-black-hair.

CHAPTER 5

80 Over time, and into the modern era, cornrows . . . were given a negative connotation:

Janice Gassam Asare, "How Hair Discrimination Affects Black Women at Work," *Harvard Business Review*, 10 May 2023, https://hbr.org/2023/05/how-hair-discrimination-affects-black-women-at-work.

David S. Joachim, "Military to Ease Hairstyle Rules After Outcry From Black Recruits," *The New York Times*, 14 August 2014, https://www.nytimes.com/2014/08/15/us/military-hairstyle-rules-dreadlocks-cornrows.html.

85 In fact, only approximately 1 percent of U of T's incoming medical classes between the years of 2010 and 2015 identified as being from African ancestry:

University of Toronto, Faculty of Medicine, *Undergraduate Medical Professions Education. Annual Report 2012–2013*, https://md.utoronto.ca/sites/default/files/UMPE%20Annual%20Report%20%282012-2013%29.pdf.

Trevor Young, "We're Not That Diverse, But We're Working On It," *Temerty Medicine*, 26 October 2016, https://temertymedicine.utoronto.ca/news/were-not-diverse-were-working-it.

CHAPTER 10

129–130 Yes, there were many non-white individuals in my class . . . but historically under-represented groups in medicine . . . matriculated in chronically low numbers:

Young, "We're Not That Diverse, But We're Working On It."

CHAPTER 11

133 Research had demonstrated that subconscious racial/anti-Black bias may permeate medical school admissions committees:

Quinn Capers IV, "How Clinicians and Educators Can Mitigate Implicit Bias in Patient Care and Candidate Selection in Medical Education," *ATS Scholar* 1, no. 3, https://www.atsjournals.org/doi/full/10.34197/ats-scholar.2020-0024PS.

Quinn Capers IV, Daniel Clinchot, Leon McDougle, and Anthony G. Greenwald, "Implicit Racial Bias in Medical School Admissions, *Academic Medicine* 92, no. 3, March 2017, https://journals.lww.com/academicmedicine/fulltext/2017/03000/implicit_racial _bias_in_medical_school_admissions.32.aspx.

134 We were asked to participate in an interview about the necessity of the initiative:

Temerty Medicine, *Black at Temerty Medicine: Addressing Anti-Black Racism at Temerty Medicine, Accountability Report, February 2022,* https://black-at-temertymedicine.ca /wp-content/uploads/2022/02/Addressing-Anti-Black-Racism-at-Temerty-Medicine -Accountability-Report-February-2022.pdf.

CHAPTER 15

181 . . . Dr. David Latter, had announced that there would be fourteen Black medical students matriculating through the BSAP program that fall:

Temerty Medicine, *Black at Temerty Medicine.*

CHAPTER 19

227 ... drapetomania, the fake psychotic label given to enslaved Black people who tried to earn their freedoms

Sonia Meerai, Idil Abdillahi, and Jennifer Poole, "An Introduction to Anti-Black Sanism," *Intersectionalities: A Global Journal of Social Work Analysis, Research, Polity, and Practice* 5, no. 3: 18–35, https://journals.library.mun.ca/ojs/index.php /IJ/article/view/1682.

227 This—coupled with the understanding that Black Canadians experiencing first episode psychosis are at greater risk:

Sommer Knight, G. Eric Jarvis, Andrew G. Ryder, Myrna Lashley, and Cécile Rousseau, "Ethnoracial Differences in Coercive Referrals and Intervention Among Patients With First-Episode Psychosis," *Psychiatric Services*, 13 July 2021: 1–7, https:// ps.psychiatryonline.org/doi/10.1176/appi.ps.202000715?url_ver=Z39.88-2003&rfr _id=ori:rid:crossref.org&rfr_dat=cr_pub%20%200pubmed.

"Mad Studies: Intersections with Disability Studies, Social Work, and 'Mental Health,'" *Intersectionalities* 5, no. 3 (Special Issue) 2016.

Meerai, Abdillahi, and Poole, "An Introduction to Anti-Black Sanism."

Tiyondah Fante-Coleman and Fatimah Jackson-Best, "Barriers and Facilitators to Accessing Mental Healthcare in Canada for Black Youth: A Scoping Review," *Adolescent Research Review*, 5 no. 2, 115–36. https://doi.org/10.1007/s40894-020-00133-2.

CHAPTER 21

251 ... U of T had recently admitted the largest class of Black, talented medical students in Canadian history:

Temerty Medicine, *Black at Temerty Medicine.*

CHAPTER 22

265 Black men ... are more likely to have physical restraints used, and higher doses of tranquilizing medications administered:

269 Black people experiencing a mental illness in the community were still more likely to have coercive and threatening force used to bring them to the ER:

Ambrose H. Wong, Travis Whitfill, Emmanuel C. Ohuabunwa, et al., "Association of Race/Ethnicity and Other Demographic Characteristics With Use of Physical Restraints in the Emergency Department," *JAMA Network Open* 4, no. 1, 25 January 2021, https://jamanetwork.com/journals/jamanetworkopen/fullarticle/2775602.

Leah Robinson, Laura D. Cramer, Jessica M. Ray, et al., "Racial and Ethnic Disparities in Use of Chemical Restraint in the Emergency Department," *Academic Emergency Medicine* 29, no. 12, December 2022: 1496–99, https://doi.org/10.1111/acem.14579.

Utsha G. Khatri, M. Kit Delgado, Eugenia South, and Ari Friedman, "Racial Disparities in the Management of Emergency Department Patients Presenting with Psychiatric Disorders," *Annals of Epidemiology* 69, May 2022: 9–16, https://doi.org/10.1016/j.annepidem.2022.02.003.

Meerai, Abdillahi, and Poole, "An Introduction to Anti-Black Sanism."

Knight, Jarvis, Ryder, Lashley, and Rousseau, "Ethnoracial Differences in Coercive Referrals and Intervention Among Patients With First-Episode Psychosis."